Illinois Central College
Learning Resource Center

# THE YOUNG WRITER AT WORK

*THE*

# Young Writer at Work

**JESSIE REHDER**
UNIVERSITY OF NORTH CAROLINA

THE ODYSSEY PRESS, INC · *New York*

# Acknowledgments

The author is grateful to the following publishers, authors, and literary agents for permission to quote from the works listed.

From "Interview with William Faulkner," *The Paris Review.* By permission of the publisher.

"The Tonsil Operation," by Cherry Parker. By permission of *The American Journal of Nursing* Company.

From *A Certain Measure*, by Ellen Glasgow. By permission of Harcourt, Brace & World.

From *A Personal Record*, by Joseph Conrad. By permission of J. M. Dent and Sons, Ltd.

From "The Celestial Omnibus," from *The Collected Tales* of E. M. Forster, published by Alfred A. Knopf, Inc.

From *Life on the Mississippi* and *The Adventures of Huckleberry Finn*, by Mark Twain. By permission of Harper & Row.

From "Bezhin Meadow." From *A Sportsman's Notebook* by Ivan Turgenev. Published by the Viking Press, Inc.

From *Ethan Frome*, by Edith Wharton. Published by Charles Scribner's Sons.

From "Silent Snow, Secret Snow," from *The Collected Short Stories of Conrad Aiken.* Published by The World Publishing Company of Cleveland and New York.

From *The Horse's Mouth*, by Joyce Cary. Published by Harper & Row.

From *A Portrait Of The Artist As A Young Man*, by James Joyce. Published by The Viking Press, Inc.

From "The Book-Bag," by W. Somerset Maugham. Reprinted by permission of Doubleday & Company, Inc.

From *A Writer's Notebook*, by W. Somerset Maugham. Copyright 1949 by W. Somerset Maugham. Reprinted by permission of Doubleday & Company, Inc.

From *The Crack-Up*, by F. Scott Fitzgerald. Copyright 1945 by New Directions. Reprinted by permission of New Directions, Publishers.

From "Winter Dreams," by F. Scott Fitzgerald. Copyright 1922 Frances Scott Fitzgerald Lanahan; renewal copyright 1950. Reprinted with the permission of Charles Scribner's Sons from *All the Sad Young Men* by F. Scott Fitzgerald.

From Flaubert's letter to de Maupassant. Quoted in Introduction to *Pierre and Jean*, by Guy de Maupassant. Published by Alfred A. Knopf, Inc.

From "A Letter To F. Scott Fitzgerald," by Thomas Wolfe. From *The Crack-Up* by F. Scott Fitzgerald. Copyright 1945 by New Directions. Reprinted by permission of New Directions.

From *A Tree Grows In Brooklyn*, by Betty Smith. Copyright 1943, 1947 by Betty Smith. Reprinted by permission of Harper & Row.

From the Foreword to *Camino Real*, by Tennessee Williams. Copyright 1948 and 1953 by Tennessee Williams. All rights reserved. Reprinted by permission of New Directions, Publishers.

"The Lost Beach," by Louise Hardeman. Copyright 1954 by Street & Smith Publications, Inc. By permission of the publisher.

"Eveline," by James Joyce. From *Dubliners* by James Joyce, Compass edition. Reprinted by permission of The Viking Press, Inc. All rights reserved.

From "I Call My Jesus," from *Dog On the Sun* by Paul Green. Published by The University of North Carolina Press.

From *Look Homeward, Angel*, by Thomas Wolfe. Copyright 1929, Charles Scribner's Sons; renewal copyright 1957 Edward C. Aswell.

From "The Story Of A Novel," by Thomas Wolfe. Copyright 1935, The Saturday Review Company, Inc. Copyright 1936 Charles Scribner's Sons.

From "Interview With Nelson Algren," *The Paris Review*. By permission of the publisher.

From "Never But Once The White Tadpole," by Leon Rooke. From *New Campus Writing No. 3*, edited by Nolan Miller and Judson Jerome, Grove Press, New York, 1959.

From "Interview With Frank O'Connor," *The Paris Review*. By permission of the publisher.

"The Use Of Force," by William Carlos Williams. From *Make Light of It*. Copyright 1938 by William Carlos Williams. Reprinted by permission of New Directions.

From "Don't Look Behind You," by Fredric Brown. Copyright 1947, The American Mercury, Inc.

From *Lie Down In Darkness*, by William Styron. Copyright 1951 by William Styron; used by special permission of the publishers, The Bobbs-Merrill Company, Inc.

From "The Open Boat," by Stephen Crane. From *Twenty Stories* by Stephen Crane. Published by Alfred A. Knopf, Inc.

From "What To Do Till The Postman Comes," by Max Steele. By permission of the author.

From a letter to E. L. Sanderson. From "The Condition Of Art," by Joseph Conrad. By permission of J. M. Dent & Sons, Ltd., Doubleday & Company, Inc., and the Trustees of the Joseph Conrad Estate.

From *The Private World of William Faulkner*, by Robert Coughlan. By permission of Harper & Row, copyright 1933.

From "An Old Manuscript," by Franz Kafka. Reprinted from *The Penal Colony*, by Franz Kafka, translated by Willa and Edwin Muir by permission of Schocken Books Inc., New York. Copyright 1948 by Schocken Books Inc.

From *Re-Birth*, by John Wyndham. Used by permission of the author and the author's agents, Scott Meredith Literary Agency, Inc.

From "The Ballad of the Sad Café," by Carson McCullers. Published by Houghton Mifflin Company.

From *The Dharma Bums*, by Jack Kerouac. Copyright 1958 by Jack Kerouac. Reprinted by permission of The Viking Press, Inc.

From *The Great Gatsby*, by F. Scott Fitzgerald. Copyright 1925 Charles Scribner's Sons; renewal copyright 1953 Frances Scott Fitzgerald Lanahan.

From *The Man With The Golden Arm*, by Nelson Algren. Copyright 1949 by Nelson Algren. Reprinted by permission of Doubleday & Company, Inc.

From "Interview With Ernest Hemingway," *The Paris Review*. By permission of the publisher.

From *Time And The Novel*, by A. A. Mendilow. By permission of The Books for Pleasure Group, Ltd.

"The Moth And The Star," by James Thurber. Permission the author; © 1939 *The New Yorker Magazine*, Inc.

From *A Farewell To Arms*, by Ernest Hemingway. Copyright 1929 Charles Scribner's Sons; renewal copyright 1957 Ernest Hemingway.

From *Far From The Madding Crowd*, by Thomas Hardy. Published by Oxford University Press.

From *Crime and Punishment*, by Feodor Dostoyevsky, translated by David Magarshack and published in Penguin Classics.

From "That Evening Sun," by William Faulkner. Copyright by Random House, Inc., and used by permission of Random House, Inc.

From *The Sound And The Fury*, by William Faulkner. Copyright by Random House, Inc., and used by permission of Random House, Inc.

"Time Schedule for *Ulysses*," by James Joyce. Adapted from *This Generation* by Anderson and Walton. Copyright 1939, 1949 by Scott Foresman and Company, Chicago.

From "Interview With Aldous Huxley," *The Paris Review*. By permission of the publisher.

"The String," by Guy de Maupassant. Reprinted from *The Collected Novels and Stories of Guy de Maupassant*, Vol. VI, *Miss Harriet and Other Stories*, by permission of Alfred A. Knopf, Inc. Copyright 1923 by Alfred A. Knopf, Inc.

"The Guardian," by Scott Griffith. By permission of *The Carolina Quarterly*.

"Miss Brill," by Katherine Mansfield. Reprinted from *The Short Stories of Katherine Mansfield*, by permission of Alfred A. Knopf, Inc. Copyright 1922, 1937 by Alfred A. Knopf, Inc.

From *Points of View*, by W. Somerset Maugham. By permission of Doubleday & Company, Inc.

From a letter to Richard Murry, by Katherine Mansfield. Reprinted from *The Letters of Katherine Mansfield*, by permission of Alfred A. Knopf, Inc.

"The Day after Tomorrow," by

Charles Nisbet. By permission of *The Carolina Quarterly*.

From "A Good Man Is Hard to Find," by Flannery O'Connor. Copyright, 1953 by Flannery O'Connor. Reprinted from the title story of the volume *A Good Man Is Hard to Find* and Other Stories by Flannery O'Connor by permission of Harcourt, Brace & World, Inc.

"The Proud and the Virtuous," by Doris Betts. Reprinted from *Mademoiselle;* © Street & Smith Publications, Inc., 1956.

From "What Is a Literary Agent?" By permission of the Society of Authors' Representatives, Inc.

From "The Writer and His Agent," by Shirley Fisher. In *The Writer Magazine*, December, 1957, by Shirley Fisher of McIntosh and Otis, Inc.

From a letter from Malcolm Cowley. By permission of Mr. Cowley.

From *Advertisements for Myself*, by Norman Mailer. By permission of the author.

From the Introduction to *Cat on a Hot Tin Roof*, by Tennessee Williams. Copyright 1945 by Tennessee Williams. All rights reserved. Reprinted by permission of New Directions, Publishers.

"The Field of Blue Children," by Tennessee Williams. From *One Arm* and Other Stories, Copyright 1948 and 1954 by Tennessee Williams, Reprinted by permission of New Directions, Publishers.

From "Young Writers," by Jean Stafford. Reprinted by permission of *Analects*.

From "Comment," by Gore Vidal. Reprinted from *Esquire*, May 1961.

From *Ulysses*, by James Joyce. Copyright by Random House, Inc., and used by permission of Random House, Inc.

From *Studies in Human Time*, by Georges Poulet. By permission of The Johns Hopkins Press.

From *Art and Reality*, by Joyce Cary. By permission of Harper & Row.

From comments on "Plot," by M. H. Abrams, *et al*, in *Glossary of Literary Terms*. By permission of Holt, Rinehart and Winston.

From *Editor to Author: The Letters of Maxwell E. Perkins*, edited by John Hall Wheelock. Copyright 1950 Charles Scribner's Sons.

From *Crime and Punishment*, by Fyodor Dostoyevsky, translated by David Magarshack and published by Penguin Books. Used by permission of the publisher.

The author wishes to thank Hugh Holman, Roberta D. Cornelius, Frances Gray Patton, and Porter Cowles for their encouragement. In particular, she is grateful to the students and to the professional writers who have allowed their work to appear in this book.

# Foreword

The disturbance which haunts a potential writer and draws him to pencil and paper is something which lies outside the range of books of instruction. It is so compelling, and so ill-defined, that philosophers of the past have called it a gift of the gods, and it is something which the writer must bring with him. Even so, when a person sits down to write he is often disheartened at the outset by questions which loom like dams between his creative urge and the bright and intricate patterns he wants to put on paper. Instead of presiding easily over the flow of words, he finds himself facing a multitude of choices he must make before he can go on. Whether he fully recognizes the nature of these choices or not, he already has before him the evidence that writing is not only creative inspiration but also a craft.

It is at this point that the present book may be helpful. Its aim is to bring the young writer—particularly the young writer on the college campus—to a sharper awareness of the processes and methods among which he must choose, without prescribing *how* he must choose. There is no single way to write a short story or a novel. If a book on writing is to be useful it should act as a companion, making clear and encouraging, without endangering the young writer's individuality. At the same time there is much which the individual writer shares with his fellow writers, and it is therefore to the common ground of fiction that this book is devoted.

The discussion, and the progressive assignments which accompany it, are purposely centered on the short story. The principles of poetry are different enough in nature to need a full and separate treatment, and it is in fiction, moreover, that most young writers are mainly interested. In the classroom, the relative brevity of the short story makes it a more manageable subject than the novel. At the same time, the person who writes a short story has inevitably laid part of the foundation for the writing of a novel. The experience he gains is thus far from wasted even if he should, eventually, discard the shorter form.

Joseph Conrad has said that a novel is a conviction of our fellow man's existence strong enough to take upon itself a form of imagined life clearer than reality. What he has said of the novel is also true of the short story. If the present book helps to ease some of the young writer's difficulties in trying to express an imagined life clearer than reality, its purpose is amply fulfilled.

J. R.

# Contents

# Assignments

## PART ONE

## A WRITER LEARNS

# 1

# The Urge to Tell a Story

The urge to communicate our experience to others is probably as old as language itself. Everyone is familiar with it and everyone obeys it to some extent, but the person who wants to be a writer feels it with particular force. The writer wants to share his awareness with others by creating a word structure that will convey as exactly as possible what he feels and knows. In doing this he must use words that have been used by people before him, but in each beginning writer the words and the urge to use them seem new.

How does this urge come? One person, using words to clarify his own thinking, may in the process stumble upon a talent he has not recognized before. Another person, even before starting to write, may already be conscious of a desire to invent a fictional world which imitates the actual one and through this imitation to compel others to a new comprehension. Many people simply want to tell a story.

Whatever your reason for writing, your obvious problem is to find a method of translating your desire to *tell what you know* into the particular kind of reality known as fiction. If this reality is achieved, it will draw life from what you yourself are —your hopes, fears, remembrances, observations, your total environment. You will go through a complex process that changes your unwritten narrative into a story, and the story will have a place of its own and people in motion who live in that place.

Getting your story down on paper is an exercise in technique and discipline. As anyone who has attempted the task will tell you, the story only *begins* in the imagination. You may want to present some variation on a common theme, as Hawthorne did in "The Birthmark," in which he shows how a small blemish in an otherwise perfect person brings tragedy. Perhaps you hope to recreate in fiction the atmosphere of a warm room in which you lived with a comrade now gone. Or, more ambitiously, you may intend to trace the path of an imaginary expedition along the ridges of a mountain that you will never see. But you will never be able just to wish your people into existence.

Wait a minute, you say—what about genius? *Genius* is a word to be used sparingly. By one definition it is a quality that enables a man to make his own way. But even for a person possessing this quality, a work of art does not just appear in finished form. The genius may find a path nobody else ever dreamed of taking. He may create a literary form unknown before he fashioned it. But he works, and in writing he learns how to command the compulsion with which he began.

One student, believing he was especially gifted, liked to call his compulsion for writing an *animal*. Curbing the animal was abhorrent to him. Any consideration of subject matter in a story, or of its potential interest to other people, was beneath him. Only after a good many months of inactivity did he even acknowledge that one function of a writer is to write.

He then began to put down whatever came from his head, still refusing to consider that ugly word *technique*—at least in the initial draft, which was the only one he made. He did not read over what he had written or make any attempt to decide whether his account of a sensitive boy left too long at a private school by careless parents said what he wanted to say. Words simply ran out of him, spilling to nothing in the end.

And yet this student had himself experienced the events he wanted to relate and had not only been deeply affected by them but also wanted others to share what had been significant to him. He had, too, a gift of words. But he was not interested in the process of writing and scorned the methods by which one learns to discipline an urge and at the same time enhance its vigor. His primary desire was to let his animal run free.

But, you ask, how do you write a story? Where do you start? Of necessity the writer of a story—like the painter, the sculptor, the musician—begins with what is meaningful in his own particular realm of knowing and feeling. There he makes his choice among the different means of expression and begins the particular process which leads to fiction. This process consists of a series of further steps, consciously taken, by which one presents certain significant aspects of experience in a guise imitative of reality. In taking these steps, the writer adds thinking to feeling.

He may hope to create a realm of fantasy or an imaginative reproduction of some aspect of real life. Whatever his fictional province, his eventual aim is to present his deepest beliefs in an esthetically harmonious structure that will be as moving and convincing for other people as it is for him. In attempting to achieve this aim, he subjects his feelings to the discipline of thought.

Of course there is always the old lady of the anecdote who was being told about the importance of process in writing. "You must think about what you are trying to say," she was told, "before you try to say it." "But," she asked, "how do I know what I think until I see what I've said?"

You may agree with her and think the best way to write a story is to sit down at a typewriter and write until you decide to stop, settling problems of fictional process as you go along. But this procedure is generally wasteful, and may frustrate the writer so greatly that he abandons his goal. Most often he ends up, not with the first draft of a story but with a mass of contradictions which merely pose the very problems he should have thought out before sitting down to write. If you agree that the first steps in a process come first, one way to start is with the idea or impression that lies behind the story.

The narrative may rise from a half-remembered impression or from the shock of an unforgettable experience. It may come to you through hearsay. Henry James, listening to a garrulous luncheon partner ramble on about the break-up of a family, created a novel from the idea given him by a "bore." Sometimes the narrative takes shape visually, appearing on the screen of your consciousness like a painting.

In *The Paris Review*, William Faulkner tells how his novel, *The Sound and the Fury*, began.

*Faulkner:* It began with a mental picture. I didn't realize at the time it was symbolical. The picture was of the muddy seat of a little girl's drawers in a pear tree, where she could see through a window where her grandmother's funeral was taking place and report what was happening to her brothers on the ground below. By the time I explained who they were and what they were doing and how her pants got muddy, I realized it would be impossible to get all of it into a short story and that it would have to be a book.

Mr. Faulkner adds that he told the story once through the eyes of an idiot child, then tried to tell it again, the same story, through the eyes of a brother. That was still not it. He told it again through the eyes of a second brother. That was still not it. He adds that he never could tell it right, though he tried hard and would like to try again. But it took the mental picture to start him at all.

One ambitious young writer came away from Faulkner's comments in *The Paris Review* with a mental-picture beginning for his own next story. He imagined the ghost of a red setter, Redlegs, roaming the Alabama hill country on a moonlit summer night. The dog and his master had been murdered in a cabin in the hills but Redlegs' ghost afterwards returned to the forest, baying into the moonlight until a friend of his dead master came to investigate and discovered the crime.

In the story-to-be, Redlegs was always at the center of the action, but the writer had a pastoral imagination. Trees lit by intermittent moonlight, and the honeysuckle of a hundred scented meadows, were all he could get on paper. He is reworking his story around an actual account of a murder, trying to forget his mental picture, but he knows that one danger of this approach is that he may produce a story stamped, "It happened this way," forgetting that fiction is both what is and what is not, a combination of fact and fancy. But his urge is a strong one—he will find a way in the end.

However you begin and whatever your urge, to be effective you must convey your impression through the senses. In calling fiction the appeal of one temperament to many temperaments, Joseph Conrad was again saying that, regardless of the method, the writer's aim is to translate what he has experienced into what many people will want to feel with him.

Suppose you sit down and remember an experience that has had meaning for you. Use an incident that has left its mark on your personality. Convey it as vividly, as sensuously, as you can.

## WRITING DOWN AN INCIDENT:   Assignment 1

Recall an experience with your parents that made you feel they had deserted you. What made this incident affect you strongly? Afterward, did you feel that your parents had come back to you or was there a wall between you and them?

Describe an encounter with a stranger in a city unfamiliar to you. You may have read the story of a boy who was warned against strangers and afterward, to his surprise, was given good advice by every stranger he met. What came of your own experience in an alien town?

Recreate on paper the strong sense-impressions that came to you during an incident that took place in a pastoral environment. Write of an encounter with a fox or a snake. Or you may have found a young bird or a squirrel and brought him home with you. Emphasize the rural surroundings and limit the time to a summer afternoon.

As a child, did you have an older and much loved friend from whom you became separated by forces beyond your control? How did the separation affect you?

Were you ever hurt by a doctor or dentist who was trying to help you but seemed to you to be an enemy? Where did the incident take place and what were your immediate reactions to it?

After you have written your own incident based on one of the preceding suggestions, read the two student sketches included in this chapter. First analyze Cherry Parker's telling of the personal story behind the outward one. She has tried through remembrance to capture the fears of a six-year-old child who must have a tonsil operation. The incident has a raw violence. Also, you may think it dated. But if the writer successfully reproduces the emotion of her "I," an incident like this becomes a narrative-seed that might flower into a story.

## THE TONSIL OPERATION (At Age Six)

### CHERRY PARKER

Probably if Mama could see me now she wouldn't know I was Cherry Cartwright. Or Daddy—or the Simpson kids. I feel so funny, not a bit the way I did when Daddy left me here and a nurse named Miss Love let me walk around on my own two feet to the big room where she put me in a high bed and told me I'd have such a good time here in this big hospital.

Since I came yesterday, I've seen the kids come and go. They roll the stretcher in and then when they bring the kid back, sometimes he's asleep and sometimes he has a big plaster cast on his leg or something like that. But always, he yells and moans and screams and you know he hurts and you hope that stretcher won't ever, ever stop at your bed.

But this morning it stopped at my bed. I didn't say anything when they lifted me on it. I just wished Mama was here—or even Daddy. But I wouldn't want the Simpson kids to see me now.

They rolled me down a long, cold hall, and they went off and left me lying there. I'm lying here now on the flat, hard stretcher wiggling my toes in the white cotton leg wrappers that are big enough for my Aunt Ora. They are too clean because they smell like iodine has been poured on them and someone must have dipped them in starch because they are scratching my legs. I have a tight white band around my head and it hurts, but there isn't even anyone around I can ask to get me an aspirin, and besides they didn't give me as much as a drink of water this morning and my stomach hurts.

After a while I hear something. I know the sound—it's a stretcher being wheeled down the hall and it sounds like it needs some of my Mother's sewing machine oil on it. A man with his face all covered is rolling it and a kid about my size is on it and I think she's dead. Her head is all over to one side and her eyes are closed and some red red blood is running all out of the side of her mouth and onto the white sheet under her. I feel like crying, but I know I won't.

I wiggle my feet again. I can still move them. I start to sit up on my stretcher. I think maybe I'll get off and go home, but I hear the wheels again, and here comes another stretcher. The little boy on this one is bloody too and he's making funny noises like he can't breathe good and threshing around with his arms like he wants to get away. His eyes are the worst though; they're half open and they look like a fish's in a meat counter.

I sit up again. I am out of my leggings and half off my stretcher and here comes this doctor and nurse after me. The nurse pushes me back down and says, "Don't worry—you'll be all right," and now it is my wheels I hear rolling. I lie there and feel the stretcher moving under me and the doctor's eyes over the top of the rag he's got wrapped over his face look like he doesn't like me very much. I can't tell about the nurse, but she's pushing me so fast she must be in a hurry.

Now, we're in a big room and I know the smell—it's ether. I don't like it and I don't like the big lights that shine down in my face like a hundred million flashlights all turned on at once. They lift me out on a big table and it's flatter and harder than the stretcher even and when I try to kick the doctor, they tie my feet and hands down and I can only pull my feet up a little way and I can't move my arms at all.

"Mama." I'm yelling now loud as I can yell. "Daddy." "Simpson kids—help me. Help me." When I see the nurse's hand pushing a cone-shaped thing toward me, I try to bite her hand, but she pushes it over my face and there isn't any air. I can't breathe. I can't breathe.

I hear someone say, "Now be a sweet girl and count to ten." I try. "One—two— Oh, the awful stuff. It stinks. It stinks. It's running in my throat and it tastes like coal-oil. Like coal-oil—can't you hear me?"

"Mama—Mama—Mama—" My head is spinning around and around. There are bright red neon lights like at the Red Pig Barbecue flashing on and off—on and off—and they're making me blind. I can't see. I can't hear. I can't breathe. Make the lights stop! Please make the lights stop!

## TURNING FACT INTO FICTION:  Assignment 2

Another way to begin is to take a dramatic incident from a newspaper and try to imbue the account with your personal emotions. Read the following paraphrase which is based on the newspaper account of a boy lost in the woods beside a wrecked plane. Afterward, write a sketch centering it around the boy's experience and presenting your work in the first person. Limit your point of view to that of the child beside the plane as the helicopter dips toward the ground.

James Allen, found beside the wreckage of a plane where he had spent fifteen days alone in a forest, was returned to the Flin Flon Hospital by helicopter and has survived his vigil in the bush. After bringing James to safety, the helicopter returned to the wreckage to get the bodies of the boy's father and the pilot of the plane who were both killed in the crash three hundred miles north of Winnipeg.

The eight-year-old survivor told his rescuers how his father, pitched from the plane and fatally injured, gave him final words of advice before he died, instructing his son to stay near the wreckage and drink lots of water. His last words were, "Your mother will come for you." The son sat under a tree when it rained. During the time he waited, he drank water which gathered in the rocks.

Fifteen days after the crash a helicopter plucked him from beside the burned plane. The helicopter pilot, Ken Snyder, had taken off with a construction worker for a final air search of the area where the plane had been lost. The construction worker asked Snyder where the plane had been when it disappeared.

"I was over Bear Lake at the time," said Snyder, "so I looked out and started to tell him that the plane had disappeared somewhere just below us."

"I never finished because directly below me I saw the skeleton framework of an aircraft. I banked sharply to get a better look and then my heart missed a beat. Below me on a flat rock surrounded by bush was a small boy frantically waving his arms and jumping up and down. I suddenly realized I had found the missing plane and the boy was alive."

Snyder said that if he had been 100 yards to either side of his course he would not have seen the boy or the wreckage.

He said he realized the number of disappointments James must have had the past two weeks as he tried to attract search planes, so he flew so low over the lad he could see the flowers on his sweater.

The sweater and other heavy clothing helped protect the boy from the cold and mosquitoes. Rescuers said he was nearly incoherent from exhaustion and hunger when found. He did not know that a package containing enough food for 25 days had been thrown clear of the wreckage.

In writing of the lost boy waiting beside the plane, you have drawn on your own emotional responses but have presented them in the framework of an experience belonging to someone else. Compare what you have written with "The Golden Eye-

ball," by G. M., included below. This sketch is based on a newspaper account of a prison break that ended in failure. It
represents an experiment in recording an impression of a dramatic movement.

The newspaper story told how a prisoner broke out of a state
farm, evaded capture for a week, and during that time added
two new crimes to those already on his roster. From a secluded
farm he secured the shotgun with which he destroyed himself.
The chase was a long one but with men and dogs beating the
woods for him the convict no longer had a chance. "The
Golden Eyeball," in which the sun may represent the eye of
heaven, attempts to capture that desperate instant just before
death.

# THE GOLDEN EYEBALL

### G. M.

The golden eyeball watched so silently that the hurried, muffled
footsteps could be heard for a great distance. Suddenly his legs
sprawled out from under him; there was the rasp of tearing denim,
then a thud. From the other side of the thicket a bluejay called, then
all was silent in the dazzling, morning sunlight.

Cautiously he pulled himself up on his haunches. A black knee
poked through the torn dungarees. Slowly, a little stream of blood
and sweat trickled down the knee and made a dark spot on the
faded pants. Quickly he bent over and sucked the wound.

The bluejay called again, and he spat out the salty mixture in his
mouth. He had known that he would not be able to run much farther, but he would have preferred to choose his own place for the
ending. However, as he rested, his resentment slowly left him and a
great tiredness crept over him. An uneasy breeze began to stir the
pine trees overhead, and its sound harmonized with the drone of a
fly that was dancing nearby. As he lay down, his hand relaxed; and
he let go of the shotgun for the first time in two days.

Through his shut eyelids the sun formed a hot red ball that
burned itself deep into his skull. He smiled. The sun was a friend
now; for months it has been his daily companion, but it had been a
sadistic comrade. Its arrival each day marked the end of his refuge
in sleep. All day it heated his sweating body with its rays, and only
when it had burned itself out could he rest.

He slept now. The sun bore down on him, and he became the sun. He dreamed of woman, and the sun forced his way through the shadows in the grove, destroying them and filling their place with his own being.

From the distance came the sound of breaking twigs, the crackle of a radio, the bay of hounds on a trail. The jay screamed a warning. He awoke. His hand grabbed the hot metal of the shotgun barrel. As he moved he felt the pain in his leg. He looked down in time to see a fly rise from the congealed blood and circle away. The sun pinpointed the black figure in the middle of the grove. Its rays played on the hot steel clutched in his fist.

As he grinned up to the sun he had to blink because of the radiant light. Casually he waved a salute to the heat above with his free hand; then he leaned over the barrel and pulled the trigger, blasting himself across last year's pine needles.

In "The Golden Eyeball," the author sacrifices detail in trying to gain a sensory effect. We know very little about place in this sketch and never actually see the convict, but we are exposed to sights and sounds that convey his plight to us. This impressionistic account could become the final incident in the narrative G. M. has not yet written. He does have something to start on.

In your account taken from the newspaper story of James Allen's vigil, you too have begun to shape a story. By translation, the boy waiting for help beside the wreckage is you. The incident written out of your own experience was a different kind of translation. There the "I" you created became both you and someone else. So far, then, you have worked on two simple patterns of narration, confining them to the point of view of a child. You have emphasized character, and that is where a story has its beginning.

But another step in writing a story is to learn how to place characters in a believable landscape. We already know that your people must carry with them, and communicate for you, the truth of your own experience. And what is true for them is true for the province in which they live. The locale of your story may be a single room, or it may embrace a river as huge as Mark Twain's Mississippi. In either case you must make your place as true as your people. Only then will you be able to stake it out in the imagination of the reader who comes to you.

## 2

# Discovering Your Province

Somerset Maugham says in his story, "The Book-Bag," that a writer gets to know the people he writes about by standing in their shoes and feeling with their hearts. In the story you want to tell and are already beginning to write, you will be wearing the clothes of your characters and feeling by proxy with the people you create. Beyond that, you will be moving with them through the fictional territory that is their home, instilling in your readers the spirit of that place. You will be establishing your *province*.

*Place, setting, scene,* or the larger *environment* of a story, should reflect your characters so truly that people, place, time elements, and the action itself merge into a single pattern in the finished narrative, with the parts of the pattern seemingly inseparable. But when you are setting out to write a story and are wondering how a writer communicates a sense of place, you might try considering scene as if it were a separate element, like a map or a blueprint.

By deliberately isolating scene from the other elements in a story you may learn how to merge it with them later in a much more effective manner. Your problem now is to create rather than merely to describe a region. Learning how to observe a hill, a field, or a precipice and then to describe what you see in precise language is always important. First, though, you need to recognize your own fictional province. Then you can begin to relate it to people in action.

For some regional writers almost the entire fabric of a narrative is woven from the locale in which the action takes place. The author presents the scene in such a way that it becomes an actor in the story. In Charles Dickens' *Bleak House*, a novel centered on the long struggle for an inheritance by characters

who are stuck in a legal fog bank, Dickens says at the very beginning: "fog everywhere, up the river, down . . . fog in the
yards, and hovering in the rigging of a great ship . . . fog cruelly
pinching the toes and fingers of the shivering little apprentice
boy on deck. . . ." This London fog permeates the entire action
of the novel.

Scene has its own importance in Ellen Glasgow's novel,
*Barren Ground*, in which the atmosphere of the Virginia she
knew so well pervades the book and in which the characters are
figures made from the soil, tempered by "the slow seasons, the
blighted crops, the long droughts. . . ." Miss Glasgow empha-
sizes every significant aspect of nature and, in discussing *Barren
Ground*, says of scene:

> The significance of this book, the quickening spirit, would not
> have varied, I believe, had I been born anywhere else. Nevertheless,
> I felt that the scene in *Barren Ground* possessed an added dimension,
> a universal rhythm more fluent than any material texture. Under
> the lights and shadows there is the brooding spirit of place, but,
> deeper still, under the spirit of place, there is the whole movement
> of life.
>
> For the setting of this novel, I went far back into the past. The
> country is as familiar to me as if the landscape unrolled both with-
> out and within. I had known every feature for years, and the satura-
> tion of my subject with the mood of sustained melancholy was
> effortless and complete. The houses, the roads, the woods, the end-
> less fields of broomsedge and scrub pine, the low, immeasurable
> horizon—all these images I had seen with the remembering eyes of a
> child. And time, like a mellow haze, had preserved the impressions
> unaltered. They are the lighter semblances folded over the heart of
> the book.

The role played by a rural community in which the vital
stream of living was running into shallows is defined in this quotation. Of course, Miss Glasgow formulated her comment after
the book was completed, but long before beginning her first
draft of *Barren Ground* she understood the importance of place
for her characters and for herself. The sense of locale is so
strong in some writers that they believe they do not choose
their literary landscape but are chosen by it.

Perhaps Joseph Conrad began to feel "called" when as a little boy in Poland he announced that he would one day go to the heart of Africa.

It was in 1868, when nine years old or thereabouts, that while looking at a map of Africa of the time and putting my finger on the black space then representing the unsolved mystery of that continent, I said to myself with absolute assurance and an amazing audacity which are no longer in my character now:
"When I grow up I shall go *there*."
And of course I thought no more about it till after a quarter of a century or so an opportunity offered to go there—as if the sin of childish audacity was to be visited on my mature head.

*A Personal Record*, Joseph Conrad

The child looked at the map and told himself, "I shall go *there*." The man later took the trip to the Congo, worked his way into the continent, made monotonous marches, and contracted an illness that had much to do with forging his destiny and turning him into a novelist. The experience in Africa affected him so acutely that material for some of his most powerful stories evolved from his stay in the region he had chosen from a map as a boy and later, in the deepest psychic sense, had been chosen by.

It is an experience common to writers to be fascinated by what you might call a *there* region to which they have been attracted through their imagination in early life. Later they visit the country, absorb its atmosphere, and reproduce it in a focus of their own. In *Of Human Bondage,* Somerset Maugham describes how this experience came to Philip Carey, a boy who resembles Maugham himself.

The lonely Philip, living in the house of his selfish uncle and ineffectual aunt, comes one day on a translation of *The Thousand Nights and a Night*. The boy is delighted by the tales of the East, as he was delighted earlier by the pictures his aunt had shown him of the bazaars, Arabs, camels of an Eastern town. For Philip, as for Maugham, books became a bulwark against the distress of real life and at the same time a beacon for a new world.

During his long writing career Maugham travelled to many

narrow corners of the earth and often described the exotic East instead of his native England. For you as for Maugham, it is important to make the people of any story you write believable in the region in which you place them. The boundary lines for character movement can be fixed only by the writer who has travelled his territory in advance until he knows every inch of the way.

Place may be *here, there,* or even *anywhere,* but in every story that fulfills its author's intent place has its own reality in the reader's mind. Edgar Allan Poe's famous black and lurid tarn that lay in unruffled luster until its waters closed over the doomed House of Usher is not on any map but readers relate it to country through which they have travelled, if only in the mind. Franz Kafka, writing symbolic fiction, creates places that are everywhere and nowhere. There is also a kind of fantasy that employs an imaginary setting but grafts it onto commonplace landmarks. This last is true of E. M. Forster's fine story of a boy who took a bus to Heaven.

At the level of ordinary reality, the locale of "The Celestial Omnibus" is the home of a lad who resides at Agathox Lodge, 28, Buckingham Park Road, Surbiton. The boy, though, is caught up into a reality of a different sort, the personal reality of imagination and wonder. On the bus he moves from the one reality into the other, taking a trip over unknown chasms before he arrives safely at journey's end. Scene is given special significance by the fact that the boy on the bus travels through a literary landscape that is recognizable to him but completely unreal to his fellow passenger, Mr. Bons.

... the omnibus had reached the summit of a moonlit hill, and there was the chasm, and there, across it, stood the old precipices, dreaming, with their feet in the everlasting river. He exclaimed, "The mountain! Listen to the new tune in the water! Look at the camp fires in the ravines," and Mr. Bons, after a hasty glance, retorted, "Water? Camp fires? Ridiculous rubbish. Hold your tongue. There is nothing at all."

Yet under his eyes a rainbow formed, compounded not of sunlight and storm, but of moonlight and the spray of the river. The three horses put their feet upon it. He thought it the finest rainbow he had seen, but did not dare to say so, since Mr. Bons said that nothing was there.

This is a country the boy sees and the reader sees, only because Mr. Forster himself knows it. The scene evolves from literature, from the books, the novels, the myths, the poetry, that had been chosen by the writer when he was young. In "The Celestial Omnibus" the author is recreating his own favorite landscape. Although his *place* is spun of fantasy, Mr. Forster is following the old advice to "write about what you know."

But, as one student asked, "How do I find out what *I* know?" Before finding his province a writer may have to go over a lot of unfamiliar ground in order to get back home. There is no "best" way to determine your own fictional territory, but there are some ways of finding out what you do know about *place* and how you can use this knowledge in your writing. We can start by describing a *here* setting.

Begin with a region you know well and care for deeply. You may object that you care for a good many places. When you have had more experience as a writer and are perhaps working on a novel, you may use a number of the locales familiar to you, but now when you are beginning to write why don't you choose one place arbitrarily and concentrate on that? It can be a street, a room, a house, a campus, a town, or a field near the town. It should be a locale you would recognize even if you were blind, and you should have a slant that makes the landscape peculiarly your own.

## MAPPING A FAMILIAR LOCALE: Assignment 3

Write not less than 500 words, selecting for use in your sketch the salient physical features of a school or a street, or a town in which you have lived. Or you may choose to describe a rural landscape. Do not emphasize character, or action, but *place*. Remember that although you are using recognizable detail your main intent is to saturate your work with the spirit of the place about which you have chosen to write.

After you have done your assignment compare what you have written with "River Bank," included below. This uncorrected sketch is written—or overwritten—in an impressionistic manner rather than as a piece of straight description. Notice how the student misuses the word "pregnant" in saying that the tree is "pregnant with Spanish moss." Notice that the author is "setting" on the river bank. Notice, too, the many similes the writer employs: the moss "like an old lady's hair," the remote lights that wink "off and on like a lightning bug sending Morse code," the boats "bobbing up and down like apples in a barrel." The quarters are far too close for so much imagery.

## RIVER BANK

D. V.

A fish jumped lazily on the smooth-surfaced Trent River. The sun hung hesitantly on the lower lip of the horizon, ready to be swallowed up for another day. The sun glinted off the surface of the river, sending its orange-yellow rays shooting into space. Setting on the river bank leaning against a massive cyprus tree pregnant with Spanish moss, I looked about me at this panoramous stage of nature.

To my left was the marsh grass looking like inverted swords interspersed with smooth brown cyprus knees. Pools of green algae played silently at the junction of the grass and the water. In the distance I could see a wooden pier. Two boys were in the water beside the pier, taking their final swim before darkness. At the foot of the pier and all along the shore line were more cyprus trees, garnished with the gray Spanish moss hanging almost to the surface of the water. The moss looked like an old lady's hair before it is rolled up.

Ahead of me a remote light winked off and on like a lightening bug sending Morse code. Several boats dotted the opposite shore line, bobbing up and down like apples in a barrel. The giant cyprus trees were reflected in the mirror-like water. Here and there a fish leaped from the water, suspended for a moment between earth and sky, before slipping again into its aquatic haven. Its readmittance into the water transmitted concentric circles shimmering in every direction.

To my right were more cyprus trees and marsh grass. Only now it was becoming dark. The marsh grass was silhouetted against the water, looking like a black picket fence against a gray house. A bull

or more, the tint has lightened to the tender young green of spring; the cape beyond that one has almost lost color, and the furthest one, miles away under the horizon, sleeps upon the water a mere dim vapor, and hardly separable from the sky above it and about it. And all this stretch of river is a mirror, and you have the shadowy reflections of the leafage and the curving shores and the receding capes pictured in it. Well, that is all beautiful; soft and rich and beautiful; and when the sun gets well up, and distributes a pink flush here and a powder of gold yonder and a purple haze where it will yield the best effect, you grant that you have seen something that is worth remembering.

## From THE ADVENTURES OF HUCKLEBERRY FINN

MARK TWAIN

It was a monstrous big river down there—sometimes a mile and a half wide; we run nights, and laid up and hid daytimes; soon as night was most gone we stopped navigating and tied up—nearly always in the dead water under a towhead; and then cut young cottonwoods and willows, and hid the raft with them. Then we set out the lines. Next we slid into the river and had a swim, so as to freshen up and cool off; then we set down on the sandy bottom where the water was about knee-deep, and watched the daylight come. Not a sound anywheres—perfectly still—just like the whole world was asleep, only sometimes the bullfrogs a-cluttering, maybe. The first thing to see, looking away over the water, was a kind of dull line—that was the woods on t'other side; you couldn't make nothing else out; then a pale place in the sky; then more paleness spreading around; then the river softened up away off, and warn't black any more, but gray; you could see little dark spots drifting along ever so far away —trading-scows, and such things, and long black streaks—rafts; sometimes you could hear a sweep screaking; or jumbled-up voices, it was so still, and sounds come so far; and by and by you could see a streak on the water which you know by the look of the streak that there's a snag there in a swift current which breaks on it and makes that streak look that way; and you see the mist curl up off of the water, and the east reddens up, and the river, and you make out a log cabin in the edge of the woods, away on the bank on t'other side of the river, being a woodyard, likely, and piled by them cheats so you can throw a dog through it anywheres; then the nice breeze springs up, and comes fanning you from over there, so cool and fresh and sweet to smell on account of the woods and the flowers; but sometimes not that way, because they've left dead fish laying around, gars and such, and they do get pretty rank; and next you've got the full day, and everything smiling in the sun, and the song-birds just going it!

In reading the passages included here from Twain, you will see that the rhythm of the writing does not vary perceptibly. Your clue to where the writer departs from fact and starts telling a story lies in his choice of point-of-view, in the reaction of the observer to what he sees. We always go back to people. Huck's personality gives the fictional scene a more intensely personal tone than the one from the river book, but over both passages lies the brooding spirit of place.

In *Huckleberry Finn*, sometimes called the book from which all modern American literature comes, scene is only one part of the whole novel, and like all great books this one is more than the sum of its parts. In the simplest analysis, it is a story about two runaways on a river, travelling through a region of our country that the author knew by heart. For an exercise, try placing a character of your own in a region you know well. Concentrate again on *place*, but this time add to it a person in motion. Let your character, like Huck, travel a little over ground you as a writer have made your own.

## THE EFFECT OF PLACE ON A CHARACTER:   Assignment 4

Pick a river, a mountain path, or a country road as a locale and try to communicate a sense of isolation, of mystery. Start at the instant the narrator discovers that he does not know his way home. See if you can recreate for your reader each step the "I" takes until he comes on a landmark he recognizes. After writing your assignment, read the following selection from "Bezhin Meadow," by Ivan Turgenev.

. . . I was shooting blackcock in the district of Chern, in the government of Tula. I had found and shot a fair quantity of game; a bulging game-bag cut mercilessly into my shoulder; but the sunset glow was already dying down, and in the air, still light, although no longer flushed with the rays of the vanished sun, cold shadows were beginning to deepen and to spread, when at last I decided to return home. At a quick pace I passed through a long brake of under-growth, climbed a hill and, instead of the familiar plateau which I expected, with a clump of oaks to the right and a little white church in the distance, I saw a completely different, unknown landscape. Below my feet ran a narrow valley; immediately opposite, a dense wood of poplar rose in a steep wall. I stopped in perplexity and looked round. . . . Aha! I thought, I've come out in quite the wrong place, I've struck too far to the right; and, amazed at my own mis-take, I went swiftly down the hill. . . . I thought to myself, I shall strike the track at once; but I've gone a good mile out of my way.

Eventually I reached the corner of the wood, but found no sign of any track there: stunted, straggling undergrowth stretched far and wide before me, and behind it, away in the distance, could be seen an empty plain. I halted again. What an extraordinary thing. . . . Where on earth was I? What I had taken for a wood turned out to be a dark, round hillock. . . . "Then where on earth am I?" I re-peated again, aloud, halted for the third time, and looked inquiringly at my piebald-yellow gun-dog Dianka, decidedly the cleverest of all the four-legged creation. But the cleverest of all the four-legged creation only wagged its tail, gave a sad twinkle of its tired eyes and had no sort of practical advice to offer. I felt ashamed in front of it, and set off ahead in desperation, as if I had suddenly guessed which way to go, skirted the hill, and found myself in a gentle hollow in the midst of cultivation. A strange feeling immediately came over me. The hollow was like an almost symmetrical cauldron with slop-ing sides. At the bottom of it rose, bolt upright, several large white stones, which seemed to have crept down there for a secret con-clave, and the whole place had such a deaf-and-dumb feeling, the sky hung so flatly and gloomily above it, that my heart shrank. Some little creature was squeaking faintly and plaintively among the stones. I hastily came out again on to the hillock. Hitherto I had not given up all hope of finding the way home; but here I finally con-vinced myself that I was completely lost and, no longer attempting to recognize the surrounding landscape, which was almost completely sunk in darkness, boldly set a straight course by the stars. . . . I went on in this way for about half an hour, plodding forward with diffi-culty. It seemed to me that I had never been in such a desert in all my life; there was not a twinkle of light to be seen, not a sound to be heard. One sloping hill succeeded another, fields stretched end-lessly one after another, bushes fairly started up from the earth under my nose. I was still walking, and already preparing to lie down somewhere until morning came, when suddenly I felt myself on the edge of a fearful precipice.

I quickly withdrew my foot in mid-air, and, through the hardly penetrable darkness of the night, I made out, far below me, an enormous plain. A broad river bounded it in a receding arc; steely gleams of water, flashing faintly here and there, marked its course. The hill on which I was standing dropped sharply in an almost perpendicular cliff; its massive outline showed up blackly against the bluishness of the airy void, and just below me, in the angle of cliff and plain, beside the river, which at this point stood in a dark and motionless mirror, right at the foot of the hill, two fires close beside each other were blazing redly and smoking. Around them, people were stirring, shadows were swaying, and sometimes the front half of a curly head was brightly illuminated. . . .

At last I recognized where I was.

Turgenev presents his narrator obliquely so that we never see the hunter's face or body, only his bag of game. But through this physically shadowy figure we respond to the region in which he exists. We notice the changes in the undergrowth, the broad river bounding in a receding arc, and the steely gleams of the water under the darkening sky. Like the hunter, we want to get to shelter but in the same moment we are aware of the mysterious beauty of our surroundings. What of the character in your own sketch? Is he truly a figure in your landscape? Can we stay with him all the way?

In writing about a person in a place, you have used a *here* setting, but once you have discovered your own territory and staked out your ground, you can change the relative position of the setting as you please. You can use a *here*, a *there*, or an *anywhere* place, either as a background for your characters or as an actor in their story. But remember again that although we have been treating place as though it stands by itself, the region you write about must always be part of a whole communication.

# 3

# Observing Your Material

An observer is someone who sees, listens, and records without actually participating in what is happening around him. In maintaining his role he stays above the anger, the sorrow, the laughter, and the pleasures of the crowd. In one sense, every writer is an observer. Whatever else he may be—and he is much else—part of him is standing back and watching. From what he sees, the writer begins to create his fictional reality.

The imaginative writer can make an entire fictional world out of the one he sees around him. He often uses not only his eyes but all his sensory perceptions, as in *Look Homeward, Angel* where Thomas Wolfe describes how a whole background of color, warmth, odor, sound, and taste established itself never to leave him. But first he sees.

A writer may observe through what he reads, viewing his people and their backgrounds through the medium of books, as Thornton Wilder did in *The Bridge of San Luis Rey*, whose setting was eighteenth-century Peru. Wilder wrote of a country he knew through reading of an incident that occurred there in 1717. More often a writer will look at a locale in which he has lived and then use it as he needs it. Edith Wharton, for example, did this in *Ethan Frome*.

In speaking of her short novel of people in a cramped New England village, Mrs. Wharton says that one literary critic used the story as an example of a successful tale about the Berkshires written by someone who knew nothing about the region. Mrs. Wharton adds that she had spent ten years in that part of New England and knew thoroughly the hill country she chose to write about. The following passage from *Ethan Frome* shows how accurately she had visualized the scene.

The village lay under two feet of snow, with drifts at the windy corners. In a sky of iron the points of the Dipper hung like icicles and Orion flashed his cold fires. The moon had set, but the night was so transparent that the white house-fronts between the elms looked gray against the snow, clumps of bushes made black stains on it, and the basement windows of the church sent shafts of yellow light far across the endless undulations.

As Ethan Frome walks along the deserted street and into the vision of the reader, the central part of the story gets under way. Mrs. Wharton has observed the frigid winter night, the white fronts of the houses, and the endless undulations of snow on the hills beyond town. Having found exactly the right frame for her story, she goes on to set up her conflict, basing the tragedy on the mental and moral attitudes of the New England people with whom she was familiar.

One of the coldest environments in any story emerges in Conrad Aiken's "Silent Snow, Secret Snow," a tale of a profound psychological change in a boy. We do not know how the story first took shape in Aiken's mind, but the vast screen of snow is so real we are tempted to believe Aiken went out and plowed through an actual blizzard before he invented a fictional one. The disturbed boy, lying in bed, is overwhelmed by the whiteness closing in on him. He thinks:

And even now it must be snowing—it was going to be a snowy day—the long white ragged lines were drifting and sifting across the street, across the faces of the old houses, whispering and hushing, making little triangles of white in the corners between the cobblestones, seething a little when the wind blew them over the ground to a drifted corner; and so it would be all day, getting deeper and deeper and silenter and silenter.

As it happens, there is no snow at all that day. The boy opens his eyes and looks through the window, wanting to hide in a secret corner where the soothing snow can cover him. Instead, he sees bright sunlight on a street paved with cobblestones. No matter—the watcher knows only the inner world of falling flakes. The reader, too, is conscious of the silent, secret snow, and of a boy travelling into a white curve of space. Conrad

Aiken has closely observed the world of illusion. He has spied out the white country of death.

You, as a writer, must spy on your own characters and their territory. Your task, like Aiken's, is to see more clearly, to observe more deeply, and to focus your sight more exactly than other men do. Even in the moment of experiencing, you always have to be on the lookout for what may be of use to you later when, as a writer, you sweep back over the scenes and characters you have known, choosing those that suit your story best.

This special sort of observing cannot be learned from any teacher. You already know that your obligation as a writer is to watch what happens around you, to select what you can use, and to use it in a way that marks it as yours alone. In a beginning writer, learning to see is a conscious effort. Later, you will become an unconscious recorder, choosing by instinct what can be useful to you and adding it to what you already know.

Like other people, writers differ in what they see. Training, habit, and even the quality of a person's eyesight go into what a given author uses in a finished story. Joyce Cary, who started out as a painter, sees in vivid colors, and his characters imitate him. Cary's novel, *The Horse's Mouth*, opens with Gulley Jimson, the painter, watching the Thames on an autumn day.

The sun had crackled into flames at the top; the mist was getting thin in places, you could see crooked lines of grey, like old cracks under spring ice. Tide on the turn. Snake broken up. Emeralds and sapphires. Water like varnish with bits of gold leaf floating thick and heavy. Gold is the metal of intellect. And all at once the sun burned through a new place at the side, and shot out a ray that hit the Eagle and Child, next the motorboat factory, right on the new signboard.

Jimson never stops looking, whether it is at a barmaid's arm or at the blank wall that calls out to be splashed with colors. At the end of the book, when the wall crashes, he still watches with that marvelous eyesight of the artist. Or rather, it is the eyesight given to this particular artist, for nobody else has ever known a London exactly like Gulley Jimson's where the stars sparkle like electric cars and the river is the color of pig iron.

Sometimes a writer makes a virtue of a limitation, as James Joyce does in *A Portrait of the Artist as a Young Man*, where he gives his fictional counterpart, Stephen Dedalus, a faulty eyesight like his own. As a result, Dedalus puts emphasis on the inner world of emotions and the attempt to mirror them in sound. The observed world disappears and words take its place in Stephen's mind.

—A day of dappled seaborne clouds.—
The phrase and the day and the scene harmonized in a chord. Words. Was it their colours? He allowed them to glow and fade, hue after hue: sunrise gold, the russet and green of apple orchards, azure of waves, the grey fringed fleece of clouds. No, it was not their colours: it was the poise and balance of the period itself. Did he then love the rhythmic rise and fall of words better than their association of legend and colour? Or was it that, being weak of sight as he was shy of mind, he drew less pleasure from the reflection of the glowing sensible world through the prism of language manycoloured and rightly storied than from the contemplation of an inner world of individual emotions mirrored perfectly in a lucid supple periodic prose?

Some writers have a keen objective vision and at the same time are compelled from within to look at the world as if they are seeing it for the first time, or are watching it just after they have given themselves up to death and then been allowed to return reborn. In an essay on D. H. Lawrence, Aldous Huxley comments on Lawrence's gift of seeing the world all new and of being able to reveal what he saw.

He looked at things with the eyes, so it seemed, of a man who had been at the brink of death and to whom, as he emerges from the darkness, the world reveals itself as unfathomably beautiful and mysterious. For Lawrence, existence was one continuous convalescence; it was as though he were newly reborn from a mortal illness every day of his life. What these convalescent eyes saw, his most casual speech would reveal. A walk with him in the country was a walk through that marvelously rich and significant landscape which is at once the background and principal personage of all his novels.

As Huxley points out, Lawrence revealed what he saw, not only in casual talk, but in the whole range of his books, in which

his observations are as fresh now as on the day he first wrote
them down. There is no substitute for a talent like Lawrence's,
but you, as a writer, can develop your own talent for seeing.
*Spying on your material* is the first step in learning to use what
you see as an essential part of a narrative pattern.

## RECORDING WHAT YOU SEE:   Assignment 5

Glance through the window nearest to you and then, without reflection, write down what you see. Take no more than two minutes for
your writing and confine what you say to one sentence.

A group of students in a writing class were asked to record in
a single sentence what they saw on the campus outside their
classroom window. It was clear from what they wrote that a
talent for words may shine through, even in a few words. It
was also clear that some of the students were already beginning
to see people and a landscape as material for a story. After reading what the students wrote, ask yourself whether your own
sentence contains material you can use later in a scene.

The first thing that attracts my attention as I look out of the
window is a pretty, dark-haired coed who is just contemplating
whether the campus will be as big a party as she has heard.

It's early fall, cold yet green, not fresh just green, almost bleak
but for the silly people and the cool personal green.

As I look out the window I see a large irregular cavity in a tree
and am now wondering where it leads.

Outside the window blur the passing figures against a slow erratic
backdrop of dull green.

Outside I see parts of trees, parts of buildings, parts of sky, but
mostly I see people—going different places, doing different things,
and having various goals within their specific walks of life: I always
am curious about people.

I see a happily ignorant, overalled yard man mowing the lawn
sleek students throw their trash on.

Through the panes and glass, I see large trees and smaller trees, large students and smaller students, a yard man, a mower, and spraying grass.

The trees and lawn form a perfect campus picture, marred only by the slashes of the window frames which distort my view.

Some of these compressed observations contain suggestions for sketches. The pretty, dark-haired coed who is just contemplating what her life on campus may be can walk into a party that is far more exciting than any she has anticipated. The "overalled yard man" also lends himself to a situation. He may resent a sleepy student throwing trash on the lawn that he is mowing and through his resentment be forced into action, thus becoming a character in a story that had its start in a glance through a window.

The students quoted here were doing no more than writing a very brief assignment. They recorded what they saw at the moment because someone told them to do it. But there is a part of the mind that records unasked and keeps unbidden what is important to a watcher. We may keep in our mind's eye the sight of a sunset from last summer, or the fright that appears in a person's face after a street accident, or the brown, swollen look of a drowned man's body. H. S. read Ernest Hemingway's comments on learning how to write of violence without physically or mentally shutting your eyes and then wrote the following sketch about a body he had seen.

## THE BODY

H. S.

We drove down the hard surfaced road for about two miles and then turned onto a dirt track. When my father stopped the car we all walked silently away from the road and through the tall grass of the river bottom. Ahead we saw men standing on the sandy bank. The men just stood there, hardly daring to speak. One of them had his hands pushed deep into the pockets of his overalls. The only sound was the slow, lazy, quiet movement of the river slipping by and now and then the rustle of the willow trees as a light breeze went through them.

Then I saw it. Across the river at the point where another stream entered was a black tangle of brush which had come to rest against a log. Lying near the bank, face down and half submerged in the muddy water was the body. A boat came into sight and two men jumped into waist deep water, putting a rope under the arms. The men climbed into the boat and began to row to our side of the river, dragging the rope behind them. They moved to the shallows where they could easily lift the body onto a waiting stretcher. When the boat was only a few feet from me, I went nearer and half hid and half peeked from behind a willow tree.

The body was all swollen. I thought about the big, fat ticks I used to pull from my dog's ears. The tan of the boy's back was even darker because of the stain from the muddy river. Huge patches of skin were peeling off, revealing a sickening white underneath. The ears were all puffed up and stood out from the head. The hair was ragged and caked with silt. When they lifted the body from the water, more of the skin came loose, slid back into the water, and was swallowed up in its ugliness.

I couldn't look any more. I turned my face away from the river, stumbling through the mass of men's legs surrounding me, and ran along the river bottom to the car, almost stifled by the choking feeling in my throat. When my father got in beside me, we drove home to the store in silence. I stumbled from the car to the front of the store yard, sat down under a tree, and looked at the sky. *I won't think about it*, I told myself. *It's too ugly*. But I did think about it.


## REPORTING A SIGHT:  Assignment 6

In a paper of not more than 500 words, report a sight you have observed. Choose the glimpse you had of a car wreck, or your remembrance of the face of a person you saw at a party. Follow H. S.'s lead in concentrating on what you saw. Limit yourself to a pattern of selected details that will enable the reader to see with you.


After you have done your assignment, read the following passage from W. Somerset Maugham's story, "The Book-Bag," in which the writer-narrator describes the process of recalling a face from the depths of his mind. He had to form a picture of a man named Tim Hardy whom he had seen only once. The first thing that came to mind was Hardy's hands. But because the habit of years had enabled the writer-narrator to store up observations, he was able to give an accurate portrait of the man.

The impression may very well be more exact than the sober truth. And now, seeking to call up from the depths of me a picture of this man I had a feeling of some ambiguity. He was cleanshaven and his face, oval but not thin, seemed strangely pale under the tan of long exposure to the tropical sun. His features were vague. I did not know whether I remembered it or only imagined now that his rounded chin gave one the impression of a certain weakness. He had thick brown hair, just turning grey, and a long wisp fell down constantly over his forehead. He pushed it back with a gesture that had become habitual. His brown eyes were rather large and gentle, but perhaps a little sad; they had a melting softness which, I could imagine, might be very appealing.

Maugham himself, like his character who conjured up the face of Tim Hardy, knew how to remember what he saw. But as many writers do, he kept *A Writer's Notebook* as a repository for much that he saw and heard. It is a chronicle of a complex personality's responses to the world, withholding almost as much about Maugham's private life as it reveals, although it tells us a great deal about how Maugham looked at places and people and how he later used what he saw.

The river is broad, yellow and turbid. At the back of the sandy shore grow the casuarinas, and when the breeze stirs their lace-like foliage they make a sound as of people talking. The natives call them talking trees and say that if you stand under them at midnight you will hear voices of unknown people telling you the secrets of the earth.

A green hill. The jungle reached to its crest, an intoxication of verdure, and the luxuriousness was such that it left you breathless and embarrassed. It was a symphony of green, as though a composer working in colour instead of with sound had sought to express something extraordinarily subtle in a barbaric medium. The greens ranged from the pallor of the aquamarine to the profundity of jade. There was an emerald that blared like a trumpet and a pale sage that trembled like a flute.

The yellow river under the breathless sun of midday had the white pallor of death. A native was paddling upstream in a frail dug-out so small that it hardly showed above the surface of the water. On the banks of the river, here and there, were Malay houses on their piles.

Toward evening a flight of egrets flew down the river, flying low, and scattered. They were like a ripple of white notes, sweet and pure and springlike, which an unseen hand drew forth, like a divine arpeggio, from an unseen harp.

S. A boy of eighteen who has just come out. A rather good-looking youth, with blue eyes and curly chestnut hair that grows thickly on his neck. He is trying to grow a moustache. He has a charming smile with him. He is ingenuous and *naïf*. He has the enthusiasm of youth and the mannerisms of a cavalry officer.

The mangrove swamp. Along the coast and at the mouth of the river grow mangroves and nipah. The nipah is a long-leafed dwarf palm, like those palms which in old pictures you see carried on Palm Sunday. They grow at the water's edge, reclaiming the soil, and when they have made fresh, fruitful earth they die down and the jungle takes their place. They are the pioneers preparing the country for the traders and the motley crowd of humanity that come after them.

The Sarawak River. The mouth is very broad. On each side are mangrove and nipah washed by the water and behind the dense green of the jungle, and in the distance, darkly silhouetted against the blue sky, the rugged outline of a mountain. You have no sense of gloom, of being shut in, but of space and freedom. The green glitters in the sunshine and the sky is blithe and cheerful. You seem to enter upon a friendly, fertile land.

This is an orderly record of impressions, no doubt useful when Maugham came to writing a story like "The Book-Bag" and could see again through his jottings the sights and the people he wanted to recreate in a Malay setting. A very different kind of record was kept by F. Scott Fitzgerald who accumulated many notes and later arranged them so that they make good reading in themselves. The charm of these notes lies in passages like the following, chosen at random and carrying the imprint of the Twenties as Fitzgerald saw them.

She was not more than eighteen—a dark little beauty with the fine crystal gloss over her that, in brunettes, takes the place of a blond's bright glow.

A taxi tipping over on a nervous night.

She stood there in the middle of an enormous quiet. The pursuing feet that had thundered in her dream had stopped. There was a steady, singing silence.

A thin young man walking in a blue coat that was like a pipe.

Story of a man trying to live down his crazy past and encountering it everywhere.

The club lay in a little valley, almost roofed over by willows, and down through their black silhouettes, in irregular blobs and patches, dripped the light of a huge harvest moon. As they parked the car, Basil's tune of tunes, *Chinatown*, drifted from the windows and dissolved into its notes, which thronged like elves through the glade.

Out of these notes, Fitzgerald may have found an idea for a plot, a clue for what he wanted to do with a character at a party, or a suggestion for a variation on the golden girl he used so often in his writing. The blond's bright glow falls on Fitzgerald's heroines—Daisy Buchanan and Judy Jones. In writing down what he saw, and selecting from among his notes, he was taking the first necessary step in formulating a scene like the one that follows from his story, "Winter Dreams."

Later in the afternoon the sun went down with a riotous swirl of gold and varying blues and scarlets, and left the dry, rustling night of Western summer. Dexter watched from the veranda of the Golf Club, watched the even overlap of the waters in the little wind, silver molasses under the harvest-moon. Then the moon held a finger to her lips and the lake became a clear pool, pale and quiet. Dexter put on his bathing-suit and swam out to the farthest raft, where he stretched dripping on the wet canvas of the springboard.

There was a fish jumping and a star shining and the lights around the lake were gleaming. Over on a dark peninsula a piano was playing the songs of last summer and of summers before that—songs from "Chin-Chin" and "The Count of Luxemburg" and "The Chocolate Soldier"—and because the sound of a piano over a stretch of water had always seemed beautiful to Dexter he lay perfectly quiet and listened.

The tune the piano was playing at that moment had been gay and new five years before when Dexter was a sophomore at college. They had played it at a prom once when he could not afford the luxury of proms, and he had stood outside the gymnasium and listened. The sound of the tune precipitated in him a sort of ecstasy and it was with that ecstasy he viewed what happened to him now. It was a mood of intense appreciation, a sense that, for once, he was magnificiently attune to life and that everything about him was radiating a brightness and a glamour he might never know again.

A low, pale oblong detached itself suddenly from the darkness of the Island, spitting forth the reverberate sound of a racing motorboat. Two white streamers of cleft water rolled themselves out behind it and almost immediately the boat was beside him, drowning out the hot tinkle of the piano in the drone of its spray. Dexter raising himself on his arms was aware of a figure standing at the wheel, of two dark eyes regarding him over the lengthening space of water—then the boat had gone by and was sweeping in an immense and purposeless circle of spray round and round in the middle of the lake. With equal eccentricity one of the circles flattened out and headed back toward the raft.

"Who's that?" she called, shutting off her motor. She was so near now that Dexter could see her bathing-suit, which consisted apparently of pink rompers.

The nose of the boat bumped the raft, and as the latter tilted rakishly he was precipitated toward her. With different degrees of interest they recognized each other.

"Aren't you one of those men we played through this afternoon?" she demanded.

He was.

"Well, do you know how to drive a motor-boat? Because if you do I wish you'd drive this one so I can ride on the surf-board behind. My name is Judy Jones"—she favored him with an absurd smirk—rather, what tried to be a smirk, for, twist her mouth as she might, it was not grotesque, it was merely beautiful—"and I live in a house over there on the Island, and in that house there is a man waiting for me. When he drove up at the door I drove out of the dock because he says I'm his ideal."

There was a fish jumping and a star shining and the lights around the lake were gleaming. Dexter sat beside Judy Jones and she explained how her boat was driven. Then she was in the water, swimming to the floating surf-board with a sinuous crawl. Watching her was without effort to the eye, watching a branch waving or a seagull flying. Her arms, burned to butternut, moved sinuously among the dull platinum ripples, elbow appearing first, casting the forearm back with a cadence of falling water, then reaching out and down, stabbing a path ahead.

They moved out into the lake; turning, Dexter saw that she was kneeling on the low rear of the now uptilted surf-board.

"Go faster," she called, "fast as it'll go."

Obediently he jammed the lever forward and the white spray mounted at the bow. When he looked around again the girl was standing up on the rushing board, her arms spread wide, her eyes lifted toward the moon.

"It's awful cold," she shouted. "What's your name?"

He told her.

"Well, why don't you come to dinner to-morrow night?"

His heart turned over like the fly-wheel of the boat, and, for the second time, her casual whim gave a new direction to his life.


## VISUALIZING A SCENE:   Assignment 7

Write an incident centered around a boy's reaction when he meets a girl. It does not have to be a romantic scene like Fitzgerald's. Choose any subject you like, concentrating on visualizing a character in a landscape. Compare your scene with Fitzgerald's and try to analyze how well you have begun to use *seeing* as an element in a story.

"Winter Dreams" takes its tone from the night on the raft, which gives Dexter Green's life a new direction. But there is much more here than tone. Fitzgerald has watched so closely, and reported so imaginatively, that his raft, this star, this girl, could not have been other than what they are in "Winter Dreams." He has seen his material in exactly the way Flaubert told his protegé de Maupassant a writer should see.

Everything you want to express must be considered so long, and so attentively, as to enable you to find some aspect of it which no one has yet seen and expressed. There is an unexplored side to everything, because we are wont never to use our eyes but with the memory of what others before us have thought of the things we see. The smallest thing has something unknown in it; we must find it. To describe a blazing fire, a tree in a plain, we must stand face to face with that fire or that tree, till to us they are wholly unlike any other fire or tree. Thus we may become original.

Then, having established the truth that there are not in the whole world two grains of sand, two flies, two hands, or two noses absolutely alike, he would make me describe in a few sentences some person or object, in such a way as to define it exactly, and distinguish it from every other of the same race or species.

But it is not enough simply to follow Flaubert's advice to observe some person or object and then define it exactly. Fitzgerald does that for the girl moving among dull platinum ripples, but in the design of his story he does more than that. Fiction is more than just seeing, and we have to consider many factors before a story or a novel is what we want it to be. But as a writer first you look, then you write.

## 4

# Ways of Creating Characters

First you look, and as a writer you usually look at people. You may glance at them as they pass by or you may draw them from your remembrance. They may flicker into life from a hint dropped to you in casual talk. They may seem to appear to you by sorcery, or to be reborn from myth. No matter how you find them, where you place them in time, or what their final appearance in your finished narrative is, the people you project to your reader are the heart of a story.

For as we know, a narrative has its start, its climax, and its ending with characters in a situation. A boy may meet a girl, lose a girl, and afterwards find her again. A central character may grow up in a novel, taking the reader with him through crucial moments of his development until he becomes mature. There are many variations in the fictional situation. As for manner or style of writing, a poetic novelist like Thomas Wolfe may preface his story with words about objects—"*a stone, a leaf, an unfound door*"—but he leads us from the door into the buried life of his central character, Eugene Gant.

You may, as many writers do, look first at yourself and then at others, trying to make your finished narrative a record of your personal response to environment, embracing many aspects of your experience. If this is your purpose, any story you write will start as autobiography. Unless you are able to go beyond the facts about yourself and give your people their proper fictional dress, your work will remain a record, never achieving the harmonious structure of a story.

How does a writer give his characters life? What is a writer's way with people? One novelist says he takes real men and women and writes them into the situations they deserve. Another claims that he discovered some relatives who lent themselves well to fiction so he let them run with him in his books. In defending himself against the charge of writing autobiography rather than fiction, Thomas Wolfe tells F. Scott Fitzgerald how one creates, selects, and fulfills an artistic purpose.

Wolfe writes:

Now you have your way of doing something and I have mine, there are a lot of ways, but you are honestly mistaken in thinking that there is a "way." I suppose I would agree with you in what you say about "the novel of selected incident" so far as it means anything. I say so far as it means anything because every novel, of course, is a novel of selected incident. There are no novels of unselected incident. You couldn't write about the inside of a telephone booth without selecting it. . . . I want to be a better artist. I want to be a more selective artist. I want to be a more restrained artist. I want to use such talent as I have, control such forces as I may own, direct such energy as I may use more cleanly, more surely and to better purpose.

Before he died, Thomas Wolfe learned to use such forces as he owned and to give us a mountain range of magnificent characters who outgrew the people upon whom they were modeled to the extent that the models sometimes seemed to be copying the traits of the people in Wolfe's books. Mrs. Julia Wolfe, for instance, often seemed in actual life trying to become Eliza Gant, attempting to live up to the illumination her son had given her in finding his own "way."

Wolfe controlled his talent too, in learning to write prose as poignant and effective as any that ever came from an American novelist. But without his characters his novels would pale, just as the story you are writing will remain a semblance of fiction unless you can create people who demand attention and evoke sympathy.

Few novelists have been more successful in writing out of autobiography than Betty Smith when she created Francie Nolan, the central character of *A Tree Grows in Brooklyn*. Miss Smith took her material from her early life, starting with her childhood, but in the process of writing she gave Francie a fictional dimension that made her a person on her own. The Christmas tree incident from the novel is reprinted here. Miss

Smith then adds comments on her "way" of converting a life experience into fiction.

# From A TREE GROWS IN BROOKLYN
BETTY SMITH

The spruce trees began coming into the neighborhood the week before Christmas. Their branches were corded to hold back the glory of their spreading and probably to make shipping easier. Vendors rented space on the curb before a store and stretched a rope from pole to pole and leaned the trees against it. All day they walked up and down this one-sided avenue of aromatic leaning trees, blowing on stiff ungloved fingers and looking with bleak hope at those people who paused. A few ordered a tree set aside for the day; others stopped to price, inspect and conjecture. But most came just to touch the boughs and surreptitiously pinch a fingerful of spruce needles together to release the fragrance. And the air was cold and still, and full of the pine smell and the smell of tangerines which appeared in the stores only at Christmas time and the mean street was truly wonderful for a little while.

There was a cruel custom in the neighborhood. It was about the trees still unsold when midnight of Christmas Eve approached. There was a saying that if you waited until then, you wouldn't have to buy a tree; that "they'd chuck 'em at you." This was literally true.

At midnight on the Eve of our dear Saviour's birth, the kids gathered where there were unsold trees. The man threw each tree in turn, starting with the biggest. Kids volunteered to stand up against the throwing. If a boy didn't fall down under the impact, the tree was his. If he fell, he forfeited his chance at winning a tree. Only the roughest boys and some of the young men elected to be hit by the big trees. The others waited shrewdly until a tree came up that they could stand against. The littlest kids waited for the tiny, foot-high trees and shrieked in delight when they won one.

On the Christmas Eve when Francie was ten and Neeley nine, mama consented to let them go down and have their first try for a tree. Francie had picked out her tree earlier in the day. She had stood near it all afternoon and evening praying that no one would buy it. To her joy, it was still there at midnight. It was the biggest tree in the neighborhood and its price was so high that no one could afford to buy it. It was ten feet high. Its branches were bound with new white rope and it came to a sure pure point at the top.

The man took this tree out first. Before Francie could speak up, a neighborhood bully, a boy of eighteen known as Punky Perkins, stepped forward and ordered the man to chuck the tree at him. The man hated the way Punky was so confident. He looked around and asked;

"Anybody else wanna take a chanct on it?"

Francie stepped forward. "Me, Mister."

A spurt of derisive laughter came from the tree man. The kids snickered. A few adults who had gathered to watch the fun, guffawed.

"Aw g'wan. You're too little," the tree man objected.

"Me and my brother—we're not too little together."

She pulled Neeley forward. The man looked at them—a thin girl of ten with starveling hollows in her cheeks but with the chin still baby-round. He looked at the little boy with his fair hair and round blue eyes—Neeley Nolan, all innocence and trust.

"Two ain't fair," yelped Punky.

"Shut your lousy trap," advised the man who held all power in that hour. "These here kids is got nerve. Stand back, the rest of youse. These kids is goin' to have a show at this tree."

The others made a wavering lane. Francie and Neeley stood at one end of it and the big man with the big tree at the other. It was a human funnel with Francie and her brother making the small end of it. The man flexed his great arms to throw the great tree. He noticed how tiny the children looked at the end of the short lane. For the split part of a moment, the tree thrower went through a kind of Gethsemane.

"Oh, Jesus Christ," his soul agonized, "why don't I just give 'em the tree, say Merry Christmas and let 'em go? What's the tree to me? I can't sell it no more this year and it won't keep till next year." The kids watched him solemnly as he stood there in his moment of thought. "But then," he rationalized, "if I did that, all the others would expect to get 'em handed to 'em. And next year, nobody a-tall would buy a tree off of me. They'd all wait to get 'em handed to 'em on a silver plate. I ain't a big enough man to give this tree away for nothin'. No, I ain't big enough. I ain't big enough to do a thing like that. I gotta think of myself and my own kids." He finally came to his conclusion. "Oh, what the hell! Them two kids is gotta live in this world. They *got* to get used to it. They got to learn to give and to take punishment. And by Jesus, it ain't give but *take, take, take* all the time in this God-damned world." As he threw the tree with all his strength, his heart wailed out, "It's a God-damned, rotten, lousy world!"

Francie saw the tree leave his hands. There was a split bit of being when time and space had no meaning. The whole world stood still as something dark and monstrous came through the air. The tree came toward her blotting out all memory of her ever having lived. There was nothing—nothing but pungent darkness and something that grew and grew as it rushed at her. She staggered as the tree hit them. Neeley went to his knees but she pulled him up fiercely before he could go down. There was a mighty swishing sound as the tree settled. Everything was dark, green and prickly. Then she felt a sharp pain at the side of her head where the trunk of the tree had hit her. She felt Neeley trembling.

When some of the older boys pulled the tree away, they found Francie and her brother standing upright, hand in hand. Blood was coming from scratches on Neeley's face. He looked more like a baby than ever with his bewildered blue eyes and the fairness of his skin made more noticeable because of the clear red blood. But they were smiling. Had they not won the biggest tree in the neighborhood? Some of the boys hollered "Horray!" A few adults clapped. The tree man eulogized them by screaming,

"And now get the hell out of here with your tree, you lousy bastards."

Francie had heard swearing since she had heard words. Obscenity and profanity had no meaning as such among those people. They were emotional expressions of inarticulate people with small vocabularies; they made a kind of dialect. The phrases could mean many things according to the expression and tone used in saying them. So now, when Francie heard themselves called lousy bastards, she smiled tremulously at the kind man. She knew that he was really saying, "Good-bye—God bless you."

## COMMENTS BY BETTY SMITH

Sure, we were poor. But we did not consider ourselves underprivileged. The world, that is, our little world, was ours. And it was a wonderful world of excitement, adventure, romance and drama. The public library, which had all the books in the world (or so I believed), was two blocks away, a boon to a reading girl like me. The living theatre, *Phillips Lyceum*, was just around the corner, a new show each week; admission, ten cents for gallery seats.

The shop windows were always wonderful, filled with all the desirable things of life. This was especially so at Christmas. The shop windows then were jammed full of dolls, bicycles, sleds, skates, blackboards—everything a child could wish for.

All the holidays were wonderful. But Christmas was the best. The very air was Christmas. There was the smell of oranges and tangerines; these fruits appeared only around Christmas time on the outdoor fruit stands. A week before Christmas, the tree vendors set up their stock along the curb. Sometimes there was a row of trees a block long and the air smelled of the cool aromatic branches.

We always had a tree for Christmas. True, it was so little, that it seemed like robbing the forest cradle. I lived for the day when I'd be old enough to win a great big tree in the tree throwing contest. Fourteen, by some unspoken rule, seemed to be the age when children were eligible for this competition. When I reached the age of eight, and my brother was six, I concluded by some weird mathematical process that we were fourteen years old, together, and were eligible to compete for a tree.

We did. And the passage published here explains how we came out and got a great big Christmas tree free.

Well, that was an incident of my childhood and it blended in with tens of thousands of other incidents and experiences. It was just one of those things among a multitude of other things.

Thirty years later, I was living in Chapel Hill, North Carolina, with my two young daughters. By that time, Brooklyn was a myth. I had married, lived in Michigan, and my two children had been born in Michigan. Then I had lived in Connecticut. Now I was living in the south. Brooklyn was just an old story to be told.

Again it was Christmas. My two girls had decided that the time had come when they could take a journey together on their own which meant, without Mama. I put them on the bus. Their grandmother would take them off the bus in Brooklyn. They were happy to leave and I was sad to see them go.

I comforted myself, however, with the thought that I'd have a whole free weekend to write. At that time I was engaged in that most exciting of all things—writing my first book.

As the day wore on, I found that I didn't want to write. I missed the children too much. And there was the somber realization that this would be the first Christmas I had spent alone in all of my life. I had a premonition that as the years went by, there would be many a Christmas I would have to spend alone. The thought made me very moody.

I had decided not to have a Christmas tree. It seemed silly to buy and decorate a tree just for myself. But as night came, I felt that I *had* to have a Christmas tree; there was no meaning to Christmas without a tree.

I went downtown but all the trees had been sold! I went back home very depressed. I wanted a tree. There was no tree to be had. It would be a dreary Christmas indeed without the children and without a tree.

Someone came to my door. It was a professor friend. He carried a small cedar tree.

"I brought you a tree," he said. "For Christmas."

"It's beautiful," I said. "Where did you buy it?"

"We don't buy trees here," he said. "I got it out of the woods."

As I dressed the tree, the thought came to me that twice in my life I had gotten a Christmas tree for nothing. The first time was that time in Brooklyn when my brother and I were big enough, together, to have a tree thrown at us. Suddenly, that Christmas tree throwing was all vivid and new again. Once more I felt the cold of that Brooklyn street, the mountain smell of balsam branches. Again I saw the street lights and heard clearly the street sounds and remembered that red knitted stocking hat pulled down over my ears. And I guess I remembered my running nose, too. Again, my little brother was standing with me, holding my hand.

I finished decorating the tree and turned the tree lights on. I prepared a simple supper. I washed the few dishes I had used, straightened the house up a bit, wrote a letter to my mother and opened the Christmas presents my girls had made for me; a couple of pot holders and some hand-hemmed dish towels. At twelve o'clock I listened to Midnight Mass on the radio, then went to bed.

I lay awake thinking of the beauty of the night. It was a beautiful night the way December nights are usually beautiful in Chapel Hill. Warm, silent and misty with the stars shining through the mist. It must have been on a night like this, I thought, when He was born; a night when the stars shone through the mist over the little town of Bethlehem.

I lay awake thinking of, and reliving, that Brooklyn Christmas Eve when my brother and I won the biggest Christmas tree in all the world! And it was as if we were children again.

I awakened Christmas morning with a feeling of quiet expectancy. After a cup of coffee, I took my manuscript out of the desk drawer and read my work. Then I put a sheet of paper in the typewriter and started to write:

*There was a cruel custom in the neighborhood* . . . I began, *It was about the trees still unsold* . . .

## A CHARACTER DRAWN FROM REMEMBRANCE:
Assignment 8

Write an incident from a recollection of your own, concentrating on giving your central character a dominant wish, such as Francie's strong desire for the tree, that will enable him to overcome the difficulties of the fictional situation in which you place him.

We already know that in creating a story one may begin with something one hears, as Henry James did in listening to the talk of the garrulous luncheon-table partner about the break-up of a family. A character too, like the tale itself, may be founded on hearsay. Doris Betts, whose *The Gentle Insurrection* and *Tall Houses in Winter* are fine books by a young writer, comments at the end of "The Alligator" on the material from which she "picked up" both a character and the story itself. In analyzing "The Alligator" she has also written the following note. After you have read it, as well as the story and the author's comments, decide whether you agree with her reasons for the failure of this particular piece of work. Do you think the story succeeds in spite of obvious faults? If so, why does it? If not, why not? Miss Betts writes,

... what one hears can be a help in writing if only one doesn't hear too much, and if one listens for the hint instead of the wholly formed situation. The curiosity ought to be more for *why* than for *what* and it seems to me that in "The Alligator," I listened for *what* and got stuck with an Emory who never came alive as I wanted him to be.

## THE ALLIGATOR

### DORIS BETTS

It was on Good Friday that Uncle Emory appeared in Waynesville with a baby alligator for his sister's children.

Since Uncle Emory had made a career of doing the unexpected no one saw anything strange in his Easter gift. This was Emory's private damnation—to be cursed with a family which now assumed that all his actions were sensible and normal.

His sister Martha met him at the door looking exactly as she had looked when he dropped in unexpectedly the year before. She barely glanced at the container, calling her two children, "Your Uncle Emory's brought you an Easter present!" Then she said, "How are you, Emory," and went back to the kitchen where she was making yeast-bread.

Emory felt somewhat dashed. But he pulled on the mischievous smile he reserved for all children as Bobby, 7, and Rita, 3, came running from the yard.

They lifted the lid and looked into the box. "Thank you, Uncle Emory," Bobby said.

He could hardly bear it. He shook the box so that the small beast scrabbled about inside. "It's an alligator!"

Bobby said dutifully that it was just what he had always wanted.

At this Uncle Emory stamped off into the house and made a speech to his sister about conformity and lack of gumption.

"You're staying for supper?" Martha said.

He had stayed for supper last year, hadn't he? "I guess I will."

Emory had to admit he had lost luster for the children on the day they discovered the souvenirs he brought had come from New York dimestores instead of dens in Singapore. Still, he'd argued to Martha, they would remember his sea-faring stories longer than the disappointment. No child should grow up without a touch of imagination.

Martha said Emory had been downright shoved by imagination; he had been plastered; he had been flattened right down.

Martha was a widow-woman. When Jed died, her window to the world had closed. Now she was no more concerned with Singapore than with an anthill at the back steps. She had a small income from insurance; she made potholders and sock-dolls for a local store; and most of the time she was letting out or taking in the seams of clothing other people gave her for the children. They never seemed to have any for Martha so she soon stopped going anywhere. The only new thing she had owned in five years was a crimson kimono covered with dragons which Emory had given her one Christmas.

She did not dread her brother's visits. When she knew he was coming she would sit on the children's beds the night before and tell them, "You be *nice* to your Uncle Emory." So they were agonizingly nice to him and he would stalk off muttering about the perils of socialized government.

Usually she did not know when he might appear.

When he and the alligator came on Good Friday Martha put the bread away to rise and stacked clean sheets and a coverlet at the foot of the living room couch where he would sleep.

"You're staying the night?"

Emory said he guessed he would.

He went along with her to the kitchen and stood in the doorway while she went quietly about her business.

"Well, Martha, how are things?"

"Pretty fair," she said.

"How's Bobby doing at school?"

"He does all right."

"That Rita sure has grown."

Martha stood on tiptoe with her head in a kitchen cabinet and did not seem to hear.

Uncle Emory stood on his head in the doorway. "Good for circulation," he puffed.

"Must be."

He clattered down. "All the time you got wasted blood settling in your feet if you don't do that," he explained. "People start aging; their feet hurt. Stay cold at night. Won't carry them as fast. Not a blame bit of wonder, I always say."

"You're aging some yourself," said Martha. She stopped the second kneading of the bread to look at him closely. "A little more weight than last time. You been at a sitting-down job?"

He said he'd been cooking for a circus down in Florida. Before that he'd caught shrimp off the Carolina coast.

"Um Hum. You want asparagus?"

"Be fine. I'm thinking of going out to Nevada with a geiger counter next. Might make us all rich."

Martha was rooting around for the canned asparagus and answered with a grunt.

"All of us rich as Croesus," he went on nervously. "Thought I might name the mine for you. The Martha Sue—how's that sound? Or just plain Martha?"

She had gotten up from the lower cabinet and he could see a small smile on her mouth. "Name it the Lazarus," she said.


Uncle Emory showed up in Waynesville four or five times in the good years, bringing odd presents and wearing the latest styles. One time it was flowered and embroidered vests, a whole suitcase full. Another time he wore walking shorts and flannel socks, with silk scarves at his throat. Word would run all through the town that the brother of Martha Sue Reep had come and little boys would climb up in trees like Nicodemus just to see him pass.

But Martha only met him at her front door with something in the hand she had just been using—a broom or a mound of dough. "How are you, Emory," she'd say without even looking up or down to catch the full-length splendor.

And some years he didn't come at all and at Christmas would mail a dingy stone with a note saying it was jade, but could only be cut and polished by one expert in America, whose name and address Emory was trying to obtain.

Martha seldom thought of him between visits. There would be postcards showing French villas (mailed in St. Louis) or Spanish bullfights (sent from Richmond) which she tacked on the wall of the children's room because Emory said they were educational.

Near Christmas she'd lay in a small supply of Brazil nuts which Emory said he'd gotten fond of while he was at Panama. And some Christmases he would come, bringing an electric icecream freezer for her present, with knight's armour for Bobby and a lace mantilla for the girl.

Now that the alligator was growing larger, Martha found her thoughts turning to Emory more often.

For one thing the alligator was always cold. It would not stay in the box unless she moved it near the kitchen stove. It ate too much and preferred raw fish, which were hard to get in Waynesville and took too much out of the budget. She had never been told that alligators barked but this one did, sometimes from hunger but usually from a bad disposition.

When the alligator was a year old it was nearly two feet long and even the largest box that was built for it would fit only with its tail forever bent. It lost teeth and grew new ones, and Bobby was saving up for a necklace of the discards.

"When you make that necklace, we'll give it to Uncle Emory for Christmas," said Martha once, with a smile that was slightly sideways on her face.

Emory never asked about the alligator. When he came home the Christmas the alligator had reached three feet and lived in a pen in the yard with a washtub sunk in the ground, he seemed amazed to see it.

"What are you doing with this beast?" he demanded.

Martha said there wasn't much anybody could *do* with it.

Emory grew thoughtful. "I didn't know they grew so much. There's a fortune to be made in selling the skin, I bet."

"He gets terribly cold out there," said Martha. "I built the pen right next to the place we burn the trash but it doesn't seem to help. He doesn't eat in the winters. I think he'll die."

And when she said it Martha found she felt faintly sad that this creature should die in the cold so far from its home.

"He hibernates," said Emory. "How about it, Bobby, you must be learning a lot, having an unusual animal like that for a pet. I bet all the other boys are envious."

They had been very envious, it was true, until their parents forbade them to play anywhere near that house that had a dangerous animal bigger than they were shut up behind flimsy walls.

"He's o.k.," said Bobby politely. "Thank you again."

By the time the alligator was four years old and some 50-odd inches long the Waynesville City Council called on Martha Sue Reep with a list of zoning laws. They couldn't have an alligator kept like that in the middle of town. What if some rash schoolboy decided to climb the fence and ride it? (Actually all schoolboys would only walk on the other side of the street and had a tendency to burst into a run from corner to corner of the block where Martha lived; not because they were *afraid*, you understand, but from high spirits.)

No, said the City Council, the alligator could not be released into a creek or river; that violated state laws.

Martha admitted something must be done. And she thought of the old well on the back of her property which had been nailed shut years ago. The alligator could go in there, she said. There was still water in the bottom in most seasons. And no alligator could climb out of a well.

Would it be better just to shoot the alligator? If Emory had been there she would have asked his advice. But the City Council was satisfied to put it down into the well.

The Waynesville National Guard Unit and the Police Force arrived at Martha's house on a Saturday afternoon to make the transfer, guns cocked in case the animal should go berserk. First they roped the alligator several times, dragged and tugged until it was pulled tail-first into a box which had both ends open. The end at its head was quickly boarded up and the ropes were slipped from the tail as the other end was closed.

Then they dragged the box by another rope (attached at the tail-end by a nervous police rookie who was hoping to prove something) down through the weeds of the back lot and pried up the covering on the old well.

No one wanted to lift the box bare-handed. A Guardsman made a quick trip to the lumberyard for boards to slide beneath it and the crowd on Martha's property grew and grew, until she and the two children were forced to watch proceedings from the back porch. She shaded her eyes.

When the two boards had been lined up evenly beneath the box, four men took hold and lifted; and a sudden shaft of sunlight made it seem to Martha like a golden scene out of old Baghdad, where some royal personage was borne on a dais by his slaves. She let out a small gasp.

"He won't get loose," said Bobby scornfully. It was the first time they had called the alligator anything but "it."

"No. Of course he won't."

The men opened the end of the box where the tail of the alligator was going back and forth and then the front end was suddenly lifted to slide him down into the dark. Silence came upon the crowd like a shock. The back feet of the alligator, four-toed and webbed and clawed, had flattened on the wood of the box, and because of the angle at which the foot was bent it (he) was literally hanging by his toes.

"Shake the box! Shake the box!" somebody yelled.

Two policemen, after first carefully donning their dark blue gloves, took hold of the top of the box and shook, and the alligator began to slide down. For one last moment it hovered, head still inside the box, most of its body flopping back and forth like a pendulum that was out of rhythm. But the five toes on each front foot were smaller and less sturdy; they could not hold on.

The alligator fell.

In that moment, Martha turned away and rushed into the kitchen where she stood in a circle of pain. I should have killed him; it would be kinder! I wish I had the courage to kill the alligator!

Bobby and Rita followed her in. "He's down," said Rita.

"Nothing to worry about, Mom; crowd's breaking up. Mom?"

Yes, she said to Bobby, there was nothing to worry about.


By the time the alligator had been in the well two years, the wooden bars which had been nailed across the well were giving way and boys who had stoked their curiosity to white-heat would come and lean on them to see inside.

Martha was quite worn out with yelling at them and once she gave in entirely and wrote her first letter to Emory in eleven years. "You HAVE to take back your alligator!" she wrote furiously.

But the oil fields of Texas mailed her letter back, marked in purple ink: UNKNOWN.

Martha and Bobby, who was now 12, rigged up a covering for the well made out of chains; but they were too flexible and would slip apart. She lived in horror of hearing the cry of a child diminish as he fell into that well. In her sleep she often heard the first terrified shriek that was then rounded by echo, and dwindled, and thinned, and was gone.

In Waynesville, it was no longer an alligator. It had become a crocodile, and some chance remark once dropped by Uncle Emory at the bus station led to the town belief that this one had hatched from mummified Egyptian eggs in an ill-fated experiment along the Nile.

So it was a monster; a crocodile-dinosaur, people said. It might grow and grow, and curl round and round that well till someday its head would be right at the top; and one dark midnight it would grow its way all the way out and be found a size that would put Loch Ness to shame. The drugstore readers said it would take a small atomic bomb to dissipate and kill that much old and tested animal energy.

Often Martha thought the alligator must be dead. She would go to the well and call, and not a slither or a sound would come up to her. She would throw small stones and listen. Each winter when she dropped horsemeat down the shaft it would be so still that she knew it was all a waste and the alligator had died from cold.

But in the spring she could hear movement at the bottom of the well and at night the alligator would sometimes bellow. He sounded like a foghorn.

The neighbors complained about the bellowing, especially when it was set off by the sunrise band which played "Christ Is Risen" through the streets on Easter morning. At night the neighbor dogs stood safely in their own yards and howled at the strange sound, but none of them ventured near the well, which was also free of rats and toads and prowling cats.

Then the story got out that the alligator (crocodile) had started to tunnel. Ed Marvin mentioned it first, the day he found water standing in his basement and the highway department denied its new culverts were responsible. There were nearby basements where contractor-guaranteed walls had developed cracks; and here and there a young tree that had been shipped from Chicago seed houses failed to root and grow; and sometimes a small puppy would find tiny depressions in the earth and would stand there barking furiously.

"It's that crocodile!" people muttered. And they knew if it had been dug up out of pyramids it might never die at all, and would still be around to plague their grandchildren with its bellowing and digging under respectable houses.

The Waynesville City Council was sheepish when it came to Martha the second time but she didn't argue. She had not heard from Emory in more than a year. She had work to do and two children to raise and feed.

"Kill him then," she said. And as soon as she had said it she knew she was losing a torment that was essential to her.

She went into her bedroom and put on the kimono with the dragons on it and went to bed. "There'll be no supper," she said to the two children. "I don't feel good."

When Emory came home that evening (he'd brought his sister a pair of golden-hoop earrings from Roumanian gypsies) the parade had reached Martha's house, and the National Guardsmen had ridden up in the obsolete World War II tank, which they never got a decent chance to use. The Waynesville police force was on hand and Boy Scouts were holding back the crowd and selling tickets to a future jamboree in the state capitol. Police Chief Holler had brought a machine gun requisitioned all the way from the State Bureau of Investigation, which even now was secretly alerting the militia that something dangerous was going on up in Waynesville.

"My God!" said Emory. "What's going on?" He could not even

get near the house and no one in the crowd would answer his questions. He thought of war and of bank bandits and he wanted to spring ahead of the crowd like Douglas Fairbanks and save his sister.

But the people were firm as a wall, and no vines or tapestries hung down nearby to help him.

"They're ready to shoot," came the crowd's murmur.

Emory began to scream. "MARTHA! MARTHA!"

There was a perfect fusilade of shots, enough to have mowed down regiments, killed herds of mammoths, won at Argonne. To Emory it was quite clear: his family has been massacred. The town had gone berserk; perhaps it had something to do with his boasting there was Indian blood in his kin; or Bobby had been making love to other little boys; or Martha had taken to unspeakable means of supporting the family.

He staggered away. One of the people in the crowd said that Martha Sue Reep had always been queer or she would never have let this thing hang on so long.

What thing? he thought. Too late.

What would he do? Where would he go?

Emory headed back to the bus station from which he had come. He would go somewhere, somewhere far away, perhaps to the edge of the world.


# COMMENTS BY DORIS BETTS
# ON "THE ALLIGATOR"

When someone offers to tell you a family anecdote that would make a good story, place each hand over each ear and one foot after the other. Escape. Somewhere, someday, a nugget may lie among all that rubble but I have yet to find it.

Yet stories—sometimes very fine ones—are suggested by ordinary conversation. They rise out of bits and pieces dropped carelessly, almost unintentionally, by speakers who wouldn't dream of wasting your time on such trivia when they can take a whole hour to relate a miraculous experience Great Aunt Maud had in 1873. Often the real seeds for stories are later repudiated. The story ("The Alligator") was, for example, written after mention of a cousin who bought a baby alligator which persisted to full maturity, and which finally had to be dumped in an unused well on the family farm.

Later I sought out the person who had told it. "I was so curious about what happened to that alligator your cousin had," I said, "that I did a story about it."

The face which turned was not only blank but positively stony. "What alligator?" And, following an explanation, "I never heard about any alligator. That must have been the *other* side of the family."

What conversation, heard and overheard, makes the eardrums vibrate to a potential story? A single scene, a line of dialogue, a place described which seems worth better events than were allotted it by reality, a quirk of character—anything that puts forth to you not only a question mark but a quick reaction of "Shush! Don't tell me anymore! I want to fill in the blanks myself!"

Too many blanks previously filled in by actual events can be restricting. Once known, they stick in the writer's mind like an unsought foundation for his house; he tends to build even on those parts which are unsatisfactory.

"The Alligator," halfway between a first and second draft as printed here, was never successful after many revisions, perhaps because this time the writer's ear took up the novelty of what one does with a full grown alligator in a Georgia town; and that very novelty became a restriction. What finally emerged was, as my agent said, more a yarn than a short story.

In subsequent revisions, I worked on the resemblance between the alligator and Uncle Emory, especially as Martha saw them—a resemblance which "happened" gradually as this early version was set down. But Emory, as a character, had already been done to death in fiction better than this one and I failed him in every new treatment. In an even later version, Emory did not return to Waynesville at all, an attempt to save the ending from being as pat as it is in this draft. When finally I reached the point of dropping Waynesville citizens down the well into waiting jaws, I knew it was really the story I was ready to bring to violent death, and I abandoned it as a yarn and an almost.

Next time, I thought, I'll listen for the situation which will be subordinate to my story, and not the other way around. So I did listen, and I do listen; and once in awhile I hear the beginning—the merest mustard seed—of a story.

## THE MUSTARD SEED OF A STORY:   Assignment 9

Drawing on a conversation you have heard about a person who might lend himself to fictional treatment, write an analysis of how he would behave in the situation you may decide to use as a foundation for a story.

Another way of forming a character, or rather allowing one to form himself, is to conjure up a person from your imagination. Of course this method does not always work. When Owen Glendower, in the Shakespeare play, says, "I can call spirits from the vasty deep," Hotspur rightly wants to know if the spirits will come when they are called. But it is true that a character will often lie dormant in the consciousness until imagination takes over to give it a concrete shape.

To "A Matter of Time," the student story which follows, E. L. has added a comment on the way Michael and his situation were born out of reverie.

# A MATTER OF TIME

E. L.

She was sitting with her back to him, rearranging multicolored bottles on the dresser. He crossed the room, sat down on the bed, and looked past her body at the mirrored reflection. She had never been beautiful, but until the child had died perhaps he had not noticed. As he sat on the bed almost a month after the funeral his heart began to apprehend her imperfections, finding them strange, remote.

His glance moved to the closet. A small boy's jacket hung out of place with his own bulky suits. "Why don't you get rid of that?" he said abruptly. She did not answer or turn around, and because he thought she was going to cry he got up and left the room.

In the living room he leaned against the wall and lit a match to a thin cigar. He took a few drags, then dug the cigar against the side of an ashtray, watching carefully until the smoke stopped making acid funnels through his fingers. After he had torn the end of it apart, into shreds like a browned corn husk, he had nothing to do. He sat down heavily and put his hands over his temples. His head hurt and he was vaguely aware that this physical pain created his least painful reality. Closing his eyes he tried not to think of his wife in the next room. He concentrated on the pain and it comforted him.

After remaining seated for a few minutes, his hands flattened over his eyes, he stood up, steadied himself, and shuffled across the room. Lillian had hung the mirror to her height and he was obliged to crouch in front of it, his dark trousers tightened at the knees, his coat flung open. He saw his eyes twitch, examining a face which seemed ages older than five years or a day before.

Backing away from the mirror, he went again to the bedroom. She was putting on her coat and he stood in the doorway with another unlit cigar in his hand watching her button it neatly down the front, miss a button, undo two, then fasten it correctly.

"What time is it?" she asked, not looking at him.

He pushed up his coat sleeve. "After 7:30, I think."

"Are you going to smoke?"

"No," he said, stopping, putting the cigar in his coat pocket, crinkling the remaining cellophane between his fingers. "Are you going out?"

"I've the laundry." She flicked powder off the surface of her black coat. She went to the closet and picked up an umbrella from where it had fallen to the floor.

"I'll take it down," he said, irritated. "The walk will be good." His head had begun to throb above the eyes.

She sighed and relaxed. "That would be wonderful," and she kissed him sadly and absently on the cheek. Michael pulled a trench coat from the closet, picked up the laundry bag, and when he left he closed the door very quietly behind him.

Once outside he did not walk after all, but decided to take the old trolley line to town. He got off at the main intersection of Orange and Church Streets and started back toward the laundromat. The air was spicy cold and it was drizzling slightly. He walked slowly along the rain-confettied streets looking into store windows, keeping pace with the other evening window shoppers. Neon lights reflected off and on in the puddles of the street, tossing color on clusters of blacks standing at doorways and laughing on the curbs.

He stopped in front of a noisy, red-neon bordered bar and looked at the Halloween displays built around Scotch bottles. Then with weary determination he went inside, deposited his bundle on the floor and sat down on a bar stool. The bartender looked at him quizzically. "Something to wash your clothes in?" he asked. "A Moscow Mule with plenty of kick. Beats starch all to hell."

"Let me have some sort of big beer in a can," said Michael, wrapping his legs around the bar stool.

"Anything particular?"

"Just a big beer in a can," said Michael. "With two holes."

"Coming up," said the bartender.

With the beer in one hand and the laundry bag in the other Michael entered the laundromat. It was steamy and smelled cleanly of soap and starch. There was almost a score of people lined up in chairs along the wall, reading magazines; most of the machines were taken. He found an empty washer near the back and dumped the clothes in, putting the laundry bag on top of the washer. When he got ready to start the machine he remembered that he had forgotten the soap and he couldn't find his wife's usual brand in the dispensing machine. He sat down by the driers and drank half his beer very quickly. Then he walked over to where a toothy pumpkin sat in the middle of the counter and queried a dumpy blond in white.

"Do you have any Ivory Soap Flakes?"

"Do you *see* any?"

"No, but I thought you might have some."

"I thought we didn't *carry* Ivory Soap," she said, getting excited. "I don't see how we could be *out* of Ivory Soap."

"I didn't say there *wasn't* Ivory Soap," said Michael. "I was just, so to speak, looking for some, but since you say there isn't any . . ."

"Well, don't take my word for it. I just work here. Go look for yourself."

Michael went back and borrowed some soap of an indiscriminate brand from a lady with a child named Margadell who was dressed like a goblin.

"Do you like Halloween?" asked the child named Margadell, after Michael had drunk all his beer, smoked half a cigar, and tired of watching the undulating window of the washer.

"Yes, I like it very much," said Michael, sitting down in a bamboo chair. "There is nothing I like better than a good glass of Halloween after a long hard day."

"Halloween," said Margadell, putting the end of a blond braid in her mouth, "does not go in a glass. Stupid."

"You are perfectly right," reconsidered Michael. "I wasn't thinking. Halloween is an effervescence not intended to be bottled. Thank you for reminding me. Hasn't your mother told you not to talk to old men with beer cans?"

"My mother tells me lots of things," said Margadell. "Do you know about Mr. Potter?"

"No," said Michael. "I was about to ask if you did."

Margadell looked at him scornfully. "He has a *dog*," she said. "It barks at night and my father says he's going to put Mr. Potter in the dog pound." She thought this hilariously funny.

"Hey," said Michael. "What have you got in that sack?"

"Do you know about the birds and the bees?" asked Margadell.

Michael said he thought he had heard them mentioned, but that he could have imagined it.

"Oh," she said. She sat down on the floor with the goblin suit hoisted above her knees and emptied the sack on the floor. "Trick 'er Treat Sack. Here are four tootsie rolls, a nickel, and two lollipops. I don't like yellow. Do you?"

"I don't believe it would go well with my drink," said Michael. The heat of the room and the beer made his face quite red. He gave Margadell the dime he was going to use for the drier and asked to be excused.

"Sure," said Margadell, starting to count candy corn.

He went to the door and let the clean night wind blow into his face. It did not chill him or clear the circus of mental images generated by heat, beer and the past month. The frumpy blond behind the counter was cleaning her nails with a bobby-pin. His headache had begun again and he felt exceedingly tired as he went back and sat down in the bamboo chair.

"I have twenty-one jelly beans and nine pieces of candy corn," said Margadell. Michael handed her a piece of corn off the floor. "That's nine and a half," she said. "It's been stepped on."

"Listen, Margadell," said Michael. "You would never know it, not to look at me, but I am an escaper. I have a deep dark sad past and I hide it in laundromats."

Margadell looked interested, so he continued.

"It's unreality I love. Everyone has tried to shake my faith, but I've stuck to it through thick and thin. Most people don't do that. I am an escaper, there is no doubt about it. But I am afraid that someday I will run out of places to escape to."

Margadell tied her braids under her chin and put one end in her mouth.

"If you continue to do that," said Michael, "you will get the Galumphing Blond Braid Disease."

"You're teasing," she said, batting her eyelashes. But she took the hair out of her mouth.

"Afraid not," said Michael. "Everything I say is the absolute truth." He held up his right hand. "A paragon of honor. And my laundry has finished flipping."

Someone had taken his laundry bag from the top of the washer. "Hey," he said to a tow-headed boy in blue jeans, "have you seen a stray laundry bag?"

"Enough of them around here," said the boy. "Just latch on to one."

"I'd like *mine*," said Michael. "The one I came in with."

"A laundry bag's a laundry bag," said the blond boy, stepping back as an overloaded machine spurted soap on the floor. "Somebody probably swiped yours. Return the favor."

Michael took the clothes out of the machine and carried them across the room to his chair. One of his wife's slips hung over the edge and he picked it up so it wouldn't drag on the floor. Then he squatted down on his heels in front of the little girl, finding himself so dizzy that he had to put one hand on the floor to steady himself.

"I have had a great loss, Margadell," he said solemnly. "I have lost my laundry bag, and I have lost my son, and I am losing my wife." He reached out quite deliberately and tugged a braid.

"Cut it out," she said. "That hurts."

"I didn't mean it to," he said.

Margadell glanced sideways to see her mother appear from behind a drier. "I've got to go," she said briskly.

"Well, goodbye," said Michael. Margadell wiped her fingers against the side of her goblin suit, dropped a piece of candy corn on his knee, and scampered off after her mother.

It was late, almost eleven, before he reached home. The lights were off except for one small T-V light and the fireplace burning slowly, like something forgotten. He left the laundry in the hall and, since the room was musty, raised a window before he went to sit by the fire. His head hurt and he wished he had the foresight to have taken something for it earlier. He sat down and leaning back with his feet toward the fire his glance fell on his wife's knitting and belt, draped over the back of a chair. He looked at these objects steadily for a long while, feeling a passive, undirected sadness. Certainly, he assured himself, he would soon understand what had happened to them. Then he could do something about it. It was all a matter of time, and most certainly things would work out.

The room was becoming chill. He put his shoes back on and poked aimlessly with one foot at the dying coals. Then he got up and turned the small light off before he went into the room with his wife.

## COMMENTS BY E. L. ON "A MATTER OF TIME"

The story is a fantasy caused by procrastination. The funeral of the son, which is omitted from the draft you have read here, was already stale from revision, and I'd lost sight of the people. I had the funeral part and a half-hearted plan to have Michael go downtown to a drug store where some object would make him realize his situation. I couldn't get any feeling about it, so I went downtown myself to get a concrete idea about the setting. Monday night, and every drug store in town was closed. I went to a laundromat, read a magazine, put the short story out of mind, and went home to bed. The next night I realized that the story was due in 19 hours, so I created a new Michael and the little girl in the laundromat out of the pure procrastination-prodded fear of having to write *something*. After I once concentrated on the characters, the setting and the dialogue came quite naturally and very quickly.

## A MAIN CHARACTER IN A SITUATION:   Assignment 10

In whatever way your character has appeared to you for your own first story, think of him as he exists in his fictional situation. Then write a comment on why you think the problem he faces will interest a reader. Ask yourself what point, or truth, you hope to emphasize through your character and his actions.

The ways suggested here for bringing your characters to life and placing them in their proper fictional situations are obviously not the only ways. As Thomas Wolfe pointed out in the letter to F. Scott Fitzgerald quoted at the beginning of this chapter, any argument for using one particular method instead of another may look knowing or imposing but there is nothing to it. Wolfe adds that often "what a man is really doing is simply rationalizing his own way of doing something, the way he has to do it, the way given him by his talent and his nature."

Your task in fiction is to find your own method of creating a character in a situation, using the suggestions here, extracting from them, improvising, and discarding what will not be workable for you. Your method will lead you to draw on remembrance, observation, and imagination—or perhaps to synthesize all three. When you find your character, you should try to write about him with the restraint and selectiveness Wolfe desired for himself. It is this restraint, this selection, this tone, that can make a story or a novel art.

## 5

# A Style of Your Own

To be effective, any language pattern you use in fiction must create through the senses an appeal from you to the reader. The work you produce may be humorous or tragic. It may carry a point for you or simply have the aim of entertainment, but its language must have the imprint of your temperament and the work must have a diction, rhythm, emphasis, and arrangement that are suited to what you want to say. In the broadest sense, style is the use of language that reveals the spirit and personality of an artist.

Speaking of what makes a writer different from other men, Aldous Huxley says, ". . . one has the urge, first of all, to order the facts one observes and to give meaning to life; and along with that goes the love of words for their own sake . . . the knack to use them effectively." "The dress of thoughts," is Lord Chesterfield's phrase for style. Neither man mentions the emotion that often generates the thought behind the words of a writer. This quality of being able to recreate emotion through language can be very much a part of style.

If you want your own style to convey not only the fact but the feeling behind the fact, you may try to project parts of your story through figurative language—simile, metaphor. The use of imagery often heightens the emotional impact of a piece of fiction. But do not decorate just for the sake of decoration. Tennessee Williams has said,

I hate writing that is a parade of images for the sake of images; I hate it so much that I close a book in disgust when it keeps on saying one thing is like another; I even get disgusted with poems that make nothing but comparisons between one thing and another.

But I repeat that symbols, when used respectfully, are the purest language of plays.

Foreword to *Camino Real*, by Tennessee Williams

When symbols are not used for their own sake they can also have purity in a short story or a novel. Sometimes imagery comes spontaneously, as in the case of a five-year-old child who recently told her mother, "Roofs look like books open." The mother herself once wrote a story that used as its central symbol a lost beach. Through imagery, the child's world, all blue and silver in the early morning, came alive for the reader.

In the story the girl, Liza, wants to go from the mainland over to an island beach in the hope that she can be accepted as a loved companion by two other girls who live there and who have, so far, refused to make her a part of their lives. The writer's language, even with its imagery, appears as an uncontrived reflection of Liza's dream of companionship, a dream that turns dim with disillusionment when her friend, the Captain, rows her to the island and the two girls turn on her with venomous cruelty. The simple similes in the following quotation are unforced even though this writer is one who can sometimes work over a comparison until she destroys it.

"... would we go down to the bottom of the ocean?"
"I guess we could."
Liza leaned toward the Captain and fixed her eyes on his face.
"Like what? Sink like what?"
"Well now, let me see," said the Captain. "We'd go down like stones."
Liza examined her hands.
"We'd go down like . . . feathers."
Liza scratched her nose.
"We'd go down like . . . like bells."
She smiled up at him and drew her arm through the water like a swinging bell.

The more complex imagery of much of the story is related in a consistent pattern so that the symbols not only stand for something else but convey to the reader the further significance that gives a symbol power. Another way of saying it is that the lost beach is not private to the author but represents for each reader the strand of his own childhood dreams.

The problem of developing a style goes far beyond the use of symbols. Language reflects the individuality of the writer and also acts as a mirror in which revelation of scene, action, or character, may appear. Displaying a character's inner thoughts to your reader without intruding yourself as an author—a technique known as stream-of-consciousness writing —is a problem of style as revelation.

James Joyce has a story, "Eveline," dealing with the situation of a young girl who cannot bring herself to exchange the mediocre routine of home and family for the exotic life her lover offers her. Until the very end of the action, Eveline is revealed only through her own inner thoughts. Joyce's language comes directly from the mind of the character, with no interference from the outside. The "she" who is Eveline could be easily changed to an "I."

She was to go away with him by the night-boat to be his wife and to live with him in Buenos Ayres where he had a home waiting for her. How well she remembered the first time she had seen him; he was lodging in a house on the main road where she used to visit. It seemed a few weeks ago. He was standing at the gate, his peaked cap punched back on his head and his hair tumbled forward over a face of bronze. Then they had come to know each other. He used to meet her outside the Stores every evening and see her home. He took her to see *The Bohemian Girl* and she felt elated as she sat in an unaccustomed part of the theatre with him. He was awfully fond of music and sang a little. People knew that they were courting and, when he sang about the lass that loves a sailor, she always felt pleasantly confused. He used to call her Poppens out of fun. First of all it had been an excitement for her to have a fellow and then she had begun to like him. He had tales of distant countries. He had started as a deck boy at a pound a month on a ship of the Allan Line going out to Canada. He told her the names of the ships he had been on and the names of the different services. He had sailed through the Straits of Magellan and he told her stories of the terrible Patagonians. He had fallen on his feet in Buenos Ayres, he said, and had come over to the old country just for a holiday. Of course, her father had found out the affair and had forbidden her to have anything to say to him.

From "Eveline," by James Joyce

Here Joyce is using "interior monologue," a reverie, not addressed to another character in the story. In actual monologue, the person formulates his words, speaking them out, perhaps in the presence of another, but he is actually talking to himself. In the following passage, a one-armed bartender, telling his troubles in the presence of a sailor, evokes the past and also reveals himself through his style of talking.

"I had a girl, too," he said quietly, "a long time ago. We were together all the time. Her name was Kathy, and she had the bluest eyes I ever saw. . . ." He moved closer to the window and, disregarding the sailor, talked out into the rain. "She'd meet me every night when I got off work and we would walk down the beach in the moonlight, making all kinds of crazy plans we both knew could never work out. We were going to get married and have a big white yacht, and sometimes we would stay up all night talking about all the places we were going to sail to. She'd go to the library while I was working and read about Nassau and Venice and places like that, then tell me about them when we were together. She made them sound so real I half believed we were going—I was pretty young then. . . ." He turned from the window and thoughtfully lit a cigarette. "It was like that for a long time—even after I lost my arm. Then one night she told me that she didn't want to see me again—that she couldn't stand this stub. She said that about the stub so I'd get mad and wouldn't feel so bad when she left me. Went off with some Chattanooga lumberman in a Bugatti roadster."
From "Dry Prints on the Pavement," by Hugh A. McEachern, Jr.

Notice that what Hugh McEachern has left out of the bartender's recollections is as important as what he has included. In monologue, and even in stream-of-consciousness writing which theoretically includes the entire realm of a character's thoughts superimposed upon each other, no writer can tell all. Since art is selective, a good style in all its phases is selective.

Hugh McEachern's character reveals through selected words the sense of dislocation that has stayed with him a long time. His talk sharpens and gives point to the past. A real-life bartender might remember the exact day he met his girl, repeat many of the remarks she made to him, and even recall the number of rounds of beer she drank with him. But in this story, every word in the bartender's monologue points to his loss.

The rule of selectivity also applies to dialogue between two or more people in a story. It is true that life itself is your model and that part of every writer's work is to listen to real people talk, but in fictional dialogue a writer sharpens the talk he has heard. Dialogue, like monologue in a story, goes more directly to the point than in life. But you start by listening to real people.

For hints on writing dialogue learn to be a spy. It is part of your role. Try to pick up the cadence of the speech you hear at a ball game, in a taxi, in a café or restaurant. Learn to absorb a language flavor, an *aaah* of approval or a brutal expletive. Listen to how people talk. Go to books. Look again, for instance, at the dialogue Betty Smith wrote about Francie trying to get a free Christmas tree.

"Anybody else wanna take a chanct on it?"
Francie stepped forward.
"Me, Mister."
A spurt of derisive laughter came from the tree man. The kids snickered. A few adults who had gathered to watch the fun guffawed.
"Aw g'wan. You're too little," the tree man objected.
"Me and my brother—we're not too little together."
She pulled Neely forward. The man looked at them—a thin girl of ten with starveling hollows in her cheeks but with the chin still baby-round. He looked at the little boy with his fair hair and round blue eyes—Neeley Nolan, all innocence and trust.
"Two ain't fair," yelped Punky.
"Shut your lousy trap," advised the man who held all power in that hour. "These here kids is got nerve. Stand back, the rest of youse. These kids is goin' to have a show at this tree."

Omitting the description and narration, look only at the words the characters actually say. Even without the identifying phrases, "starveling hollows" and "chin still baby-round," we know Francie and we know the tree man. He is a minor character used to reveal Francie, but by reflection he reveals his own impulse toward kindness in every word he speaks.

In blending dialogue into your own narrative pattern, and thinking of it as part of your style, remember not only the need for character revelation but the importance of place. Does the following dialogue in a student story have the stamp of a defi-

nite place? Do the cigarette smoke and the painted women fix
the atmosphere of one particular party?

Jim Turnage weaved through the painted women and the starch
shirted men, cutting his way through the suffocating and foggy
cigarette smoke. She sat with her back to him, posing as though
listening for certain footsteps.

"Suzanne," he shouted. "Suzanne Johnson, how are you?"

She turned expectantly and gave him a smile.

"Jim—how are you?"

Watching her, Jim saw at once that she had changed little physically. Oh, she wore an air of worldliness, of sophistication, but
basically she was the same.

"Look," he said. "Let's find some place where we can talk."

Suzanne smiled, nodded, and found herself being ushered through
the crowd and out of the front door.

"Still the same Susie," he was saying. "Gad, I thought you'd have
stopped fiddling with that piece of hair by now."

She chuckled softly. They grew silent as she waited for him to
speak.

Finally:

"I looked forward to this party because I knew you'd be here
and I wanted to see what two years had done. Susie, you look
great!"

From "Reunion," by K. S.

The quality of the talk itself does help evoke the atmosphere
in which the boy and girl meet each other after a separation
of two years. He knows her well enough to remember her
old habit of fiddling with her hair and reminds us that he remembers. This reveals something about both of the characters.
Also, we escape "he said" and "she replied," since the words
identify each speaker.

Nevertheless, the dialogue in this passage does not quite give
us the illusion that the people who are speaking it are themselves and only themselves—this Jim, this Susie—and that they
are in one specific and recognizable place. You cannot write
true talk for people who seem to live anywhere, however good
the talk is in itself.

Paul Green, the author of *The Lost Colony, In Abraham's
Bosom,* and many fine short stories, says that he likes to write
the dialogue of his southern characters because he knows the

region and finds the talk of its people easy for him. He once said that talk grows into a story as naturally as a leaf grows into a tobacco plant, almost springing up of itself. Green's dialogue in the following sequence about a gang of convicts working near a college community, seems natural and yet is focused to show the effect of cruelty in man.

"Rain or shine, the old dog flies stay with you," he said.

The second guard lighted a cigarette and passed the package on to the first. "And the damned muskeeters allus drilling for water," he said.

"Heigh you, Sterling, raise up that pick and let her come down," the first guard called. And the convicts dug on, accompanying every blow with their everlasting "hanh," saying never a word. "You hear me, I say, putt some pep in that digging."

After a moment the tougher Bantam called out of the side of his mouth without looking around, his pick still going, "He sick. Ain't able to work."

"You bastard monkey runt, who's talking to you?" snapped the first guard.

"Hell'll be froze over 'fore you get this little digging done," said the second guard.

"That's right," said the first guard, "Let the road grow—bricks and mortar and rivers of iron, let it flow on."

And the two keepers of the law drowsed into silence.

From "I Call My Jesus" in *Dog on the Sun*, by Paul Green

This talk is more intense, more crude, than most words that just happen. It has the blending of anger and sunlight that permeates all of Paul Green's work. His people talk for him in different ways. They speak to reveal themselves, and to reveal their relationships to each other. Moreover, their talk is a revelation not only of their own character traits but of the mind and personality of the man who created them. Paul Green's dialogue illustrates the saying: style is the man.

## TESTING YOUR DIALOGUE:  Assignment 11

Write a passage of dialogue that has its inception in the opening situation of the story on which you are working. Then ask yourself:

A. Does the talk reveal the identity of your speaker?

B. Is the idiom, or manner of talking, natural to the person who is speaking and to the situation in which he finds himself?

C. Does the talk, blending with narration and description, establish the setting in which the story and this particular scene take place?

D. Does the talk project as exactly as possible the relationship between the people involved in it? Does it establish the relationship they have with each other at the moment in which their conversation is taking place?

E. Does the talk point toward a new situation in which these same characters will find themselves as the story progresses?

F. Is the dialogue free of trite phrases, aimless or repetitious sentences that mar the effect you are trying to gain in this particular situation?

In your dialogue, and in every element of your story, trying for naturalness may result in a lapse into mediocrity. On my desk is a sketch about a nun who performs a miracle by giving courage to an uncertain boy who wants to impress his school fellows. The plot is skillfully constructed, the dialogue lively, but one of the characters is "frozen with horror" and another "casts his eyes on the ground." In your own work, make it a habit to go over what you have written to find the clichés and replace them. A straightforward phrase will always work better than a trite one.

In forming a style you may want to experiment in an effort to gain the command of language a writer like John Dos Passos shows in his documentary novels about America during the first half of our century. Dos Passos can produce a jumbled and apparently senseless paragraph directly from the mind of a character and a page or so later, with equal facility, can write an entirely objective account of the actions of the same person. A writer must work to gain this further range in style.

It may be best to stick at first to *one* way of using language and try, within such a limitation, to develop a style so individual that it is at once discernible. Some styles are as recognizable as the face of the writer to whom they belong. The laconic, not easily imitated style of Ernest Hemingway is one of these. Hemingway knows how to vary his techniques of understatement; he can write lyrically or realistically. But as one student said, "The language always comes out Hemingway."

Your own untrained style is the habit of language that has become native to you over the years. To sharpen and develop it, you may choose to imitate an author you admire or, as I have suggested, to experiment with many forms. Regardless of your choice, the way to improve is by rigorously seeking out your own most apparent faults. Any improvement at all, of course, demands constant practice in writing.

The usual advice to a young writer is to find specific rather than abstract words. He should beware of using adjectives in a series; he should use adverbs sparingly; he should make his verbs active wherever possible. He is told that the great virtue is simplicity of language and that the best way to begin forming a style is to learn how to write a direct sentence. As for straight exposition, the only possible course is to avoid it.

This last is most certainly true. Never tell *about* what is happening, what is going to happen, and what has already happened. Let the scenes emerge through the characters and their actions. As for keeping sentences simple, pruning away adjectives, and letting your verbs carry the action, the rules are probably good although many distinguished writers ignore them. They can help the young writer avoid the excess of immaturity, but perhaps he should have some excesses, at least at the start.

Sometimes a richness of language, which at first appears as a fault, becomes the ground out of which a true style flowers. The charge of intemperance in expression has often, and sometimes rightly, been thrown at Thomas Wolfe. But his devotion to language and to the multiple sensations it can evoke when a style is at its best, as in the following passage, has given him a place among the best prose writers of our time.

He remembered yet the East India Tea House at the Fair, the sandalwood, the turbans, and the robes, the cool interior and the smell of India tea; and he had felt now the nostalgic thrill of dew-wet mornings in Spring, the cherry scent, the cool clarion earth, the wet loaminess of the garden, the pungent breakfast smells and the floating show of blossoms. He knew the inchoate sharp excitement of hot dandelions in young Spring grass at noon; the smell of cellars, cobwebs, and built-on secret earth; in July, of watermelons bedded in sweet hay, inside a farmer's covered wagon; of canteloupe and crated peaches; and the scent of orange rind, bitter-sweet, before a fire of coals. He knew the good male smell of his father's sitting-room; of the smooth worn leather sofa, with the gaping horse-hair rent; of the blistered varnished wood upon the hearth; of the heated calf-skin bindings; of the flat moist plug of apple tobacco, stuck with a red flag; of wood-smoke and burnt leaves in October; of the brown tired autumn earth; of honey-suckle at night; of warm nasturtiums; of a clean ruddy farmer who comes weekly with printed butter, eggs and milk; of fat limp under-done bacon and of coffee; of a bakery-oven in the wind; of large deep-hued string-beans smoking-hot and seasoned well with salt and butter; of a room of old pine boards in which books and carpets have been stored, long closed; of Concord grapes in their long white baskets.

Yes, and the exciting smell of chalk and varnished desks; the smell of heavy bread-sandwiches of cold fried meat and butter; the smell of new leather in a saddler's shop, or of a warm leather chair; of honey and of unground coffee; of barrelled sweet-pickles and cheese and all the fragrant compost of the grocer's; the smell of stored apples in the cellar, and of orchard-apple smells, of pressed-cider pulp; of pears ripening on a sunny shelf, and of ripe cherries stewing with sugar on hot stoves before preserving; the smell of whittled wood, of all young lumber, of sawdust and shavings; of peaches stuck with cloves and pickled in brandy; of pine-sap, and green pine-needles; of a horse's pared hoof; of chestnuts roasting, of bowls of nuts and raisins; of hot cracklin, and of young roast pork; of butter and cinnamon melting on hot candied yams.

Yes, and of the rank slow river, and of tomatoes rotten on the vine; the smell of rain-wet plums and boiling quinces; of rotten lily-pads; and of foul weeds rotting in green marsh scum; and the exquisite smell of the South, clean but funky, like a big woman; of soaking trees and the earth after heavy rain.

Yes, and the smell of hot daisy-fields in the morning; of melted puddling-iron in a foundry; the winter smell of horse-warm stables and smoking dung; of old oak and walnut; and the butcher's smell of meat, of strong slaughtered lamb, plump gouty liver, ground pasty sausages, and red beef; and of brown sugar melted with slivered bitter chocolate; and of crushed mint leaves, and of a wet lilac bush; of magnolia beneath the heavy moon, of dogwood and laurel; of an old caked pipe and Bourbon rye, aged in kegs of charred oak; the sharp smell of tobacco; of carbolic and nitric acids; the coarse true smell of a dog; of old imprisoned books; and the cool fern-smell near springs; of vanilla in cake-dough; and of cloven ponderous cheeses.

Yes, and of a hardware store, but mostly the good smell of nails; of the developing chemicals in a photographer's darkroom; and the young-life smell of paint and turpentine; of buckwheat batter and black sorghum; and of a negro and his horse, together; of boiling fudge; the brine smell of pickling vats; and the lush undergrowth smell of southern hills; of a slimy oyster-can, of chilled gutted fish; of a hot kitchen negress; of kerosene and linoleum; of sarsaparilla and guavas; and of ripe autumn persimmons; and the smell of the wind and the rain; and of the acrid thunder; of cold starlight, and the brittle-bladed frozen grass; of fog and the misted winter sun; of seed-time, bloom, and mellow dropping harvest.

And now, whetted intemperately by what he had felt, he began, at school, in that fecund romance, the geography, to breathe the mixed colors of the earth, sensing in every squat keg piled on a pier-head a treasure of golden rum, rich port, fat Burgundy; smelling the jungle growth of the tropics, the heavy odor of plantations, the salt-fish smell of harbors, voyaging in the vast, enchanting, but unperplexing world.

Now the innumerable archipelago had been threaded, and he stood, firm planted, upon the unknown but waiting continent.

He learned to read almost at once, printing the shapes of words immediately with his strong visual memory; but it was weeks later before he learned to write, or even to copy, words. The ragged spume and wrack of fantasy and the lost world still floated from time to time through his clear schoolday morning brain, and although he followed accurately all the other instruction of his teacher, he was walled in his ancient unknowing world when they made letters. The children made their sprawling alphabets below a line of models, but all he accomplished was a line of jagged wavering spear-points on his sheet, which he repeated endlessly and rapturously, unable to see or understand the difference.

"I have learned to write," he thought.

Then, one day, Max Isaacs looked suddenly, from his exercise, on Eugene's sheet, and saw the jagged line.

"That ain't writin'," said he.

And clubbing his pencil in his warted grimy hand, he scrawled a copy of the exercise across the page.

The line of life, that beautiful developing structure of language that he saw  flowing from his comrade's pencil, cut the knot in him that all instruction failed to do, and instantly he seized the pencil, and wrote the words in letters fairer and finer than his friend's. And he turned, with a cry in his throat, to the next page, and copied it without hesitation, and the next, the next. They looked at each other a moment with that clear wonder by which children accept miracles, and they never spoke of it again.

"That's writin' now," said Max.

From *Look Homeward, Angel,* by Thomas Wolfe

In "The Story of a Novel," Thomas Wolfe comments on his own attempts to find his style.

I know the door is not yet open. I know the tongue, the speech, the language that I seek is not yet found, but I believe with all my heart that I have found the way, have made a channel, am started on my first beginning. And I believe with all my heart, also, that each man for himself and in his own way, each man who ever hopes to make a living thing out of the substances of his one life, must find that way, that language, and that door—must find it for himself as I have tried to do.

Thomas Wolfe's work is full of remembered sensations; his words are heavy, rich, suggestive. Nelson Algren, creating characters who move along Division Street in Chicago, opens his own door of language on a police line-up or a department store robbery, catching the idiom of the hustlers along city sidewalks that usually lead to jail. An interviewer, questioning Algren about having consciously developed a style, got the following reply:

Well, I haven't consciously tried to develop it. The only thing I've consciously tried to do was put myself in a position to hear the people I wanted to hear talk talk. I used the police line-up for I don't know how many years. But that was accidental too, like that junky deal—you don't exactly seek it out, you're there and it dawns on you. I got a newspaper man to loan me his card, but that was only good for one night. But then I finally got rolled. I didn't get myself deliberately rolled; I was just over on the South Side and got rolled. But they gave me a card, you know, to look for the guys in the line-up, and I used that card for something like seven years. They finally stopped me—the card got ragged as hell, pasted here and there, you couldn't read it—the detective at the door stopped me and said, "What happened, you mean you're still looking for the guy?" This was like seven years later, and I said, "Hell yes, I lost fourteen dollars," so he let me go ahead.

Nelson Algren in *The Paris Review*

Sometimes, by one of the many paradoxes that exist in writing, an author who is seriously searching, opens a door that does not lead him where he expects to go. Thomas Wolfe said that he wanted to restrain his language and yet is known for his exuberance. Henry James, who had a tremendous interest in passion, usually wrote out of mirrored emotions and always out of long reflection. Each man deviated from his expressed goals, but the important thing was that each had a tremendous talent for words.

As for your own style, no matter how hard you try to improve it, or how great your desire to be a better writer, without a talent for words your work is wasted. If you do have that gift, then you must learn to improve on what you possess. The poetic novelist should beware of writing lyrics into his scenes. The person trained as a reporter must try to make the language of his story convey not only the fact but the emotion behind the fact.

The writers of the following four passages have begun to develop their own individual patterns of language. One author seems often to be deliberately obscure while another uses words casually and informally. A third suggests more than he actually tells you, while a fourth hands his reader a bouquet of words. As you read, look for an individual writing trait that already seems native to each author.

He had lain in bed for weeks with pneumonia, but the worst time, more terrible even than the corn-dust season, was the time when he was at the funeral and got sick. Sick and in the middle of a crowded brown room of people who were singing a slow death song. Sick and dizzy and out of breath, wanting air, he swayed on his heels, rocked back and forth as the people sang the slow death song. Before the verses were finished he was wondering who the person was who was dead and who the person was whose hand was holding, squeezing his own; wondering who and why and where and isn't it silly and how little air there was, how hot it was; and why he couldn't see, or think, or swallow, but only rock and weave and

get halfway through a thought then lose and regain and lose it
again and clutch a new thought. "Eight o'clock," someone said and
the words bounded about, rammed here and there in his head;
it didn't seem like eight o'clock, rather like a hot afternoon in a
fiery hot sun or furnace. He heard the words "she died at eight
o'clock" and this sound echoed too, echoed high and low; he asked
who who who who died at eight o'clock. His mouth held a bitter
taste and in his head his heart skated on ice; there was a pressure
on his hand and a sound in his ear that wasn't the song, but a bird,
a buzzard's noise, a sound like *Fooo-l-oofoooll* which arched
through his ears and down his spine. It was difficult distinguishing
sound from song or the pressure on his hand from the pain in his
throat and on his tongue, and he thought his eyes would fall out
and roll on his tongue—his eyes were that huge and his tongue that
hot and swollen and his throat tighter than a cord of rope around
a dying man's neck.

From New Campus Writing, by Leon Rooke

I learned to play Fish that summer. It was a little colored kid—
older than me, but smaller—who taught me. I can't remember his
name . . . I'll call him Robert. Robert and I would sit out in front
of his house, which was about, maybe, a hundred yards down a
tractor road from the main house and the highway, and we'd sit
in the shade of a great big Chinaberry tree that stuck partly out
into the road and play Fish and Rummy right after lunch, usually.
And a tractor would go by and raise a lot of dust and we'd wait
till it had all settled again, and sometimes talk about how we were
going to buy tractors someday when we got big. And one day
two pigs got loose when it was raining. The pen was right next to
Robert's house, and we got out in the rain with no coats—it was
as warm as a showerbath—and our job was to open the gate so it
stretched all the way across the road and blocked it so the two pigs
wouldn't get past when the men chased them back, but one of us
had to keep the others from getting out, too, and then we had to
close the gate quick when they ran in.

Wally Kuralt

It was mid-afternoon on the beach and in the tavern the air was
still stale from last night's spilled beer. The laughter of the tourists
had gone with the summer, and the street outside lay empty under
the steady October rain.

Light from a neon sign strove periodically through streaks of
water on the tavern window and reflected red and green on rows
of glasses behind the bar. A cowboy rode across the screen of a

television beside the window, accompanied by the sound of the William Tell Overture.

Irwin Glenn sat on his bartender's stool between the bar and the rows of glasses thinking of what a bad summer it had been and wondering, more with curiosity than anxiety, how he was going to live through the winter.

Hugh A. McEachern, Jr.

And you were there just as big and grand, living in your ornate castle, trying too hard for a kiss from the lips you were bruising. But before you could think you were on stage again dancing hard, smiling at the grotesque, zooming in the night, leaving your trail and your crystal deeds. You saw yourself once too often but you loved the reflection even more and off you flew again, still fascinated and floating on a bubble. You sailed up with them knowing their suicide and you kissed and wept, still drunk from refusal and invitation. But how clever you were among them all, holding to the perfume of the time, marching with it under alien arches and past the past. From the day you were born you were dying slowly and sweetly. Death could not blind you. It added color to your hour, your thrills were minute blossoms. Each shock of truth became personal and elevating until you broke camp again.

Leon Capetanos

## IDENTIFYING THE CHARACTERISTICS OF A STYLE:
Assignment 12

1. Which of the preceding passages seems to be most similar in diction to your own mode of expression in language?

2. Taking the chosen passage as a point of departure, comment on an individual language trait you have singled out for its excellence, relating it to a passage in a story of your own.

3. Read the following story by Anne Tyler and afterwards write a comment on the success she has achieved in suiting the language to the action of the story in dialogue, character, narration, and description of landscape.

"The Saints in Caesar's Household" was written by Anne Tyler at Duke University. It first appeared in the campus magazine, *The Archive*, in April, 1961.

# THE SAINTS IN CAESAR'S HOUSEHOLD

ANNE TYLER

Mary Robinson did not come home until that fall. People said she was coming mainly because of Laura (they'd been best friends all through school) but Mary's mother said Mary didn't know about Laura at all; no one wanted to tell her. Mary's mother was the sort of woman who bought brooms from the Knights of Columbus, and wrote letters to the little boy who was on the March of Dimes poster, and cried when she sang Christmas carols to the County Home; everyone said she was exactly the one to tell Mary. But every week she spent one morning trying to think of something to write Mary and she always ended up with nothing but how is your work (Mary was with a publishing firm in New York) and have you met any nice young men, and then something about whom she'd seen lately. She believed in telling bad news in three letters, gradually. And she had it planned to send Mary a clipping first, saying Miss Laura Gates had left her job in Chicago for a brief stay with her parents, and to pencil in the margin a note asking if she remembered Laura (although that was a silly question). Next would come a letter telling how she'd seen her on the street, and she was looking a little nervous and thinner than usual and had asked how Mary was; and finally the third letter, saying something was wrong with Laura Gates, something in her mind, and it was the saddest thing she'd yet seen and she was sorry to be the one to tell her.

That was how she had it planned. But summer came and went with her somehow forgetting all about Laura every time she sat down to write Mary, and in the fall Mary came home herself and there was no need to write it. She came on the noon bus and one of the first things she said after she walked in the door was, "Clemson Roberts on the bus said Laura Gates was home."

And Mary's mother looked at Mary's father and wrapped one hand up in her apron as if it were a gift and said, "Yes, she has been since May." When she said that she watched to see if Mary were going to say something else, like why didn't you tell me sooner when you knew there wasn't ever another person who made as much difference as Laura. But she didn't ask that.

She said, "She didn't write from Chicago. I thought she had forgotten all about us and wasn't ever coming back."

"Well, she's back now," her mother said.

And after that Mary went upstairs to wash and didn't say anything about Laura at all, just handed little presents to her parents and talked to her aunt on the phone and put sheets on her old bed. "What I heard," she said at dinner, "about Laura Gates throwing her little sister's clothes away, was that true?"

And her mother said, "Yes, I think I heard that too."

But when Mary didn't ask anything after that, or even mention it, they knew it must have all been said by Clemson Roberts on the bus and they didn't try to explain any more, or tell about the mailman or the Catholic confessional or any of the rest of it, or even comfort her.

Mary's aunt said (this was on the second day she was home) that she could remember when Mary and Laura spent all of their seventh summer stealing smudgepots from the road construction and storing them in the garage. "Somebody found them," she said. "I can't remember who."

"It was you that found us," Mary said.

"Maybe it was. Maybe it was and maybe it wasn't, I can't remember now. But I know I must have been near, because I can still see you standing there, the two of you, sticking up for your rights and defending your smudgepots."

She said later that that should have done it, if Mary had forgotten about how she and Laura were in the old days it wasn't because she hadn't tried to prod her memory. "You might also say it's her *duty*, to go see her," she said. "People are wondering, and asking, and whispering amongst themselves."

And they were. Even Mary's mother knew that; Mary's mother spent her Fridays visiting the sick and she said to Mary's father, on the fourth evening, "I would have gone to see Laura Gates myself, every day of her life, but she's never been able to abide me and it was Mary who was close to her, Mary was the one who never let a day pass without her going there or Laura coming here. I don't know, I just don't know," and trailed off and stared into the twilight, while upstairs Mary sat at her window and fiddled with the ruffles on the organdy curtains and watched the black trees against the dark autumn sky.

On the fifth day Mary got up early; it was raining and even her room was grey and misty. She put on warm clothes and at breakfast she asked her mother if she could have the car, just for the morning. Her mother was reading the paper. She said, "Take it for the day, I'm not going anywhere," and turned another page and asked if she would bring her some teabags if she went near the grocery store.

"I doubt if I'll be going near the grocery store," Mary said.

She had already put a scarf over her head and left before her mother had really thought about her going. When she was talking to Mary's aunt later she said, "It might be she's going to Laura's, but today of all days I almost hope not, she was so grim when she left I don't think she'd be much cheer."

"Well, you never can tell. Maybe it was just because she *was* going to see Laura, we don't know."

"Now, that's no reason," Mary's mother said.

And Mary parked the car in front of the Gates', and walked up through cold driving rain and rang the bell. A wet cat rubbed against her. She took off the scarf and shook out her hair, and then the door opened and Laura stood there with her face made thinner by the shadows behind her and a cup of coffee in the hand that wasn't holding the door. She was in dark blue, an old dark blue sweater and a dark blue pleated skirt that needed cleaning. She must have had them a long time for them to look so shabby, but Mary could never remember seeing them before; she had always remembered Laura in red and orange and green and peacock, sometimes all together because Laura said the way some people believed about colors practically amounted to superstition and there wasn't any reason why you couldn't jumble colors up.

All this time, while Mary was trying to get used to everything all over again, the world was as silent as an empty building and there was only the hushing sound of the rain. And then Laura stepped aside and said, "Who did you come to see?" which was what she always asked, even if she knew.

"I came to see you," Mary said.

"Well, come in."

The smells in the house were of wet wood and dry dust, the way they were any time of year. Laura led the way to the dining room and in her navy blue she was like another shadow in the house, or a dark flower on the living room rug. "I haven't eaten breakfast," she said. "Have you?"

"Yes."

Laura sat down at the head of the table. "I always have coffee," she said, "and two rolls. That's my breakfast. You might want to know, if you came to watch me. But I'm all right now, I'm getting better, and there's nothing much to watch any more."

She buttered a roll, and then put it down.

"But if you'd come to watch me," she said, "you'd have come before. You've been home five days now."

"Yes, I have," Mary said.

Laura pushed her rolls away and stretched, smiling, with her arms far above her head. "Have a roll," she said, "and say what you're doing in New York. I can still *hear* all right."

"I'm not doing anything," Mary said. "I'm on vacation."

She put sugar in her coffee and Laura handed her the cream; she handed it as if she were a judge handing the witness a glass of water and telling her to go on, but Mary didn't say any more. She just put the cream pitcher down and stared absently at the brown wallpaper, the wallpaper with the edges darker and tangled vines as thin and dark as Laura.

"Saturday night I heard a funny noise," Laura said. She sounded as if she were prompting Mary, waiting for her to take the story up. Mary looked at her. "It was at midnight I heard it," Laura said. "A sound like a loudspeaker in a railroad station, frightened and hurrying, with that kind of background of chattering voices blurring together."

"In your house you heard it?"

"Yes. And a man said, 'All right, Laura,' and I sat straight up in bed with my heart beating so loud I couldn't have heard him again if I'd tried. I kept waiting for my family to come bursting out of bedrooms saying, 'What was that? Did you hear that?' and comforting each other. But no one came. Somewhere there was a little creak, and I waited a while longer, but no one came."

Mary turned a fork over and over in her hands.

"At breakfast I asked my family, I said, 'Did you hear anything in the night?' But their faces were funny and blurred, all turned toward me while I stared hard at the dining room wallpaper and waited for my mother to say, 'Now, Laura, there wasn't a sound,' and she did, and she passed me the toast."

"It was probably the house," Mary said. "That you heard, I mean. That or you being half-asleep, or maybe both."

"Of course it was," Laura said. "Do you think I hear *voices?*"

"No. I was explaining more for your mother, I guess."

"My mother's so old. She's touched people who've touched other people all the way back to Babylon, all those generations touching hands."

"So have you," Mary said.

"No, I haven't, I don't feel that way. My mother can remember back to when ballpoint pens were a miracle. Mrs. Parry was the envy of all the women in the neighborhood; she had a fur coat down to her ankles and a ballpoint pen."

She threw back her head and laughed, and Mary laughed too, just to see her; the whole day seemed better. Mary pushed her chair back and said, "Let's go to the amphitheatre, it's always nice in the rain," and Laura said, "All right," and pulled a brown jacket from the hall closet.

They went outdoors and the rain had turned into a fine spray, just enough to make their faces shine under the wet leaves that hung over the sidewalk.

"Things are supposed to seem little when you come back to a place," Laura said. "But everything seems big to me."

"Me too," Mary said.

"Did your aunt remind you about the smudgepots?"

"Yes."

"She reminded me too; she called up my mother and asked did I remember. My mother said *she* did even if I didn't, and I said I did too. But she asked as if it were long ago and tiny, and I still remember it as being as near and big as this morning, or bigger."

"Well, not bigger," Mary said.

"To me it's bigger."

They walked to the end of the block and then turned off into the trees that were to the right of them. Laura led the way. She held out her arms to balance herself down narrow slippery stones that were laid down like steps, and when they were through the trees there was the little amphitheatre, deserted in the rain, with the stone wall around it and the parking lot completely empty at the rear and the stone seats sloping down in semicircles to the stage. "I never can imagine what this place is like when the plays are going," Laura said, "I don't think we've ever been here then."

"I have," Mary said.

Laura climbed down toward the stage, leaping from one semicircle to the other in great wide steps and sometimes almost missing because it was a long way to jump, while Mary sat on the top row and watched her. Halfway down Laura stopped and turned back so she was facing Mary.

"Why do you think she reminded you about the smudgepots?" she called.

"Why did she?"

"Because your mother visits the sick in the County Home and lends her heating pad out, that's why. Don't you want to be reminded how it was when we were seven, and remember and come visit like your mother with her jar of chicken broth? Don't you want to be like your mother?"

"No," Mary said.

"And remember the aged and understand the insane?"

"No," Mary said.

"Were you afraid to come?"

"No."

Laura turned and spread her arms like wings, looking up at the grey sky and letting the spray fall flat on her face. "Well, that's why she told you," she said after a minute. "So you would remember the aged and understand the insane." And she leapt down one more semicircle and sat down, with Mary sitting almost directly behind her and seven rows back. They stayed that way for ten minutes; all that time Mary sat staring straight ahead at Laura and the stage below her, and Laura rested her chin in her hands and looked at her shoes. At the end of that time she raised her head and looked at the stage and said, "But your aunt was trying, all the same, and those smudgepots *were* fun, I do remember that."

"I do too," Mary said.

The rain started coming in drops. They both sat waiting for each drop, because it splashed large and cool and was different from the spray, with a cleaner feeling to it. Laura stood up again and started turning around and around with her hands raised to keep her hair away from the back of her neck and let the rain splash on it. "Your aunt," she said, "and your mother, and the nuns in Our Lady, and the Salvation Army . . ." and to Mary her voice came echoing across through the raining world like a chant. After she stopped spinning she started walking calmly down the hill, one foot on the stone and the other on the ground; stone, ground, stone ground, while her voice swam back to Mary. "You even ask them, you go to Catholic confessional when you've never set foot in mass even, and offer to let the priest confess to you, poor man, but people won't hear of it."

"I hear thunder," Mary said.

"People won't hear of it," Laura repeated; she was far away now. "They won't hear of it, they won't even listen. I don't know my sister. Do you know my sister, Jennifer Gates?"

"Yes, a little."

"I said, 'Stay and talk,' but she's always away. Even when she's home, she's a little bit away; I woke up at seven and put all her clothes in the garbage can, so she would have to stay and talk, she couldn't just go walking off. That was silly, but there was some sense to it."

She stopped on the front row, far below Mary, and turned, standing on tiptoe, and reached high up with both hands and shouted, "Can't you just *see* my sister, without a stitch on, sitting down and *finally* getting into a really good *talk?*"

Mary smiled, and then she began laughing and leaned forward with her hands on the stone and laughed.

"That's right," Laura said. "Now you know; there isn't anything to be afraid of now."

And after that she seemed to be finished worrying; she turned again and started climbing the little side steps to the stage. "You can't stop a soul; you lean out of windows and say, 'Don't you even want to talk about it?' but they don't bother trying . . . why did I do that? I should have known it wouldn't work." And then she smiled, while Mary on the back row stood up and tightened her scarf.

"Stay where you are," Laura said, "it's better there." She wandered onto the stage. "Can you hear me?"

"I can hear you fine," Mary said.

"Even with the rain?"

"If you speak loudly."

"Well, then, listen. Because some April you'll go up to someone—an old woman on a bus, a man selling pencils, a little boy with a turtle—and you'll think about how you understand even the littlest thing inside them; you're even the same people, and you run after them quick and catch them—"

She stopped and looked up at Mary. Mary was sitting in the rain and frowning at the ground.

"The saints salute you," Laura said.

Mary looked up at her.

"And especially they that are of Caesar's household; that's a Bible verse and the only one I know, but I think I will all my life remember that feeling you get in the front of your head when you catch people and say, 'Wait,' and they look at you and pull their arm gently away from you and go on—Nowadays there is too much love in the world; it goes floating around and nobody wants it. Are you getting cold?"

"No," Mary said. "A goose walked over my grave."

"You can go home."

"I'm not cold."

"Go *home!*" she shouted suddenly, and it echoed around the seats. "It's none of your *business* being here, up on top row so far away I couldn't touch you with a bamboo pole; who did *you* ever reach out for as they went by? And what are you *doing* here?"

And she stood with her fists clenched beside her and shouted, while Mary stood up and wrapped her coat around her and climbed back up through the trees to the sidewalk. Once she looked back, and smiled at Laura, but Laura had turned away and it wasn't any use. Mary left her that way, her dark blue clothes heavy with rain and her back to everything.

People say (and Mary's mother also) that it was a heartless thing to leave a disturbed person out there alone in the rain, with the stones all around her and the grey sky pressing in. Mary's aunt said she didn't care *what* Laura Gates had done, or what had been said between them, you still have to make allowances for a nervous person. She said all this straight to Mary, whom she found standing at her bedroom window the afternoon of the day it all happened. She said, "Sometimes it takes an effort, Mary, to understand people who are mentally disturbed." And then she clicked her teeth and stared over Mary's shoulder into the street below. "I don't understand you," she said after a minute. "I would have thought you should be very worried about Laura Gates."

But Mary only smiled and said, "No, I'm not worried," and then grew serious again and leaned her head against the windowframe.

After a while the aunt left, but Mary stood there with her eyes closed and for a minute she thought that even through her eyelids

she could see, down on the street, the grass pressed flat by the wind
and the people blurred by the rain.


## COMMENT

The first quiet sentence, "Mary Robinson did not come home
until that fall," presents her as a member of the small community in which the story takes place. We are given hints of what
the saints of her town are like through the early references to
the March of Dimes and the weeping at the County Home
during the singing of the Christmas carols. Finally, we are
led gently to the realization that Mary's friend, Laura Gates,
has something wrong with her mind. Even at the beginning,
the mother's concern over Laura's difficulties is "professional."

Laura herself derides the local, orthodox attitude toward
mental illness and at the same time suspects that the old, fixed
symbols of order are impossible to overthrow. It is in this am-
bivalence that the story rests. The smudgepots, for instance,
represent a time of childhood before conventional attitudes
have interfered with the direct relationship between one person
and another. For the aunt, they merely symbolize the fact that
there was a relationship and that as a result it is Mary's duty
to go visit her friend.

The mistiness of the day intensifies the mood of the visitor.
Mary sets out on a gray, rainy morning. In the vague landscape
the trees are black against the sky. A scarf covers her face, and
also her intention, as she starts on what is only *perhaps* an
errand of mercy. Her mother declares that Mary is grim, but
her true mood, like the true nature of the meeting with Laura,
is still to be discovered.

Laura's house is framed in a setting of cold, driving rain. She
appears at the door, her face in a half light, her sweater dark.
Her skirt, as does its wearer, needs cleaning. Inside the room,
where Laura once strutted in peacock colors, she is now like
another shadow or a dark flower on the living room rug. These

sensuous details are in themselves dark flowers of words projecting the atmosphere of illness.

When the dialogue begins, the talk between the two girls
heightens the estrangement. In suggesting that Mary has come
to "watch" her, Laura implies that everyone is a watcher, that
the world is one big prying eye. There are many prying eyes
but no ears at all—only Laura has heard the voice in the night,
the man in the loudspeaker who may be God. Even in confiding
that she heard him say, "All right, Laura," Laura Gates knows
that Mary, like the others, will think nobody was there at all.

Then, moving by surprise out of the blur of estrangement,
Laura is the one who brings them both back to the present by
a specific repudiation of the past. No more old-time ballpoint
pens that seemed to be miracles, or fur coats that went all the
way down to the ankles. Laura does not want to feed on what
is gone and neither does Mary Robinson. The laughter between
them initiates the key scene in the amphitheatre and the central
event of the story.

As they walk through the rain which is now only a spray,
the whole day seems better until it is again dimmed by the
reminder of the smudgepots. For a moment it seems that there
will be no drama in the story, that no connection at all can
exist between the two people in the theater. Then, the smudgepots intrude again and we see that now they are tied in with
the conventional idea of duty—a jar of chicken broth brought
to the sick.

Laura underscores her hatred of conventional help for the
needy by making it plain that those pots are a signal of an obligation to remember the insane. For the first time, she speaks
the word. By now its connotation has been so powerfully suggested by the imagery that the word *insane* has a heightened
meaning. It is not just a sign we might see on a ward door. It
is Laura Gates.

The ritual on the stones begins with a confessional in which
Laura reveals how she tried to communicate with the postman,
the priest, and the sister whose clothes she put in the garbage
thinking Jennifer would stay and talk to her. Throwing the

clothes away may have been a gesture of wanting everyone else to become a poor, bare, forked animal like herself. But she cannot share her nakedness. She cannot make people stay with her.

The story turns sharply when Laura calls out to Mary, "Go home!" At last she is convinced that she must stop reaching, since you cannot hold anyone no matter how hard you grab them. She is apart from Mary now, on the stage of the amphitheater. When Mary, after starting toward home, looks again, Laura has turned away.

At the end, the people are arrested where we found them earlier. The saints still have their certitude and Mary Robinson will never follow them. The word *saints*, like *insane*, now has a new connotation. As for Laura, we are away from her and from her too-much-love world, which is not a practical one. Like Mary Robinson, we have left her in the dark, her clothes heavy with rain and her back to everything.

Throughout the story, Mary's behavior represents a protest that is conveyed through varying patterns of language. A muted ending that shows us Mary at the window thinking for a minute that with her eyes shut she can see the people in the street through a blur of rain. What she does see, and what any one of us sees of the people with whom we try to communicate, must be decided in the lingering aftereffects of Anne Tyler's fine story.

## WORKING WITH LANGUAGE PATTERNS:
Assignment 13

1. From the working draft of your own story, try to isolate paragraphs that display a command of language in each of the following areas:

 a. An objective passage reporting the actions of a character.

 b. The thoughts of a character revealed through his own point of view.

    c. A passage projecting the setting of your story.

    d. A paragraph that hints at the idea of your story.

  **2.** Commenting on "The Saints in Caesar's Household," say whether you think Anne Tyler's story could be put into a category such as *realistic* or *impressionistic,* so far as her manner of writing goes.

The word *style* can be used to put a writer into a class with other writers whose language resembles his own. We can say that certain writers are symbolic or that they are documentary in manner. We can call an author lucid or obscure in his language. But for the measure of your own style that is in the process of becoming what you want it to be, you need more delicate tests than these.

An understanding of *category* in style is necessary for a critic and helpful for a reader. But for anyone who is trying to find out how to *tell what he knows* in his own language, too intensive a study of literary terminology will hamper the freedom of expression that must always exist when a person commits himself to the act of writing.

# 6

# But What Is a Story?

This book began by discussing the desire to write a story, for without this desire no writer has ever been able to create his own world in fiction. It is this primary need that compels a man to overcome his problems in technique in order to fashion a story or a novel. We return to it again before trying to bring together the elements that make up fiction.

We already know that the urge does not lend itself to analysis and is even difficult to name. You can call it a daemon, linking it with myth, or designate it as a compulsion. D. H. Lawrence thought of it as therapeutic, remarking that "we shed our sickness in books." Some say it is a matter of madness, others of genes. All we really know is that this instinct is unique in each writer but that by necessity it links him, through his work, to other men.

The force also exists strongly in the engineer who arches a bridge across a bay and the architect who raises a tower over a city. It can appear in different guises in the same man, making of a Leonardo a sculptor, a painter, an architect, and an engineer. It sometimes withers early as in Wordsworth, or flowers late and for a second time as in Verdi, who composed *Otello* long after *Aïda* had been accepted as the crown of his career. The important thing is that the instinct does exist in you and that it compels you to write your story.

But what is a story? The dictionaries try to tell us. One says that a story is a narrative of events which happened or might have happened. Another calls it an account of some incident but fails to mention plot, place, or theme. The archaic meaning of fiction as a *lie* may be misleading but it is appropriate, too, in that it stresses the need for invention.

It is easier to tell what fiction is about than to define it, and also easier to define it than to produce a good story within the limits of the definition. In some fictional experiments, as in the early stream-of-consciousness novels, we can derive a different definition from each finished book. Nor is any story, whatever technique it employs, exact in the sense of having a stringently fixed form.

We start again with the fact that each story has its beginnings in your urge to tell what you know and that its roots are deep in the experiences that have meaning for you. We know, too, that a story has varied sources. It may come directly out of your experience. It may come from a book you have read, or from a scene you have watched, or have invented. Whatever the source, a narrative structure must be imposed upon it if it is to have a life of its own as a story. It must have form.

Fiction, as Aristotle has said of tragedy, is an imitation of an action. Furthermore, it is an imitation of *people* in action, and this imitation must be expressed in words. The people and the action generate the words you write and determine the pattern into which they flow. But the people are yours. You have observed them so well that they as characters, together with their situations and surroundings, truly belong to you. In a sense, then, fictional form, like style, is a reflection of your own personality and a result of your own invention.

Form also refers, more narrowly, to the interrelationships among the various parts of a work, to the manner in which the style, the setting, the action, and the characters are joined in the pattern. Form is thus used to designate both the organization of content and the structure of thought in fiction.

We will put aside further attempts at definition for a moment and say that in the strictest personal sense the story you write is you but that it must simultaneously live beyond you. A young writer in my class has claimed, "Any story I ever write is between *you* and *me*. The exact details, such as plot, characters, and style are trivial and uninteresting except in view of this end."

We can take it still further by saying that you as a writer

are unique. Your work is a jewel unlike any ever cut before and so much your own that nobody else could mine it in the dark reaches of the imagination or bring it into the open and polish it into shape. It is a possession you would like to keep. My student added, when we were talking together about fiction, "My story belongs to me and I don't want it taken away."

When reminded of the *you* he had included before, he admitted wanting *one* reader but would go no further except to say again, "A story is between you and me." He was exactly right in that a story does first have to be yours and belong to you. But after its lonely beginning it must belong to other people or perish. To do this it must resemble other fiction and grow in common ground. It must share a recognizable form.

The common ground of fiction is very wide. In the novel, as E. M. Forster says, it occasionally degenerates into a swamp. He goes on slyly to call a novel a work of prose fiction of 50,-000 words. The short story covers much less ground, at the least a yard, at the most a mile. It is "a piece of prose fiction that may be a 1000 words long or run to as many as 7000 words." Length, though, is only one aspect of the common ground on which your story must stand.

As for subject matter, you can write a parable, which is a story in its own way, like the tale of the people who came late to the vineyard. They were paid as much as the people who came early and made a lot of enemies who remained resentful even when the owner of the vineyard explained that many are called but few chosen. You can write a long, involved narrative, as Henry James did in *The Turn of the Screw*, in which we never really know the nature of the governess or of the children, and in which the conflict to this day remains a shadowy one. Within such a range, you must, as my student said, pick a subject that has meaning for at least one other person.

Whatever you write must have a place to start, a place to make its point, and a place to stop; or, as Aristotle demanded, it must have a beginning, a middle, and an end. Although in many modern stories the start, and sometimes the end, are implied rather than stated, every work of fiction must have a complication and a subsequent resolution, or at least the suggestion of a resolution emerging from forces at work within the framework of the narrative. Some people call this double requirement a *plot*.

You will hear that a story always starts with a person wanting something and ends with his getting it or not getting it. He may be a Hemingway hero who wants to learn a code for facing life in a God-abandoned world and learns it through defeat in battle. He may be a Huck Finn who hates the idea of being "sivilized" and so wants to light out for the territory. But he must be a person for whom your reader cares and this caring usually depends on the truth, or the point, your characters make for you.

We say, then, that a story contains a truth which you know and understand and think important enough to share with other people. Through your characters and their actions, and in the fictional form by which you present them, your point becomes important for the reader. Frank O'Connor, the Irish writer, believes that this truth, or point, which he calls a theme, is the most vital part of a story.

*Interviewer:* What is the greatest essential of a story?

*O'Connor:* You have to have a theme, a story to tell. Here's a man at the other side of the table and I'm talking to him; I'm going to tell him something that will interest him. As you know perfectly well, our principal difficulty at Harvard was a number of people who'd had affairs with girls or had had another interesting experience, and wanted to come in and tell about it, straight away. That is not a theme. A theme is something that is worth something to everybody. In fact, you wouldn't, if you'd ever been involved in a thing like this, grab a man in a pub and say, "Look, I had a girl out last night, under the Charles Bridge." That's the last thing you'd do. You grab somebody and say, "Look, an extraordinary thing happened to me yesterday—I met a man—he said this to me—" and that, to me, is a theme. The moment you grab somebody by the lapels and you've got something to tell, that's real story. It means you want to tell him and think the story is interesting in itself. If you start describing your own personal experiences, something that's only of interest to yourself, then you can't express yourself, you cannot say, ultimately, what you think about human beings. The moment you say this, you're committed.

This "extraordinary thing," which to Frank O'Connor is a theme, links you to other story tellers and to the people who read what you write. It is not a theme at all in the sense of being about love, death, or politics because you think you ought to write about some significant subject. As we are using the terms here, *theme*, *truth*, or *point* mean the extraordinary quality in the human situation of your characters.

Nor do you have to imitate what other writers have said before. A Sherwood Anderson may do a free-flowing, unplanned tale about a boy who wants to know why life is not what he thought it to be, or a Graham Greene may write a tight-rope entertainment about an old man who has been so psychologically crippled by a murder he witnessed long ago that he has never been able to face life at all. You may find ground that is entirely your own.

J. H., the student whose "Christmas" appears below, told me that in his home town, he heard how a neighbor brought home a billy goat on Christmas Eve and kept the goat in the house against the wishes of his wife. The student wanted to tell a story of a man who quarreled with his wife on Christmas Eve but found a new meaning for the holiday in a final moment of understanding. Our writer framed his events in a pattern and put them in a time sequence, but he intended to do more, and so we will judge him on his intentions.

## CHRISTMAS

J. H.

May sat at the kitchen table, her elbows on the bare wood. Leaning over, she snatched a straw from the broom which stood against the sink. As she picked her teeth she hummed along with the boiling kettle.

Through the passageway to the front room she saw a glint of the lamplight on tinsel. The tinsel was hung on the dwarfed cedar standing in the corner by the door.

She and the kettle hummed something akin to a discordant "Silent Night," and she wondered again where Henry was.

Along the dirt road which ran past the house, and perhaps a

quarter-mile away, an awkward hulk stumbled toward the light ahead. The base of this shadowy form was Henry, and across his shoulders he carried a full-grown goat—a billy. The horns crested the stumbling, grunting, cursing form. Occasionally this stumbling, grunting, cursing form would emit a sharp "BAA-A-A."

The night was clear and bitterly cold, and the moon silvered the landscape. Turning into the yard, he saw the icicles still hanging from the outhouse eaves. "I'll just wait until the ground thaws to move it."

As he came around the house to the back porch the billy struggled. "BAA-A-A!" Inside the house May called, "You Henry?"

"No dammit! Open the door."

She did, and he stopped to put the animal on the floor. "Christmas," he explained.

They stood a moment, May surveying the goat, the goat staring at Henry, Henry looking anxiously at his wife. "Christmas," she said finally.

Henry shuddered at the room's warmth, and she moved to fill two cups from the musical coffee pot. They sat and watched the animal just becoming used to the room.

"Kids in bed?" he asked. It was 2 o'clock.

"Yeah."

They sat for a minute. "Let's wake em up," he said.

"No."

"Why?"

"A few hours won't hurt."

They sat again in silence. The kettle droned lower as the fire died. Again he spoke:

"I remember when I got a goat when I was a kid. Had a cart and harness with bells, and he had a beard . . . as long as that one. We used to play with him ever day; all the kids around. . . ." He looked at May.

"No!" she said with finality. "They can wait till morning."

Silence again. Then:

"May?"

She rose and walked to the bedroom door. She hesitated a moment, then smiled broadly and burst into the bedroom.

"Wake up, wake UP, Santa Claus's come! Wake up, Santa Claus is been here! Wake UP!"

The sleeping forms stirred in bed. One asked, "Why?"

"Santa Claus!"

"Santa Claus? Santa Claus!" The covers flew back, and three little boys tumbled out onto the floor. They stumbled into the kitchen and saw the goat. He was chewing on a dish towel. The youngest one screamed with terror and buried his face in his mother's apron.

The two advanced on the animal timidly, and the little one peeped cautiously from the apron's folds.

"BAA-A-A!"

The little one shrieked again, the other jumped back in fear. Henry laughed and leaned over to pat the goat. The animal spread his hind legs. From his hindquarters issued a stream of pellets which rolled across the floor.

The two older boys laughed hysterically. Henry pushed the door open and swept the dry dung through it. He turned, caught his wife's eye, and walked outside to sweep the dung from the porch and steps.

Frank, the oldest boy, came out of the front room, buckling on his pants.

"Did you get a cart, Pop?"

"No. We can build one out of the wagon tomorrow."

"Yeah."

The two larger children crowded around the animal's head, wondering at the fearsome horns which spiraled outward. The youngest toddled up to the group and gingerly touched the long beard.

"Time to go to bed," May commanded.

"No."

"No!"

"Nooooo!"

"Bed!"

The three boys turned silently toward their room. Frank paused a moment; "Merry Christmas, Pop"; and went back into the front room.

May walked to the bedroom door. The three were already huddled under the quilt asleep. She closed the door. "Get that dam thing out of here," she said quietly.

"Where?"

"In the barn."

"Can I keep him on the porch tonight? May?"

"OK . . . tonight."

## FINDING THE ESSENTIAL POINT:  Assignment 14

In reading through "Christmas," ask yourself what essential point is lacking in the tale. Suggest one change the author could make in the action of the story to make the reader aware of a theme that is lacking here. Add a comment on how the change would strengthen the ending.

"Christmas" does have its virtues. The people live in a believable little world and they have a small, brash liveliness. It
is true that in presenting them, the author has attempted no
plot development and offered almost no suspense, but he does
have a situation. The sketch also gives us a look into what
develops when Henry brings home a present for May and the
boys that is actually a gift for himself. The trouble is that we
do not get more than a look.

A deeper trouble is that the characters' reactions in the situation never catch us and hold us. The sketch never jumps the
gap from the author to us and makes us want it entirely for
ourselves. The possible point, that Henry reaches an understanding of the significance of the gift to his wife, is not embodied
in the narration or displayed by its people.

J. H. needs to look particularly at the central section of his
work for it is here that the flaws in technique are most apparent, and in the shallows of the story the hoped-for truth is lost.
By analyzing more deeply the character relationship between
Henry and May the author may be able to begin the process
of giving "Christmas" a design that will carry his point for
him. Certainly, a close look at the center will reveal the fuzzi-
ness of the ending.

You may say, "But I like the story. I like Henry and May just
as they are." One student who saw "Christmas" as a small
"entertainment" felt that to attempt any change would be
ruinous, and he was right in his own vision of the story. Like
everyone else, he judged by what appealed to his taste. Still,
when a reader becomes aware of what we are calling *truth* in
fiction, he will in the end not settle for less than what the author
really wants to tell him.

## BLOCKING OUT A STORY:   Assignment 15

1. Work out an exact statement of the point or theme you find important enough to want your reader to share with you in your first
story to be written for this class.

2. Write out a brief comment on the narrative framework you intend to use. Specifically, answer the questions of who will tell your story and of its boundaries in time and space. Write a brief description of your central characters and their conflict.

3. At what point in the narrative will your truth emerge from the story you intend to write?

4. Read through "The Use of Force," which follows here, and find the point that Williams makes in his narrative.

## THE USE OF FORCE

### WILLIAM CARLOS WILLIAMS

They were new patients to me, all I had was the name, Olson. Please come down as soon as you can, my daughter is very sick.

When I arrived I was met by the mother, a big startled looking woman, very clean and apologetic who merely said, Is this the doctor? and let me in. In the back, she added. You must excuse us, doctor, we have her in the kitchen where it is warm. It is very damp here sometimes.

The child was fully dressed and sitting on her father's lap near the kitchen table. He tried to get up, but I motioned for him not to bother, took off my overcoat and started to look things over. I could see that they were all very nervous, eyeing me up and down distrustfully. As often, in such cases, they weren't telling me more than they had to, it was up to me to tell them; that's why they were spending three dollars on me.

The child was fairly eating me up with her cold, steady eyes, and no expression to her face whatever. She did not move and seemed, inwardly, quiet; an unusually attractive little thing, and as strong as a heifer in appearance. But her face was flushed, she was breathing rapidly, and I realized that she had a high fever. She had magnificent blond hair, in profusion. One of those picture children often reproduced in advertising leaflets and the photogravure sections of the Sunday papers.

She's had a fever for three days, began the father and we don't know what it comes from. My wife has given her things, you know, like people do, but it don't do no good. And there's been a lot of sickness around. So we tho't you'd better look her over and tell us what is the matter.

As doctors often do I took a trial shot at it as a point of departure. Has she had a sore throat?

Both parents answered me together, No . . . No, she says her throat don't hurt her.

Does your throat hurt you? added the mother to the child. But the little girl's expression didn't change nor did she move her eyes from my face.

Have you looked?

I tried to, said the mother, but I couldn't see.

As it happens we had been having a number of cases of diphtheria in the school to which this child went during that month and we were all, quite apparently, thinking of that, though no one had as yet spoken of the thing.

Well, I said, suppose we take a look at the throat first. I smiled in my best professional manner and asking for the child's first name I said, come on, Mathilda, open your mouth and let's take a look at your throat.

Nothing doing.

Aw, come on, I coaxed, just open your mouth wide and let me take a look. Look, I said opening both hands wide, I haven't anything in my hands. Just open up and let me see.

Such a nice man, put in the mother. Look how kind he is to you. Come on, do what he tells you to. He won't hurt you.

At that I ground my teeth in disgust. If only they wouldn't use the word "hurt" I might be able to get somewhere. But I did not allow myself to be hurried or disturbed but speaking quietly and slowly I approached the child again.

As I moved my chair a little nearer suddenly with one catlike movement both her hands clawed instinctively for my eyes and she almost reached them too. In fact she knocked my glasses flying and they fell, though unbroken, several feet away from me on the kitchen floor.

Both the mother and father almost turned themselves inside out in embarrassment and apology. You bad girl, said the mother, taking her and shaking her by one arm. Look what you've done. The nice man . . .

For heaven's sake, I broke in. Don't call me a nice man to her. I'm here to look at her throat on the chance that she might have diphtheria and possibly die of it. But that's nothing to her. Look here, I said to the child, we're going to look at your throat. You're old enough to understand what I'm saying. Will you open it now by yourself or shall we have to open it for you?

Not a move. Even her expression hadn't changed. Her breaths however were coming faster and faster. Then the battle began. I had to do it. I had to have a throat culture for her own protection. But first I told the parents that it was entirely up to them. I explained the danger but said that I would not insist on a throat examination so long as they would take the responsibility.

If you don't do what the doctor says you'll have to go to the hospital, the mother admonished her severely.

Oh yeah? I had to smile to myself. After all, I had already fallen in love with the savage brat, the parents were contemptible to me. In the ensuing struggle they grew more and more abject, crushed, exhausted while she surely rose to magnificent heights of insane fury of effort bred of her terror of me.

The father tried his best, and he was a big man but the fact that she was his daughter, his shame at her behavior and his dread of hurting her made him release her just at the critical times when I had almost achieved success, till I wanted to kill him. But his dread also that she might have diphtheria made him tell me to go on, go on though he himself was almost fainting, while the mother moved back and forth behind us raising and lowering her hands in an agony of apprehension.

Put her in front of you on your lap, I ordered, and hold both her wrists.

But as soon as he did the child let out a scream. Don't, you're hurting me. Let go of my hands. Let them go I tell you. Then she shrieked terrifyingly, hysterically. Stop it! Stop it! You're killing me!

Do you think she can stand it, doctor! said the mother.

You get out, said the husband to his wife. Do you want her to die of diphtheria?

Come on now, hold her, I said.

Then I grasped the child's head with my left hand and tried to get the wooden tongue depressor between her teeth. She fought, with clenched teeth, desperately! But now I also had grown furious—at a child. I tried to hold myself down but I couldn't. I know how to expose a throat for inspection. And I did my best. When finally I got the wooden spatula behind the last teeth and just the point of it into the mouth cavity, she opened up for an instant but before I could see anything she came down again and gripping the wooden blade between her molars she reduced it to splinters before I could get it out again.

Aren't you ashamed, the mother yelled at her. Aren't you ashamed to act like that in front of the doctor?

Get me a smooth-handled spoon of some sort, I told the mother. We're going through with this. The child's mouth was already bleeding. Her tongue was cut and she was screaming in wild hysterical shrieks. Perhaps I should have desisted and come back in an hour or more. No doubt it would have been better. But I have seen at least two children lying dead in bed of neglect in such cases, and feeling that I must get a diagnosis now or never I went at it again. But the worst of it was that I too had got beyond reason. I could have torn the child apart in my own fury and enjoyed it. It was a pleasure to attack her. My face was burning with it.

The damned little brat must be protected against her own idiocy, one says to one's self at such times. Others must be protected against her. It is a social necessity. And all these things are true. But a blind fury, a feeling of adult shame, bred of a longing for muscular release are the operatives. One goes on to the end.

In a final unreasoning assault I overpowered the child's neck and jaws. I forced the heavy silver spoon back of her teeth and down her throat till she gagged. And there it was—both tonsils covered with membrane. She had fought valiantly to keep me from knowing her secret. She had been hiding that sore throat for three days at least and lying to her parents in order to escape just such an outcome as this.

Now truly she was furious. She had been on the defensive before but now she attacked. Tried to get off her father's lap and fly at me while tears of defeat blinded her eyes.

Williams fulfills the demands of a short story in that he has written of an experience that is meaningful and has framed his events in a narrative pattern. He shows how a doctor is driven into a primitive fury in trying to rip from a child patient the secret of a hidden killer. We see that force can brutalize the person who must use it. The war between the doctor and the child, which is the specific representation of the point or truth, is defined in terms of the actions of the characters and occurs near the end of the story.

The truth which you as a writer want to show and want the reader to take for his own should emerge, as in "The Use of Force," through the narrative form you impose on your initial idea. As we already know, form is a process of objectifying what is personal to you and giving it an esthetic structure to carry the meaning of what you want to say about human beings and their relationship to each other.

Form, in the construction of a narrative, embraces, too, the way you decide to tell your story, whether by designating a character as your narrator or by seeing with your own "god eye" and being your own reporter. It is a container for the people, the struggle, the theme, and the style which is the dress of your thought. It dictates the selection of events and it has not changed basically since Edgar Allan Poe wrote the following.

A skilful artist has constructed a tale. He has not fashioned his thoughts to accommodate his incidents, but having deliberately conceived a certain *single* effect to be wrought, he then invents such incidents, he then combines such events, and discusses them in such tone as may best serve him in establishing this preconceived effect. If his very first sentence tend not to the outbringing of this effect, then in his very first step he has committed a blunder. In the whole composition there should be no word written of which the tendency, direct or indirect, is not to the one pre-established design. And by such means, with such care and skill, a picture is at length painted which leaves in the mind of him who contemplates it with a kindred art, a sense of the fullest satisfaction.

And as Joyce Cary, a later artist representing our own time, has pointed out, in any creative work the great difficulty of the writer is to preserve "the force of his intuition, his germ, what is sometimes called his inspiration through the long process of technical construction." In the giant step from the story that is *you* to the story that gives the reader a sense of fullest satisfaction, the greatest problem is to keep the strength and freshness of the initial urge.

And so before we start the study of specific techniques in fiction writing, we come back to the creative instinct with which we began, to the desire to tell what you know. If your writing is based on this need to impart your own comprehension to others, then, as Thornton Wilder has pointed out, "Well, that telling is as difficult an exercise in technique as it is in honesty; but it should emerge as immediately, as spontaneously, as undeliberately, as possible."

## THE FIRST VERSION OF YOUR STORY:   Assignment 16

Without attempting to do more toward preparing for your first story than you have done in your prevoius assignment, sit down and write as complete a first draft as you can, finishing it at a date designated by your instructor.

## PART TWO

---

## A WRITER WORKS

# 7

# Narrative Point of View

Point of view may refer to the general philosophical position from which a story is written, or it may refer to the person or agency through whose eyes the events are seen. In the more restricted sense, it is referred to as a verb form, varying from first to third person and from singular to plural, which functions as a control over the action in your short story or novel. Your choice of a fictional point of view is particularly important since it contributes to the impact and to the lingering aftereffects of the story on your reader.

This chapter offers a technical explanation of those narrative points of view which, together with their variations, are commonly used by writers: First-Person Narrator, Second-Person Narrator, Third-Person Narrator, and Omniscient Author. You, as a writer, may feel that such matters unduly limit your freedom of expression. The hope is, rather, that this discussion will help you choose the point of view through which your story can best be filtered and so lead you to a more effective and harmonious control of your material.

First-Person Narrator and variations.   In a story written from this point of view, the narrating character begins by saying, in effect, "This is what happened to *me*." He is thus made responsible for reporting his own actions and responses and those of the characters surrounding him. The "I" is at the center of the action and passes on to the reader what he as a direct participant feels, knows, experiences.

The narrator who says, "This is what happened to me," should appear on the scene naturally during the entire action. It is by virtue of his own direct involvement, through the recording of his own experiences, that he convinces the reader of his own reality, the reality of his fellow characters, and the reality of the actions which draw them together. This *First-Person-Involved* is both self-limiting and self-revealing.

This particular choice is a natural one for a story that can be told by an "I" who resembles you, the writer, in feeling, thought, and experience, but that has its own fictional need for an on-the-spot narrator. You can present your "I" as addressing his story to a listener, or as writing it down in a letter or a diary.

One of the main difficulties with the this-is-what-happened-to-me narrator is to place him correctly in the structure of the story. The person who is telling the tale must appear in every scene and must seem to appear there naturally. If he is awkwardly pulled into a situation to report what he has no right to see, hear, or comprehend, then the story itself becomes awkward and not only the "I" but the author behind him is in trouble.

If, for instance, you are writing from the "I-Involved" viewpoint and the story ends with the death of this "I," it will be difficult for him to report the manner of his own death believably. Love, that other fundamental, also offers trouble. The first-person "I" would seldom be present as a third person when a love situation develops between two people other than himself. If your "I" forces himself into crucial scenes of love or death then the story will be in danger of losing credibility.

Again, should the "I-Involved" see himself as other than he is in reality, the viewpoint can become complicated. If the "I" of a particular story is irrational, then somewhere along the line the reader must be allowed to see that the viewpoint is ironic. Suppose the "I" announces in church that he has just had a letter from the King of Thailand asking him to convert Thailand to Methodism. Then you must find a way of establishing your "I" as tragic, ridiculous, or fantastic, depending on how you wish to present him.

## Illustration of an *"I-Involved" Narrator: Tragic*

I had known for almost a month that I would grab the first chance

of shooting Augie when dusk came to the woods behind Blue Clay
Road. I had known since the first night with Marietta when Augie
was away in Tennessee. I had gone to her then, the fire singeing my
heart. Near the pond, I thought of how it had been that night and
then of how it would be soon with the gun blasting away into a
darkening sky.

Student story

## Illustration of an *"I-Involved" Narrator: Fantastic*

For I had changed now. Or they believed I had. One of them
looked at me and called me Fox. I felt his eyes watching for the
moment of my making a move toward my burrow. And where?
But the hole for which I must make opened near the log under the
cypress tree. And in it were my foxlets.

Student story

*First-Person Watcher* is a variation on the First-Person Narrator, one who tells your story for you but is not himself
directly affected by the action. His role may be, and usually
is, that of a minor character, but the personal bias he brings to
the story gives him a very real importance. This "I" has the
advantage of being a spectator and of supposedly being able
to evaluate events, but he has the disadvantage of not being
immediate to the action. He can, however, tell what he has
heard, report what he has seen, and make his own judgments.
He is especially valuable as a narrator if your story comes from
a distance in time or in space.

In a novel this watcher, this I-saw-in-passing-by narrator,
may also consist of a number of witnesses each giving his own
report on events. Joseph Conrad, for instance, liked to use
the "cloud of witnesses" point of view, each witness giving a
different report of a developing situation. The single "I-
Watcher," almost always preferable to many watchers in a
short story, may start as an observer and then change his role
to that of an actor in the events.

## Illustration of an *"I-Watcher"*

I hailed Serval. He came up with his long strides like a crane.
I asked him: "What's become of those people?"

And he told me this story:
When the war was declared, the son Sauvage, who was then thirty-three years old, enlisted, leaving his mother alone in the house. . . .

From "La Mere Sauvage," by Guy de Maupassant

SECOND-PERSON NARRATOR. Your story may be pointed at an individual "you" or may be directed toward a generic "you" who, as a minor character, appears occasionally and draws the reader into the action with him. The particular "you" often turns out to be the victim of a joke or a crime, or the perpetrator. For the serious short story this single-person "you" is a choice almost impossible to sustain. Many writers feel that both the universal and the particular "you" should be used sparingly, and not be held to through an entire short story. A "you" narrator cannot be sustained throughout a novel without some variation of viewpoint.

Illustration of the *Individual You*

Don't look around; you'll be happier if you don't know, if you don't see the knife coming. I've killed people from behind and they don't seem to mind so much.
Go on, just a little while, thinking this is just another fiction story. Don't look behind you. Don't believe this—*until you feel the knife.*

From "Don't Look Behind You," by Fredric Brown

At the beginning of a novel, or as an occasional passage in fiction, the second-person point of view draws a generic "you" into the action and through him establishes intimacy with the reader. The person addressed begins to feel that he has a real identification with the story. This generic "you" works well in the following passage.

Riding down to Port Warwick from Richmond, the train begins to pick up speed on the outskirts of the city, past the tobacco factories with their ever-present haze of acrid, sweetish dust and past the rows of uniformly brown clapboard houses which stretch down the hilly streets for miles, it seems, the hundreds of rooftops all reflecting the pale light of dawn; past the suburban roads still sluggish and sleepy with early morning traffic, and rattling swiftly now over the bridge which separates the last two hills where in the valley below you can see the James River winding beneath its acid-green crust of scum out beside the chemical plants and more rows of clapboard houses and into the woods beyond.

Suddenly the train is burrowing through the pinewoods, and the conductor, who looks middle-aged and respectable like someone's favorite uncle, lurches through the car asking for tickets. If you are particularly alert at that unconscionable hour you notice his voice, which is somewhat guttural and negroid—oddly fatuous-sounding after the accents of Columbus or Detroit or wherever you came from—and when you ask him how far it is to Port Warwick and he says, "Ab*oot* eighty miles," you know for sure that you're in the Tidewater. Then you settle back in your seat, your face feeling unwashed and swollen from the intermittent sleep you got sitting up the night before and your gums sore from too many cigarettes, and you try to doze off, but the nap of the blue felt seat prickles your neck and so you sit up once more and cross your legs, gazing drowsily at the novelty salesman from Allentown P-a, next to you, who told you last night about his hobby, model trains, and the joke about the two college girls at the Hotel Astor, and whose sleek face, sprouting a faint gray crop of stubble, one day old, is now peacefully relaxed, immobile in sleep, his breath issuing from slightly parted lips in delicate sighs. Or, turning away, you look out at the pinewoods sweeping past at sixty miles an hour, the trees standing close together green and somnolent, and the brown-needled carpet of the forest floor dappled brightly in the early morning light, until the white fog of smoke from the engine ahead swirls and dips against the window like a tattered scarf and obscures the view.

Now the sun is up and you can see the mist lifting off the fields and in the middle of the fields the solitary cabins with their slim threads of smoke unwinding out of plastered chimneys and the faint glint of fire through an open door and, at a crossing, the sudden, swift tableau of a Negro and his hay-wagon and a lop-eared mule: the Negro with his mouth agape, exposing pink gums, staring at the speeding train until the smoke obscures him, too, from view, and the one dark-brown hand held cataleptic in the air.

Stirring, the novelty salesman looks drowsily out of the window and grunts, "Where are we?" and you murmur, "Not far from Port Warwick, I hope," and as he turns on his side to sleep some more you finger your copy of the *Times-Dispatch* which the newsboy sold you an hour ago, and which you haven't read and won't read because maybe you have things on your mind; and instead you look out once more at the late summer landscape and the low, sorrowful beauty of tideland streams winding through marshes full of small, darting, frightened noises and glistening and dead silent at noon, except for a whistle, far off, and a distant rumble on the rails.

From *Lie Down in Darkness*, by William Styron

THIRD-PERSON NARRATOR. The writer may feel that the sense of personal immediacy conveyed by the use of "I" and "you" is not appropriate to his story. He may then choose to cast the story in a third-person framework, where again he has several alternatives.

*Third-Person-Limited Narrator.* Like the first-person choice, this one keeps your story circled inside the world of a character who functions in the action as part of what is happening, showing your reader only what this single character hears, sees, knows, or experiences. It offers the unity that comes with a restricted viewpoint.

In many cases, the Third-Person-Limited resembles a First-Person Narrator so closely that in using it you can write a version of your narrative in the "I" form and then adapt it to the "he" viewpoint, with little variation. In the following versions of the same story-passage, the "I" conveniently disappears to be replaced by an Alma who has almost the identical effect of the First-Person Narrator.

Every Saturday morning I would place the six dozen carefully selected eggs in one basket, and the six pounds of rich, yellow butter in another basket and leave for town. Sometimes I would walk the three miles to the village, sometimes I would take the bus, particularly if the weather were cold, but often someone I knew came along and stopped for me.

Every Saturday morning Alma would place the six dozen carefully selected eggs in one basket, and the six pounds of rich, yellow butter in another basket and leave for town. Sometimes Alma would walk the three miles to the village, sometimes she would take the bus, particularly if the weather were cold, but often someone she knew came along and stopped for her.

Student story

*Third-Person Interpreter.* One character in your story sees his fellows and what is happening to them, projecting them to the reader. He differs from the Third-Person-Limited in that he reports the story through analyzing the thoughts of the other characters instead of filtering the events only through his own experiences and responses. In theory he is not unlike a person gifted with a power of absorbing thought and action from others, tuning in on other people's responses, giving a believable version of their individual and related behavior patterns. Like the correspondent in the following passage, he is an intelligence which overcasts the entire story and yet he remains a character in himself. He is an excellent means of revealing the nuances and subtleties of other characters which might not be apparent to the reader.

## Illustration of a *Third-Person Interpreter*

The correspondent wondered ingenuously how in the name of all that was sane could there be people who thought it amusing to row a boat. It was not an amusement; it was a diabolical punishment, and even a genius of mental aberrations could never conclude that it was anything but a horror to the muscles and a crime against the back. He mentioned to the boat in general how the amusement of rowing struck him, and the weary-faced oiler smiled in full sympathy. Previously to the foundering, by the way, the oiler had worked double-watch in the engine-room of the ship.

"Take her easy, now, boys," said the captain. "Don't spend yourselves. If we have to run a surf you'll need all your strength, because we'll sure have to swim for it. Take your time."

Slowly the land arose from the sea. From a black line it became a line of black and a line of white, trees and sand. Finally, the captain said that he could make out a house on the shore. "That's the house of refuge, sure," said the cook. "They'll see us before long, and come out after us."

The distant lighthouse reared high. "The keeper ought to be able to make us out now, if he's looking through a glass," said the captain. "He'll notify the life-saving people."

"None of those other boats could have got ashore to give word of the wreck," said the oiler, in a low voice. "Else the lifeboat would be out hunting us."

Slowly and beautifully the land loomed out of the sea. The wind came again. It had veered from the north-east to the south-east. Finally, a new sound struck the ears of the men in the boat. It was the low thunder of the surf on the shore. "We'll never be able to make the lighthouse now," said the captain. "Swing her head a little more north, Billie," said he.

"A little more north, sir," said the oiler.

Whereupon the little boat turned her nose once more down the wind, and all but the oarsman watched the shore grow. Under the influence of this expansion doubt and direful apprehension was leaving the minds of the men. The management of the boat was still most absorbing, but it could not prevent a quiet cheerfulness. In an hour, perhaps, they would be ashore.

Their backbones had become thoroughly used to balancing in the boat, and they now rode this wild colt of a dingey like circus men. The correspondent thought that he had been drenched to the skin, but happening to feel in the top pocket of his coat, he found therein eight cigars. Four of them were soaked with sea-water; four were perfectly scathless. After a search, somebody produced three dry matches, and thereupon the four waifs rode impudently in their little boat, and with an assurance of an impending rescue shining in their eyes, puffed at the big cigars and judged well and ill of all men. Everybody took a drink of water.

From "The Open Boat," by Stephen Crane

*Third-Person-Effaced.* In this method you are working as a dramatist works, letting the story tell itself without any open comment of your own. As the writer, you act your part by displaying the characters' behavior and showing their situations without adding your personal views or those of your narrator. You adopt a newspaper technique, never revealing your opinion directly, never asking the reader to share a secret opinion, nor ever permitting one of your fictional group to analyze his thoughts. From a hidden vantage point, you and your objective narrator tell only what takes place. Ernest Hemingway's "The Killers," is a fine example of this point of view.

### Illustration of an *Effaced Narrator*

A wagon drawn by a pepper-colored horse stood near the feed house door. On the wagon sat a hatless boy. His rich black hair glistened in the sunlight. The boy was naked from the waist up, wearing only an old and faded pair of dungarees. Dark brown freckles covered his face, ears, neck, back, and arms. Mike came from behind the feed house as he spoke to the boy.

"Hello," he said.

Student Story

THE OMNISCIENT AUTHOR. This know-all point of view

is the oldest one in storytelling, a classic in fiction, particularly in the novel form. Using it, you have no need to efface yourself. As the writer, you are fully in charge of your narrative and your people. You can appear in the narrative. You can tell your reader what your characters are thinking, where they have been, where you intend to send them, and what their destiny will be. You can comment on them as you desire since they are your puppets and you their master.

This point of view is usually scorned by authors whose primary interest is the realm of feeling rather than the world of action. If you want to reproduce a mood, a feeling, or an instant of revelation in an inner world of a character, perhaps a subjective approach will suit you best. If, though, you wish instead to manipulate a world in which action is dominant, then the omniscient might well be best. Be careful to keep your limitations of time, place, and of the action itself in an organic pattern.

The omniscient offers a sliding scale so that you can switch your attention from one character to another; you can show your people in a close-up shot or make them distant figures in a landscape. You can present them flatly or show them in depth, revealing their outer masks and inner conflicts. Time and space are at your disposal to use as you will. But again, be sure to observe time, space, and action limits that will draw your reader into the story. You will exclude him if you manipulate your fictional world so openly that it is obviously artificial.

When you use the omniscient in a short story, try never to be obtrusive in shifting from one place to another. Go from one action to another without jarring your reader by too quick or too clumsy a movement. And do not tell him so much that he has nothing left to infer for himself. He will respond to a storyteller who shows him rather than informs him directly.

Example of a *Blatantly Omniscient Point of View*

It had been about six months ago when Walter Devereaux had learned of his sister's intention to be married to a Monstead of the Charleston family. Mr. Monstead had expressed a desire to meet his future brother-in-law and was on his way now to the apartment where Walter sat near the terrace waiting. Mr. Monstead was slightly over thirty and not unhandsome. He was to be the last product of two hundred years of careful breeding begun in South Carolina when the first Monstead had produced a son at Lorton Plantation before the Revolution.

Student Story

## Example of an *Unobtrusive Omniscient Point of View*

The two old men met early each afternoon on the pleasant wide porch and waited for the postman. The porch faced the park, the water and the afternoon sun. There were glass jalousie windows which could be rolled shut when the winter wind came up across the Tampa Bay.

The two old men, Mr. Beattle, who had been a professor and Mr. Kelley, a retired manufacturer, were as different in character as one could imagine; and yet this was the time of day they both waited for all morning. It was a time of easy comradeship, free from solitude, and safe from the inquisition of strangers who had no notion of privacy. There was, too, and more important, the possibility of mail.

From "What To Do Till the Postman Comes," by Max Steele

## Example of *Classic Use of the Omniscient Point of View*

A throng of bearded men, in sad-colored garments, and gray, steeple-crowned hats, intermixed with women, some wearing hoods and others bareheaded, was assembled in front of a wooden edifice, the door of which was heavily timbered with oak, and studded with iron spikes.

The founders of a new colony, whatever Utopia of human virtue and happiness they might originally project, have invariably recognized it among their earliest practical necessities to allot a portion of the virgin soil as a cemetery, and another portion as the site of a prison. In accordance with this rule, it may safely be assumed that the forefathers of Boston had built the first prison-house somewhere in the vicinity of Cornhill, almost as seasonably as they marked out the first burial-ground, on Isaac Johnson's lot, and round about his grave, which subsequently became the nucleus of all the congregated sepulchres in the old churchyard of King's Chapel. Certain it is, that, some fifteen or twenty years after the settlement of the town, the wooden jail was already marked with weather-stains and other indications of age, which gave a yet darker aspect to its beetle-browed and gloomy front. The rust on the ponderous iron-work of its oaken door looked more antique than anything else in the New World. Like all that pertains to crime, it seemed never to have known a youthful era. Before this ugly edifice, and between it and the wheel-track of the street, was a grass-plot, much overgrown with burdock, pigweed, apple-peru, and such unsightly vegetation, which evidently found something congenial in the soil that had so early borne the black flower of civilized society, a prison. But, on one side of the portal, and rooted almost at the threshold, was a wild rose-bush, covered, in this month of June, with its delicate gems, which might be imagined to offer their fragrance and fragile beauty to the prisoner as he went in, and to the condemned criminal as he came forth to his doom, in token that the deep heart of Nature could pity and be kind to him.

This rose-bush, by a strange chance, has been kept alive in history; but whether it had merely survived out of the stern old wilderness, so long after the fall of the gigantic pines and oaks that originally overshadowed it—or whether, as there is fair authority for believing, it had sprung up under the footsteps of the sainted Anne Hutchinson, as she entered the prison door,—we shall not take upon us to determine. Finding it so directly on the threshold of our narrative, which is now about to issue from that inauspicious portal, we could hardly do otherwise than pluck one of its flowers, and present it to the reader. It may serve, let us hope, to symbolize some sweet moral blossom, that may be found along the track, or relieve the darkening close of a tale of human frailty and sorrow.

From *The Scarlet Letter*, by Nathaniel Hawthorne

In present-day novels, unlike those of Hawthorne's time, some writers use the omniscient point of view as a hook on which to hang many kinds of authority in narration. If you are working in a fiction form where the time span and the action are long, you can use a know-all narrator as your over-all authority, as a kaleidoscopic control shifting the viewpoint to a third-person character or into monologue and then back to the old-fashioned omniscient at will.

In this kaleidoscopic point of view you can change your authority whenever you want to alter the contour of an apparently fixed narrative point of view. You may present a day or a year in the lives of the people in the story, or work inside the time-span of a day in which the residual actions of years are caught. You may use an "I-Involved," an Effaced Narrator, or a god-in-the-wings, employing them separately in varying sequences. The omniscient method thus can become a container for all the other points of view discussed here.

## CHOOSING A POINT OF VIEW FOR A NARRATIVE:
Assignment 17

Write an opening paragraph for a story and in it define clearly the point of view you would like to use throughout the narrative.

Comment on your reasons for choosing this point of view for this particular story and why you think it will be the best means of presenting the pattern of events you intend to display.

## DAY DREAMS

D. V.

I used to walk under the oak trees behind the house, past the cornfield beside the creek. I'd look up at the branches, beyond the branches to the sky with clouds that were shaped like elephants, trees, knives or streetcars. I'd look down at the stubs of roots under the oak trees, the place where that city boy was killed last year. It was in all the papers and on the radio, the boy being killed, and dozens of men and boys searched all night for him.

(Found anything Clem? Nope, not yet, got th' boys scattered out pretty well tho. . . . Ef he's anywhere near 'ere we find 'im.)

Must be pretty awful to get shot in the head. But he was already unconscious so I don't guess he knew anything about it. It was pitch black then, darker than the middle of the swamps in November. He'd been missing for about two days and his parents were pretty much disturbed, but they were stoic folks so they didn't let their anxiety show.

(Clem, hits put near two o'clock, what ya say we call it off till daylight? Can't see nuthin nohow unless you're kin to an old hoot owl or something. . . . Naw, let's try 'bout nother hour, we're bound to be pretty close. Ef nuthin shows up we'll call it off.)

Paper said he was a good kid, went to Sunday school regularly and all that. Imagine, I used to walk on the very spot where he was killed, might have even stepped in his dried-up blood for all I know. Of course the weeds and dead leaves have covered the spot now but I still kinda get an erry feeling whenever I go there, the place where he was killed.

I used to walk under the big oak trees behind the house past the cornfield beside the little creek at dusk. There's a time between day and night when everything takes on a double body and shadow, especially in the woods when you are alone. I used to see little city boys with bloody heads and screaming eyes behind every tree-trunk and lying down in every patch of weeds. It made me shudder.

(Clem, over here, the dawgs 'ave found somethin, quick, bring your light. Shine it over there by that big tree—there, there he is.)

There was a writeup of the funeral in the paper, a picture of the city boy with his sophisticated parents and cocker spaniel, another picture of him in his tee-shirt at summer camp. Funny thing, being dead, and so young. He didn't have much time to do anything worth doing, poor kid. But we all have to die sometime. When, we don't know. Today, tomorrow, next year, we don't know. Wonder when I'll die?

## JUSTIFYING A POINT OF VIEW:   Assignment 18

Read D. V.'s sketch above, then write a paragraph commenting on the point of view he has chosen to convey to the reader the narrator's attitude toward death. Justify the narrator's inclusion of the dialogue that brings the past events into the present for the reader. Does this time-change mean that D. V. has changed point of view?

In summing up, point of view, once again, is the choice of the authority by whom a tale should be related. You may present your story in the first person. You may—although it is unlikely—decide to use the second person throughout, addressing the reader directly. You may employ a third-person narrator to establish his own focus on the story or to present your events within a dramatic framework. You may decide to be a know-all for your characters, an omniscient author who moves them at will. Whatever your choice, first try to discover the viewpoint which is organic to the story you want to tell.

## 8

# People and Their Fictional Traits

Even after you find a way to make a character come alive in a world of fictional reality, you still have the task of controlling him in the particular story you are writing. And though you may believe, as many beginning writers do, that your people appear from your imagination fully-clothed in their proper fictional dress, you might want to test your handling of them against the following suggestions.

Fiction, unlike life itself, is first of all selective. Even if you are writing naturalistically and using a wide focus for your material, you simply cannot tell *everything* about any one person, or about any group of people. To make an individual stand out and so draw the reader and hold his interest, you must stamp a character with strong qualities and help him keep the stamp. Let him grow from his dominant traits.

One way to present a main character is to start with what he is. He may be a farmer, an engineer, or a man who makes a career of doing nothing at all; but like any effective fictional man he will have some trait, or a particular kind of background, or a way of seeing himself, by which you can show that he is different from everyone else. This does not mean that he is grotesque. It means that one of the elements of fiction is exaggeration.

Or you may want to start with what a man does, with his primary desire. He may be trying to recapture the past, or he may be pushing other people aside in order to fulfill his own longings. He may want to find love, or commit a crime, or reform the world. But he must have some need, even if it is only to escape the work of the day just ahead. You have then given him a motive that will lead him into action.

He is your main character, your protagonist, and—whatever

his motivation—you will have to differentiate him from other characters. One way is to contrast him with an antagonist, or opposing force, but in a story you cannot let the antagonist steal too much attention or he may win the role of protagonist for himself.

The obvious way to differentiate your main character from the others is to describe him fully, though selectively, or let him talk and act for himself at the forefront of your fictional stage. Again, you can present him through a narrator who, by his own concern with your hero, arouses the concern of the reader. You can also set a main character apart by showing his relationship to the minor characters, revealing his nature by the treatment he gives them.

The minor characters can often be brought vividly to life by one stroke or by a few strokes of description. In working with one of them you can give him a tag, a trait, a name, that is the badge of his nature. You do not have to show him as good or bad. He can be tall or have a stutter, or he may cringe when given an order, although his tag should never be so obtrusive that it distracts the reader's attention from the protagonist. He can be part of a list, as the following minor characters watching a parade for a football hero are listed in a student story: "The students, the campus policeman, and the dean of students, waved at him. The hunchbacked janitor, sweeping the sidewalk, gave a whistle. But Tammy, thinking of the game ahead, responded to nobody."

In a sketch in which the main character reveals himself and the people around him through an interior monologue as he passes along a street, another student author shows us a minor character in the following capsule description: ". . . what a face. Help the blind. Coins clink in bottom of tin cup; smile shows red gums; ough!" The narrator then walks along the block with no more reference to the beggar.

One function of a minor character is to enhance the attention that must be focussed naturally on the central person and his close associates. In presenting a minor character, try to see him as a response to others who are more outstanding than he. Think of him as a necessary detail in a whole picture which must be projected clearly but still be kept in scale.

But what are the specific ways in which you can set a major character apart? How do you go about making his face different from other faces, or his thoughts more arresting than those that go through anybody's head? The ways suggested here are only clues. The student writers of the following sketches are, like you, in the process of trying to find ways of creating characters for themselves.

I. A CHARACTER EMERGES THROUGH HIS OWN STREAM OF THOUGHTS

## OH! !

M. G.

Oh! !
. . . a wreck (my time stops). An interruption from—nothing and I am glad how horrible! How awful it is oh a woman lying down she's tangled up in it blood on her arm oh God. People are gaping they come to all wrecks and gape they can't help it, is that woman alive? Is she dead? I can see her blood is she dead? I have to go close and look and take it all in.

That was a pretty blue car going fast, where is somebody else . . . There must be a man, that woman is 35 older than me, she might have children in the car and not her husband. That woman is dead. She hasn't moved; I can't look in the car window I'm ashamed. Those people coming are talking loud in front of a dead woman . . . they don't know. Help is coming . . . all they will do is clean up. There is nothing else to do . . . SHUT UP would be one thing.

That woman was by herself; if there were children they would be crying, unless they were dead but I don't think they would be. She's dead, she's dead, she was by herself. Is by herself. Lying not moving, look at her eyes, just glass. By herself. I am by myself. She's gone, don't tremble, no, keep quiet, it's not your own death. I can't help her at all even if I touch her . . . and nobody will help me then. Get away, tear your mind away. Not now but one day. (My time starts) Oh! !

M. G. attempts to establish the personality of her narrator who is also her main character:

1. By letting the narrator speak for herself. It seems that this sketch is about the fate of a woman in a wreck, but it is actually the revelation of an onlooker's concern with her own death revealed through the stream of thoughts that come as she witnesses the stranger's death.

2. By working in a subjective pattern of responses. The wreck has already taken place so we know only the effect of the violence. Revelation comes through the fragmentation of emotion as the narrator reacts to what she sees.

II. A CHARACTER EMERGES WHEN A NARRATOR SPEAKS DIRECTLY TO HIM

## A LETTER TO BUDDY

D. L. H.

You are sixteen, Buddy. You don't have a beard and your face is still smooth. There aren't any wrinkles. Life has just begun to touch you.

Once in a hotel you confided to me your dearest wish—to be a bellboy. Then you saw a man riding on the bumper of a truck; you wanted to be a garbage man. The best dream of all began when you studied chemistry in junior high. You found an ideal. While other boys shot marbles you studied and worked through the afternoons and at night. After our house was dark, I used to see your bedroom light.

You were using your own formulas for your experiments. "Ah," I thought as I lay in bed, "my brother's the smartest boy around." I bragged to my friends about you. Then came a day when you put aside your cracked test tubes and worn notebooks. The files you had kept that year were discarded. The apparatus, the books, the papers—you threw them in the trash. They burned in the rusty can standing in our backyard.

Your grades at school fell. All things scientific were forgotten. Mother, Daddy and I worried about you as we watched you turn your room into a monk's retreat; only your bed, a table, and a Bible were kept.

You'll never know how many nights I worried about you. I even prayed for you—something I hadn't done for almost four years. "God," I said, "help Buddy!"

Then in a light moment Mother told me a joke that made me remember your old ambition to be a bellhop. That year in junior high, she told me, you were searching for the ultimate weapon. A bomb to end all war was the purpose of your experiments. Even while she laughed, I felt that yours was an understandable goal for the time you live in with the rest of us. The Cold War. The nuclear one. That year you worked on plans that would one day enable you to help develop the absolute weapon. Then you threw away your books, your papers, your apparatus. You had told mother why. "There is no absolute weapon. I know now that the only thing in any world that can save humanity is love."

She did not understand. A joke. Or it was one to her. And to father. They do not understand you now but if you are patient they will learn to see that your new dream is the only one and that you have already begun to go ahead in your career of finding it, that you are right, of course. The only ultimate weapon is the love that each person finds new, as you did, Buddy.

You are right. And you are only sixteen.

### D. L. H. attempts to establish character:

1. Through talking to him directly. She is able to say what she thinks of her main character and thus evaluate him for the reader.

2. By establishing her own relationship with him. The fact that she is his sister gives her an intimate knowledge of this younger member of the family.

3. By showing us what he does over a period of years. The seeming inconsistency in Buddy's character is explained in the sixth paragraph, where it is shown that the boy's aim has not changed but that he has chosen another means for attaining it.

4. By appealing to the reader's sympathy. The writer of the "letter" speaks for him in every sentence and begs us to share her understanding of her brother.

III.   A CHARACTER EMERGES THROUGH A CONCEALED NARRATOR

## OLD SMOKY JOE

J. H.

He came off of the dredge boat, and no one had ever seen him before.

He had dark curly hair and dark skin. Some of the dark skin may have been grease, and his beard was a stubble. He was short, heavily built, and his arms hung low at his sides.

When the little work boat docked in the afternoon he would climb the hill and walk across the open field to where the kids played ball.

The first afternoon they saw him he stood well back of home. No one noticed him until Sammy tipped a foul in his direction and he caught it.

"Here you are, kid." He tossed the ball to the catcher.

"Thanks, mister."

The next afternoon he came again. He stood this time under the old cedar with the boys waiting for their "bat."

On the field, the first and second basemen had a runner trapped between bases. They stood, threw, ran, threw, then one fell and the runner reached second.

He grunted. "Should of chased him back to first."

"Yeah?" someone asked.

"Never let 'im get the base. Don't try for the out. Just get 'im back."

He began commenting on almost every play. The players who were "in" gathered around to listen. Even the older ones were silent. "Don't mind the runner, play the batter . . . back 'im up there!"

That evening, Sammy was late for supper.

"Where've you been?" his mother asked.

"Talkin' with Joe."

"We were talkin' about baseball. Joe's on the dredge boat. He's real smart. 'Bout baseball, I mean."

Sammy's mother spoke to her husband later: "Sam, This man who's been playing with the kids . . . Should we let Sammy . . . ?"

"Sure. I think it'd be OK."

"Well, if you say so."

The next afternoon the boys offered Joe a turn at bat.

"No," he said. "I ain't played in a long time. You kids go ahead— Hey there! Back up the catcher."

He became manager and chief adviser.

"Do I hold the bat right, Joe?"

"How do you oil a glove?"

"Can you help tape this bat?"

Always he had a willing hand. The invitation to play stood.

The boys would sit around the cedar, some in it, waiting for the midday sun to relent. They pounded their gloves. They talked about Joe.

"I'll bet he can put it 'cross the street."

"Hang. He can put it over the oaks, I bet." All eyes would turn to the three oaks in deep right. Some of the larger boys could hit the lower branches. But no one could hit a ball over them. Yet each one secretly wondered.

One afternoon Joe showed up earlier than usual. The boys swarmed from the cedar to meet him.

"Gonna play today, Joe?"

"Need an extra fielder, Joe."

"OK," he said. "Today."

"Your first bat, Joe!"

"No. I'll play in the field first."

Taking one of the gloves offered him he trotted out to short. The second man up hit him a grounder. He fielded the ball well, but the throw was wild. His motion was stiff and awkward.

"OK, Joe. That's a'right."

The side was retired.

Joe was the leadoff batter. He stood at the plate.

The first pitch was in the dirt. The pitcher stroked his brow.

"Oh come on, pitch it up!" both sides called.

The next pitch was inside, and Joe fell back.

"Come on. Come on and pitch to 'im!"

"Lay it over the oaks, Joe."

The third pitch was straight across, belt high. Joe switched the bat, but took the pitch. Everyone was silent.

The pitcher took a long windup, reared back, and let fly. Joe's arms came back. His legs bent. His forearms tightened and he swung.

"Crack!" The ball cleared the first baseman ten feet. It covered the distance to the oaks in an instant, and rose above them. The boys gasped. Joe trotted around the bases and stomped the plate.

"Gee, Joe, that was some swat."

"Yeah," he agreed. "I gotta go now."

That evening Sammy could hardly eat.

"Dad. You ever heard of a big league player called Smoky Joe Somebody?"

"I don't think so."

"But there could of been, couldn't it? Dad?"

"I suppose so."

He ate slowly and thoughtfully.

After awhile, his father spoke. "Sammy, want to run get me some cigarettes at Mac's?"

"OK Mom?"

"Sam, do you think he should go to Mac's Bar?"

"It's OK, dear."

Sammy walked into the bar and faced up to the counter. "Luckies."

"Little young aren't you, Sammy?"

"For Dad."

"OK."

He took the change and the cigarettes and turned to go.

At a table, half lying among some empty beer bottles, was a drunk asleep. Two men were bending over him.

"Come on, Joe. Let's go. Get up, Joe. We've got to get back."

The drunk's head moved slightly, then fell back on the table.

The two men helped him out the door.

Sammy followed slowly and caught the door as it swung shut. He stood watching for a minute, then walked home.

Joe didn't show up the next day, and Sammy never told the boys about the night at Mac's.

## J. H. establishes Smoky Joe as a character:

1. By concealing the narrator. The writer could have employed a first-person point of view by one of the boys, or he could have used some other narrative focus. Instead, appropriately enough in view of Smoky's personality, the writer lets Smoky show himself to us through his own actions, supplementing our view by the responses of the boys to whom the bum is temporarily a hero.

2. By his name. Smoky Joe is a person who fades out; Smoke is misty. "Smoky" is also appropriate for a baseball player, especially if he is fast. Someone who runs fast "burns up the trail." A fast pitcher "scorches the air." A ball "travels so fast it smokes." If you will go back and look at some of the other stories that have been read in the class you will see the importance of names. A name is what we have to go by. When you take a man's name away you lessen his identity, and conversely, in fiction, when you give a man a name, you give him identity. The name should convey to the reader, without great exaggeration and without sounding forced, the feeling you want: the emotion, the reaction, the response you want the character himself to arouse in the other characters.

A name can be just as definitive for a character as his main trait. A man may be called Aubrey Vere De Vere Smith because his mother has been addicted to Tennyson and has therefore saddled him with the result of her poetic inclinations. This name suggests a comic character, where plain John Smith, until we come to know him, is just any person from any town or city.

A cruel story can be told in the disguise of the ordinary, and names at first glance may appear to be ordinary, too. In a tale of a family killed by a maniac, the grandmother, who is the archetype of hypocrites, is just Grandmother. The others are John Wesley, Bailey, and June Star. Notice that each name sets the character apart, giving him his own identity. In "Smoky Joe" J. H. is working toward this definitive effect.

3. Through physical description. The bum is described as an "old man." Right at the beginning of the story, when he comes off the barge, we are given physical details that set him apart from the boys.

4. By what he says. If you check the story, you will see that in his first dialogue with the boys Smoky shows himself as a leader.

5. Through what he does. Smoky proves himself in the eyes of the boys by hitting a home run.

6. By what happens to him in the end. We see Smoky drunk at the table. But the character in the story is never definitely resolved, for one reader may feel that Smoky has failed for himself and the boys while another may take a different view. Smoky did hit the home run and so vindicated himself in the eyes of the other players. In this light, his failure to show up on the playing field next day may prove very little since he did not know that one of the boys saw him in the café.

In the examples of student writing, we are asked to accept a spectator at a wreck who is a victim of sudden fear, a boy who becomes aware of the tremendous power of love, and an old bum turning hero before he disappears.

As sketches, the first two examples have obvious shortcomings. The situations are trite, and any justification for writing lies in presenting characters in a way that is fresh and vivid. The girl at the wreck is nobody. The boy who learns love is a sentimental figment. Only in the sketch of Smoky Joe do we have a character who has breath in him. In that sketch, the spontaneity of the author's style gives Smoky a special quality. He is not just any person but *one* person. It is possible to feel a sympathy for him on the playing field and in the bar.

People seldom change basically in fiction. As in life, they retain their fundamental personality traits until the final problem is solved. But in the action of a story a main character must undergo a change, or a series of changes. He may become mature, or learn to respond to the idea of death without fear, or conquer a flaw in himself. He may change in circumstance, meeting a girl, losing her, then marrying her. He may change in what the reader comes to know about him. In the following story, Eveline changes through the psychological pressures that are displayed in her thoughts.


# EVELINE

## JAMES JOYCE

She sat at the window watching the evening invade the avenue. Her head was leaned against the window curtains and in her nostrils was the odour of dusty cretonne. She was tired.

Few people passed. The man out of the last house passed on his way home; she heard his footsteps clacking along the concrete pavement and afterwards crunching on the cinder path before the new red houses. One time there used to be a field there in which they used to play every evening with other people's children. Then a man from Belfast bought the field and built houses in it—not like their little brown houses but bright brick houses with shining roofs. The children of the avenue used to play together in that field—the Devines, the Waters, the Dunns, little Keogh the cripple, she and her brothers and sisters. Ernest, however, never played: he was too grown up. Her father used often to hunt them in out of the field with his blackthorn stick; but usually little Keogh used to keep *nix* and call out when he saw her father coming. Still they seemed to have been rather happy then. Her father was not so bad then; and besides, her mother was alive. That was a long time ago; she and her brothers and sisters were all grown up; her mother was dead. Tizzie Dunn was dead, too, and the Waters had gone back to England. Everything changes. Now she was going to go away like the others, to leave her home.

Home! She looked round the room, reviewing all its familiar objects which she had dusted once a week for so many years, wondering where on earth all the dust came from. Perhaps she would never see again those familiar objects from which she had never dreamed of being divided. And yet during all those years she had never found out the name of the priest whose yellowing photograph hung on the wall above the broken harmonium beside the coloured print of the promises made to Blessed Margaret Mary Alacoque. He had been a school friend of her father. Whenever he showed the photograph to a visitor her father used to pass it with a casual word:

"He is in Melbourne now."

She had consented to go away, to leave her home. Was that wise?
She tried to weigh each side of the question. In her home anyway
she had shelter and food; she had those whom she had known all
her life about her. Of course she had to work hard, both in the
house and at business. What would they say of her in the Stores
when they found out that she had run away with a fellow? Say she
was a fool, perhaps; and her place would be filled up by advertise-
ment. Miss Gavan would be glad. She had always had an edge on
her, especially whenever there were people listening.

"Miss Hill, don't you see these ladies are waiting?"

"Look lively, Miss Hill, please."

She would not cry many tears at leaving the Stores.

But in her new home, in a distant unknown country, it would not
be like that. Then she would be married—she, Eveline. People
would treat her with respect then. She would not be treated as her
mother had been. Even now, though she was over nineteen, she
sometimes felt herself in danger of her father's violence. She knew
it was that that had given her the palpitations. When they were
growing up he had never gone for her, like he used to go for Harry
and Ernest, because she was a girl; but latterly he had begun to
threaten her and say what he would do to her only for her dead
mother's sake. And now she had nobody to protect her. Ernest
was dead and Harry, who was in the church decorating business,
was nearly always somewhere in the country. Besides, the invari-
able squabble for money on Saturday nights had begun to weary
her unspeakably. She always gave her entire wages—seven shillings
—and Harry always sent up what he could but the trouble was to
get any money from her father. He said she used to squander the
money, that she had no head, that he wasn't going to give her his
hard-earned money to throw about the streets, and much more,
for he was usually fairly bad on Saturday night. In the end he would
give her the money and ask her had she any intention of buying
Sunday's dinner. Then she had to rush out as quickly as she could
and do her marketing, holding her black leather purse tightly in
her hand as she elbowed her way through the crowds and returning
home late under her load of provisions. She had hard work to keep
the house together and to see that the two young children who had
been left to her charge went to school regularly and got their meals
regularly. It was hard work—a hard life—but now that she was
about to leave it she did not find it a wholly undesirable life.

She was about to explore another life with Frank. Frank was
very kind, manly, open-hearted. She was to go away with him by
the night-boat to be his wife and to live with him in Buenos Ayres
where he had a home waiting for her. How well she remembered
the first time she had seen him; he was lodging in a house on the

main road where she used to visit. It seemed a few weeks ago. He was standing at the gate, his peaked cap punched back on his head and his hair tumbled forward over a face of bronze. Then they had come to know each other. He used to meet her outside the Stores every evening and see her home. He took her to see *The Bohemian Girl* and she felt elated as she sat in an unaccustomed part of the theatre with him. He was awfully fond of music and sang a little. People knew that they were courting and, when he sang about the lass that loves a sailor, she always felt pleasantly confused. He used to call her Poppens out of fun. First of all it had been an excitement for her to have a fellow and then she had begun to like him. He had tales of distant countries. He had started as a deck boy at a pound a month on a ship of the Allan Line going out to Canada. He told her the names of the ships he had been on and the names of the different services. He had sailed through the Straits of Magellan and he told her stories of the terrible Patagonians. He had fallen on his feet in Buenos Ayres, he said, and had come over to the old country just for a holiday. Of course, her father had found out the affair and had forbidden her to have anything to say to him.

"I know these sailor chaps," he said.

One day he had quarreled with Frank and after that she had to meet her lover secretly.

The evening deepened in the avenue. The white of two letters in her lap grew indistinct. One was to Harry; the other was to her father. Ernest had been her favourite but she liked Harry too. Her father was becoming old lately, she noticed; he would miss her. Sometimes he could be very nice. Not long before, when she had been laid up for a day, he had read her out a ghost story and made toast for her at the fire. Another day, when their mother was alive, they had all gone for a picnic to the Hill of Howth. She remembered her father putting on her mother's bonnet to make the children laugh.

Her time was running out but she continued to sit by the window, leaning her head against the window curtain, inhaling the odour of dusty cretonne. Down far in the avenue she could hear a street organ playing. She knew the air. Strange that it should come that very night to remind her of the promise to her mother, her promise to keep the home together as long as she could. She remembered the last night of her mother's illness; she was again in the close dark room at the other side of the hall and outside she heard a melancholy air of Italy. The organ-player had been ordered to go away and given sixpence. She remembered her father strutting back into the sickroom saying:

"Damned Italians! Coming over here!"

As she mused the pitiful vision of her mother's life laid its spell on the very quick of her being—that life of commonplace sacrifices closing in final craziness. She trembled as she heard again her mother's voice saying constantly with foolish insistence:

"Derevaun Seraun! Derevaun Seraun!"

She stood up in a sudden impulse of terror. Escape! She must escape! Frank would save her. He would give her life, perhaps love, too. But she wanted to live. Why should she be unhappy? She had a right to happiness. Frank would take her in his arms, fold her in his arms. He would save her.

. . . . . . . . . .

She stood among the swaying crowd in the station at the North Wall. He held her hand and she knew that he was speaking to her, saying something about the passage over and over again. The station was full of soldiers with brown baggages. Through the wide doors of the sheds she caught a glimpse of the black mass of the boat, lying in beside the quay wall, with illumined portholes. She answered nothing. She felt her cheek pale and cold and, out of a maze of distress, she prayed to God to direct her, to show her what was her duty. The boat blew a long mournful whistle into the mist. If she went, tomorrow she would be on the sea with Frank, steaming towards Buenos Ayres. Their passage had been booked. Could she still draw back after all he had done for her? Her distress awoke a nausea in her body and she kept moving her lips in silent fervent prayer.

A bell clanged upon her heart. She felt him seize her hand:

"Come!"

All the seas of the world tumbled about her heart. He was drawing her into them: he would drown her. She gripped with both hands at the iron railing.

"Come!"

No! No! No! It was impossible. Her hands clutched the iron in frenzy. Amid the seas she sent a cry of anguish.

"Eveline! Evvy!"

He rushed beyond the barrier and called to her to follow. He was shouted at to go on but he still called to her. She set her white face to him, passive, like a helpless animal. Her eyes gave him no sign of love or farewell or recognition.

In "Eveline," Joyce reveals the meaning of the character's entire existence by showing how she thought about an escape from her family. The story gets its effect primarily through the character's subjective responses, which Joyce ties to objects and people of the outer world she viewed from behind the curtains of dusty cretonne. The action is there. But it is a peg for her thoughts and only at the end of the story do we move outside of her, *see* her white face, her eyes that give no sign of love, recognition, or farewell.

Joyce established the dominant trait of fear of the unknown in Eveline by:

1. Showing her in relationship to the past. We see her remembering the children who were once her companions and we feel that she is frightened to leave home as some of them did. Notice that in her reverie she couples leaving home with the idea of dying as some of her remembered friends have died.

2. By showing her present status. She thinks of her duty to her father, to the children of the family who are under her care, and of her work at the Stores.

3. By revealing her to us through her relationship with Frank who represents romance, far places, the very opposite of the home to which she has been tied so long. Joyce never really shows her in an intimate relationship with Frank. He remains in her thoughts as the symbol of an alien, attractive, and frightening world.

4. By revealing her through herself. Each one of her thoughts shows us another particle of her personality. The memories which play such a tremendous role in the beginning of the story dominate it again at its climax when she remembers her promise to her mother and is more affected than she knows.

5. By displaying her through an exact and effective choice of details about her life that appear to us on the screen of her thoughts and keep intruding on us every moment of the story: the wages she gives away, the curses of the father, and her prayer as she hears the long, mourning whistle of the boat.

6. By showing her final action, at the moment of leaving when she cannot take the passage that has been booked for her. In this instant, we are jerked out of her thoughts to see her as she never sees herself: shocked, pained, oblivious, alone.

As we have seen, Joyce is working in the realm of his character's thoughts. His method is to show us what she thinks rather than to comment on the workings of her mind. He never really thrusts a fact at us directly. The character does all her own revealing, gains sympathy, pity, or disgust for herself through her own web of remembrance set against the pressures of present time.

In "The Saints in Caesar's Household," which was discussed

earlier, Anne Tyler presented her characters primarily through the consciousness of Mary Robinson, who leaves her disturbed friend standing alone in the rain at the amphitheatre. But near the end of the narrative, the author brings in a "chorus" reminder.

People say (and Mary's mother also) that it was a heartless thing to leave a disturbed person out there alone in the rain, with the stones all around her and the grey sky pressing in.

For just a moment, we come out of the consciousness of Mary and get what almost amounts to an author comment, or perhaps even an indictment, of Mary Robinson's conduct. This is a very different approach to character revelation from the approach used by a stream-of-consciousness writer like James Joyce. Louise Hardeman's, "The Lost Beach," the story which follows, employs neither stream of consciousness nor author comment. Instead, Liza and her problem are subtly revealed through action and dialogue.

## THE LOST BEACH

LOUISE HARDEMAN

The rays of the sun fell down on the brown water and on the island that clung to the mainland with a long, steel arm. On the side of the island away from the mainland, you could see smaller islands beyond and after them the sea.

The pot plants that sat on the LaBays' front porch and the vines that twined around its banisters were bent and heavy with dust. They shook a little when the door banged and a small girl ran onto the porch, holding a large, white towel around her head. She went over to the banister and with a quick, impatient movement, pulled the towel away. A mass of wet, red hair fell down about her shoulders. She bent backward and jerked suddenly forward again, so that all the red hair hung over the banister. Glancing around to see if anyone were watching, she let her arms hang limp, and began to make hoarse, gagging sounds from her throat.

Old Mrs. LaBay came to the front door.

"Liza, are you sick?" she asked.

"No. Come and see my hair."

"Well what on earth do you want to make those noises for? You sure you not sick?"

There was a long silence. Mrs. LaBay put down her bowl of half-shelled peas and walked out on the porch.

"Liza?" She tapped the child on her shoulder.

"Look, Mrs. LaBay. Look at my hair."

Mrs. LaBay looked at the thick strands of hair that in one place were dark and wet and in another were bright with the sun.

"It's pretty. It's mighty pretty."

"What does it look like?" the child asked.

Mrs. LaBay searched the sky and the river and her own yard and house.

"It looks like . . . like a pretty red pot plant that has just grown all out of itself."

"And I'm the flowerpot," said Liza, chuckling and patting herself with both hands.

Mrs. LaBay contorted her face appreciatively and went back into the house.

An upstairs window creaked open and a voice called down, "Liza?"

"Yes, ma'am?"

"When your hair's dry, you come right on back up here and I'll plait it for you."

"Let me wear it down," Liza whined.

"No." The window was closed.

Alone again Liza stood up and felt her hair. It was still damp. She leaned back and cut her eyes around sharply to see it swing near the floor. One of the curved posts that supported the porch roof caught her eye. She looked at it closely, then shook her head from side to side in mock amorousness.

"I love you," she said. "Oh, darling, darling, darling."

She scratched her stomach with all ten fingers and burped. Down near the beach a rowboat was pulling into shore. Liza crowed and pointed a finger at the boat.

"Look, Henrietta, there's Captain LaBay. Wouldn't you like to see him?" It was more of a confirmation than a question.

Holding her arms in front of her as though she were carrying an object the size of a beach ball, she ran down the steps and across the gravel road and met the boat as it thumped against the sand.

"Captain LaBay! Hello!"

A bearded old man in a shabby uniform stepped out of the boat.

"Hello, Liza. Hello, Henrietta. How're you both?"

Liza grinned at him.

"We're good," she said. "Look at my hair."

The old man pulled his boat well up on the beach and turned

back to the child. He took her face in his hand and scrutinized her from different angles.

"Um huh!" He held up long strands of hair. "Liza," he began, "Liza, I have never seen anything to equal the sight of your hair. It is the most beautiful . . ."

"It's long," she interrupted.

"The longest I ever saw," he agreed.

"I'm a flower pot."

"A little, round flower pot," said the Captain.

Liza stuck out her bottom lip and looked down at her short, fat body.

"Round?" she asked.

"Well, not really round," he mused, "sort of round*ed*, nicely rounded."

"Oh," she said. "I wish we could go for a ride."

She spoke shyly, twisting her hair around her finger, and adding quickly, "And then we could ride by the pier and take the twins to ride maybe."

The Captain frowned out at the sea and patted Liza on the head.

"Haven't you met those little girls yet?" he asked quietly.

Liza twisted away and leaned over the boat.

"I can row."

"I guess we can take a little ride." He held up his large pocket watch . . . "Mrs. LaBay won't mind and I guess your mama won't either. Well, get in now and let's go."

The Captain yanked his hat down and grunted as he pushed the boat off with one of the oars. When they were well away from the shore, he picked up both oars and the boat moved smoothly over the water. Liza hid her face in her hands.

"You sat on Henrietta!"

The Captain held the oars in mid-air. The boat rocked gently for a while; then the Captain leaned over to one side and reached gingerly underneath himself. He saw laughter behind the hands.

"She wasn't there, Captain LaBay," Liza said consolingly. "I was just teasing."

She grinned delightedly at him, and he smiled back at her pleasure.

"Has Henrietta laid an egg yet?"

"Not a one."

"Well, when she does, you'll tell me about it?"

"I'll give it to you," said Liza and laughed again.

Now they were well away from the island and heading toward a white pier that extended a long way over the water. Liza turned and held her hand to her eyes as a sun shade. She tried to see into the screened pavilion at the end of the walkway.

"Wouldn't you like to ask the girls to come for a ride?" asked the Captain.

"I can't see if they are there."

They rowed in closer to the pavilion. Sounds of talk and laughter could be heard, and then two young girls could be seen, sprawled on the floor. Liza looked up at the Captain and ran her hand through the water.

"I don't want to," she said in a low voice.

The old man raised his eyebrows and frowned for a minute, then rowed on beyond the pier. They rowed silently for all the time that it took to get out to the little islands. The water began to get rough.

"And there's the sea," said the Captain.

"Do you get seasick?"

"You mean did I get seasick?" he informed her with a scowl. She nodded.

"I never got seasick a day in my life, not one out of ten thousand."

"I got seasick."

The Captain was watching the waves.

"I said I got seasick."

"Uh? Oh yes. Is that so? And when was that?"

"Today I was playing like I was aboard a ship and the waves came so high and I was sick over the side."

"And you might be sick over the side now. Look at those waves out there."

She held up her hand to measure them and wrinkled her square nose at him.

"Oh, they're high, all right. They just aren't close to us."

Liza studied the waves.

"If they knocked us over would we sink?"

"No, we'd swim."

"But if we didn't swim, would we sink?"

"I guess we would." The Captain looked thoughtful.

"And would we go down to the bottom of the ocean?"

"I guess we would."

Liza leaned toward the Captain and fixed her eyes on his face. "Like what? Sink like what?"

"Well now, let me see," said the Captain. "We'd go down like stones."

Liza examined her hands.

"We'd go down like . . . feathers."

Liza scratched her nose.

"We'd go down like . . . like bells."

She smiled up at him and drew her arm through the water like a swinging bell. And he drew out his handkerchief and pretended to mop his brow.

They started rowing back toward the island, and Liza threw her head back and sang one of the ballads she had learned in the second grade.

> Oh the days of the Kerry dancing,
> Oh the ring of the piper's tune,
> Oh for one of those hours of gladness,
> Gone, alas, from my life too soon.

She sang in a deep, hoarse voice.

When they came near the island, the Captain stopped rowing and bent over to Liza.

"Don't you think we could take the twins to ride now?"

Liza squirmed around on the seat. "I don't believe they can go. They probably have something else to do."

"We could ask, though. You said you wanted to take them to ride."

Liza began pulling the tangles out of her hair. The Captain watched her for a few minutes, then he leaned down until his face was close to hers.

"Liza, look here at me."

She offered him the corners of her eyes.

"Now Liza, you haven't lived here very long and I've been living on this island the good part of my life. And I know that the people here are sometimes slow to take newcomers in. Those Jarvis twins have lived here all their lives and they know everybody on the island. Just because they haven't played with you as much as some of the other children doesn't mean they don't like you. They think now they're up in grammar school, they're grown up. When you get to be a little bit older, too, it'll make all the difference in the world. It just takes a while."

Her mouth curved down at the sides like a small, curled sea shell.

"They haven't played with me at all."

The Captain cleared his throat with a burst of sound and clamped down on his bottom lip with his teeth.

"Everybody wants to be liked, Liza. It's easier for some than for others."

He picked up the oars again. "Shall we ask them to take a ride?"

"All right," she said and started arranging her hair around her shoulders.

When they came up to the pavilion, the girls stopped talking and peered over the side. Liza was very small in the boat. The Captain waved a hand.

"Hello, there. Come and have a ride with us."

The twins looked at each other.

"We can't," they said. "Mother is punishing us."

"Well, that's too bad," called the Captain. He sat back down in the boat. The twins bent toward each other and whispered.

"Let her come up here."

The Captain looked at Liza closely before he answered. "You mean Liza?" he called up to the twins. "Liza, would you like to go up on the pavilion for a while?"

"All right."

The Captain took her hand and held it while she wobbled over to the ladder. "Have a good time."

She gave him a wide smile and began awkwardly to climb up to the pavilion.

The twins opened the door for her and she walked over to the board that ran around the inside of it and sat down. Nobody said anything.

"Has the Captain gone?" one of the twins asked her.

She looked out toward the LaBay house but she didn't see the rowboat.

"I guess so," she said. "What were you playing?"

"We weren't playing; we were talking."

"Oh," said Liza.

The twins were huddled together, and starting at Liza's feet they stared all the way up to her head and then all the way down again.

"Who do you play with?" they asked.

"Henrietta," she said, laughing and warming toward them.

The twins shrugged their shoulders at each other.

"Who?"

"Henrietta. She's a chicken."

"A chicken!" the twins cried scornfully.

Liza laughed with deep, catching noises.

"You can't see her. She's a play chicken."

"How silly," said a twin.

Liza looked startled, but she said nothing.

"Why do you and your mother live at the LaBay's house?" asked one of the twins.

"It's nice."

The twin held her nose tightly between her fingers.

"It is not nice. It's old and ugly. And you live there 'cause it's cheap. And they're poor, too."

"And so are you," added the other twin, her eyes bulging with excitement as she watched Liza.

She looked back toward the house, but still she did not see the Captain's boat. She rose and started for the screen door that led to the walkway.

"I have to go," she said.

"No, wait," said a twin, standing in front of her. "Can you swim?"

"No," said Liza quizzically.

"She can't swim," the twin told her sister.

"Oh well," she said, making a face.

Liza looked up at them and hesitated a moment before she spoke.

"But if I sank do you know what it would be like?" she said hopefully.

They waited. She put her hands out, palms up, and leaned her head on her shoulder.

"Like a bell," she said simply.

The twins stood rigid and glass-eyed and then they bent away from each other laughing.

"A bell! A bell! Whoever heard of such a ridiculous thing! A bell!"

Liza darted around the twins and headed for the door, but before she got there, one of them pushed her back and then both of them ran out and locked the door. She put her hands on the screen and stared at them wide-eyed.

"We aren't gonna letcha out," they said. "We're gonna leave you there all night and terrible things will happen to you."

Liza pressed her face against the screen.

"You and your ole ugly clothes and your ole ugly hair. Don't your mama ever comb your hair? And it smells bad too, just like that old house of the LaBays', smells just like fish, and our daddy says . . ."

"Look," said her sister. "Look at the old cry baby."

"I want to go home," Liza said in a choking voice.

"I wanna go home," the twins mimicked. "What will you give us if we let you go?"

Liza clung to the door handle. Her face was screwed into a confused knot. She waited a long time to answer.

"I'll give you my doll."

"Pooh, who wants a doll!"

"What do you want?" she implored.

"No," they said, "you have to name something and we'll tell you if it's all right."

Liza rubbed her hair against her cheek and wrinkled her forehead in distress. Finally she looked up at the girls with a grave face and in a low, unsteady voice she said, "I'll tell you all the dirty words I know."

The twins' eyes were shining and they moved back and unlocked the door.

"All right," they said warningly.

Liza ran onto the walkway. She began to cry then, putting her hands over her ears, and shouting out all the childish words heard in the girls' bathroom at school, and all the words carved furtively on the desks—all the words that had no meaning and couldn't be asked about without a reprimand. She flung away from the twins and ran up the walkway toward the road.

Underneath the pier the captain waited until the twins were talking and laughing again before he started rowing quietly home.

And Liza ran all the way to the house. Mrs. LaBay was waiting on the porch for her with a brush and comb in her hand.

"Liza!" she chided, "where on earth have you been, child? Your mama's gone down town and she asked me to tell you not to run off like that and to plait your hair for you."

She looked down into the small, unhappy face.

"You been crying?" she asked kindly.

The tears rose up and spilled over again.

"There now, that's all right. You just sit right down here on the floor and we'll have your hair all plaited by the time your mama gets back."

Liza sat down and leaned on Mrs. LaBay's legs. The brush pulled her head back in short jerks.

When they started on the second plait, Captain LaBay came up through the yard. The stairs creaked as he came up on the porch and sat in the rocking chair next to his wife and the child.

"That's done!" said Mrs. LaBay, snapping a rubber band onto the plait. "Would you two like a peach cobbler and a glass of milk?"

"I think we would," said the Captain, and rubbed his hands briskly.

The door clicked gently shut behind Mrs. LaBay. The Captain leaned over and spoke to Liza.

"Do you know what I wish you would do?"

"What?" she asked in a flat voice.

"I wish you'd come up here and sit on my lap."

She rose and climbed obediently onto his lap.

"Woops!" he cried, "you sat on Henrietta!"

She looked around at him with a sober face.

"I was just teasing," he said softly.

They rocked back and forth in the big chair for a time. Now and then the Captain drew in a deep breath and let it out slowly, so that Liza rose and fell like a piece of bright seaweed on a wave.

Mrs. LaBay returned with a tray and put it down in front of them on a low table. The three of them ate cobblers and drank milk in silence. When they had finished, Mrs. LaBay poured them more milk and took the empty dishes back into the house.

The Captain wiped his mouth and hands with his handkerchief and looked at the horizon.

"Liza," he said, "look at that sky!" He slapped her on the hip. She looked up.

"It's blue and silver," the Captain said and waited for the question. It didn't come.

"Like what?" he asked himself aloud. "Blue . . . and silver," he struggled with the words, "blue and silver like . . . the beach in the early morning."

The Captain smiled to himself.

"Like a beach I used to play on when I was a boy."

He looked down at the small head with its carefully plaited hair and placed his hand on top of it.

"Like a lost beach," he said thoughtfully, sadly.

Liza held her glass of milk out in front of them and saw the shadowy reflection of a little girl with a large hand on top of her head. Then something like a smile began at the corners of her mouth and ran upward as she took the last big swallow of milk and looked over the rim of the glass out to sea.

## REVEALING A CHARACTER:   Assignment 19

1. Using "The Lost Beach" as your reference, find the section of dialogue in the story through which the crisis that Liza faces is revealed. Does her response to the twins' demand for payment if they let her go represent a defeat that makes this day typical of other days that will follow in her life?

2. In the same story comment on four minor actions by Liza that give us a clue to her character. Start with the scene in which she goes with the Captain in the row boat in an effort to make contact with the twins.

In "The Lost Beach" the world loses its early morning look when a child comes in contact with the cruelty of other children. We see Liza in the one definitive hour when she realizes that she is not going to be accepted. This is a story in which the character herself carries the idea or theme without thrusting it at the reader. The whole effect comes through the revelation of the child's personality.

Whenever you yourself are revealing character, you should know more about your fictional person than you are going to tell your reader and then select the details that make an artistic whole. You may show a man or a woman or a child in a crucial moment that works an inevitable change, or you may show the summation of many moments in a person's life. Whatever your character's narrative circumstances you yourself must know all about him and then reveal that "all" by careful selection.

## GIVING A CHARACTER HIS DOMINANT FICTIONAL TRAIT: Assignment 20

1. Write a 500-word sketch giving a background of facts about the main character for your second story and explain your attitude toward those facts. Include whatever knowledge comes to your mind regarding the man or woman's personality and history.

2. Designate from your sketch those facts that may best be used to reveal a dominant or salient trait that will determine his course of action in the story.

3. Select a method of revealing your character, not necessarily from those presented here. If you evolve a pattern of character revelation for yourself, tell why you think it will work effectively in your second story.

# 9

## The Uses of Place and Time

The aim of the artist, Joseph Conrad says, is

to arrest, for the space of a breath, the hands busy about the work of the earth, and compel men entranced by the sight of distant goals to glance for a moment at the surrounding vision of form and color, of sunshine and shadows; to make them pause for a look, for a sigh, for a smile—such is the aim . . . and when it is accomplished—behold! —all the truth of life is there. . . .

This truth, as every writer comes to know, is conveyed through the senses. The writer uses the strength of the written word to make the reader hear, feel, see, perceive, what the story teller has already felt, known, been moved by, and hopes to communicate. According to Conrad, every writer of fiction which in any way aspires to be art, makes his appeal through his own temperament to "all those innumerable temperaments whose subtle and resistless power endows passing events with their true meaning and creates the moral, the emotional, atmosphere of place and time."

Through place and time Conrad wanted to fix what we can call setting, atmosphere, or, by extension, environment in a story, environment being all those external conditions and influences which affect the lives of our characters. Of course Conrad knew the importance of character, action, and theme, but in wanting to find the truth of life through fiction he is particularly interested in the role of time and place.

Place, or setting, as we have thought of it before, is your territory. It is that segment of a created world which helps you project your whole communication to the reader. It may appear as a virtual actor in your story or as a background for your people and their actions. It must be unmistakably your own province, reflecting what you are as a writer and where you began. For as William Faulkner says, every writer must have somewhere to start from.

> I learned that, to be a writer, one has first got to be what he is, what he was born. . . . You have to have somewhere to start from: then you begin to learn. It don't matter where it was, just so you remember it and ain't ashamed of it. Because one place to start from is just as important as any other. You're a country boy; all you know is that little patch up there in Miss. where you started from.

For the moment, instead of saying place is somewhere to start from and represents what you are, we are going to approach it as a specifically designated setting, and afterward consider it briefly as environment. For a start, suppose we say that setting is any definite place, including its objects, items, and furnishings, that any writer sets out to present in a piece of fiction.

Scene as we approach it here can contain all the items of a room or a landscape, viewed as in a theater or on television. Unlike environment, it can be a street, a meadow, a sea, or a mountain where your characters appear and act. It is part, but not all, of the total climate of a story and like any other fictional element must have its proper proportions before it can be effective.

Scene has always been part of parable, verse, or storytelling. Jesus says, "There was in a city a judge. . . ." Poe entitles one of his poems, "The City in the Sea." You yourself, writing of the characters who come to life in your imagination, must give them what the poet called a local habitation. Often at the very start of your narrative it can set the tone and mood for you and go on to pervade the entire story.

In the fables that came to us from our ancestors, a setting often seemed to be nowhere and yet diffused itself everywhere. As children we heard of a "far land," or an "island in the sea," or a "dark tower," or a "cave." A magic carpet took us over one land after another and across the desert to a green spot that sheltered a caravan. Those stories with their remarkable geography still appeal to the child in all of us.

Some modern writers, using the technique of fable, like to

present an indefinable scene resembling that of a fairy tale to
create an atmosphere of cosmic chaos. In a story by the German writer, Franz Kafka, we never know the name of the
country he uses or see the actual boundaries of the land that
belongs to the emperor who rules a people invaded by nomads,
but through a deliberate, frighteningly vague presentation of
place, we sense the onslaught of barbarism.

I fancied I actually saw the Emperor himself at a window of the
palace; usually he never enters these outer rooms but spends all
his time in the innermost garden; yet on this occasion he was
standing, or so at least it seemed to me, at one of the windows,
watching with bent head the ongoings before his residence.
"What is going to happen?" we all ask ourselves. "How long
can we endure this burden and torment? The Emperor's palace
has drawn the nomads here but does not know how to drive them
away again. The gate stays shut; the guards, who used to be always
marching out and in with ceremony, keep close behind barred
windows. It is left to us artisans and tradesmen to save our country; but we are not equal to such a task; nor have we ever claimed
to be capable of it. This is a misunderstanding of some kind; and
it will be the ruin of us."
                                    From "An Old Page," by Franz Kafka

Notice the shut gates, the barred windows, and the fancy
of seeing the emperor at one of them. The reference to "our
country" is to a Hades in our own time. Kafka's is an inner
world of fear, projected by vague and often allegorical settings.
His is the inverted delight of a Freudian fairy tale.
   The other extreme from this nebulous presentation of scene
appears in a novel by John Wyndham. In writing of our own
century from the viewpoint of a man of the future, living in
perhaps 2300, and in creating the scene of a world still unborn,
Wyndham describes a house as factually as if it were the dwell-
ing next door.

Our house is not easy to describe. My grandfather, Elias Strorm,
built the first part of it over fifty years before; since then it had
grown new rooms and extensions at various times. By now, it
rambled off on one side into stock-sheds, stores, stables, and barns,
and on the other into washhouses, dairies, cheese-rooms, farmhands'
rooms, and so on until it three-quarters enclosed a large, beaten-

earth yard which lay to leeward of the main house and had a midden for its central feature. . . .

.    .    .    .    .    .    .    .    .    .    .

Within the house, life centered, as was the local custom, upon the large living room which was also the kitchen.

. . . My mother saw to it that the big room was kept very clean and tidy. The floor was composed of pieces of brick and stone and artificial stone cleverly fitted together. The furniture was whitely scrubbed tables and stools, with a few chairs. The walls were whitewashed. Several burnished pans, too big to go in the cupboard, hung against them. The nearest approach to decoration was a number of wooden panels with sayings, mostly from *Repentances*, artistically burnt into them.

From *Re-Birth*, by John Wyndham

Wyndham creates his imaginary scene by an enumeration of realistic details. Whether your setting is real or fanciful, you can characterize it, if you like, by choosing one or two salient aspects and emphasizing them by their position in a paragraph, or by repetition, rather than by giving many related details. For instance, if a writer notes that a leopard skin hangs near a Kikuyu spear in a Manhattan apartment, the feeling of the entire scene is suggested and we also learn something about the man to whom the room belongs.

A student writer used the repetition of "blue façade" for emphasis in the following passages as a way of giving scene an effective role.

It was snowing hard but I could make no effort to move in the cold. I was nearly blinded and didn't know the number of the apartment though I had been there before. Walking head down against the snow, I should never have found the place. But for some reason the lower façade of the building was painted blue. A light vivid blue, defiant between somber grays. I recognized it instantly. Blue. I walked down the steps below the level of the street into an alcove inside and shook the snow from my coat, and paused before the bright blue façade.

C. H.

Try never to write a bland physical description of a place: select what it is important for your reader to see. Do not simply put down everything about a room, a road, a house, without regard for the actions or responses of your characters. Unless you have a very special reason, do not write an expository paragraph describing scene without relating it to the action and the characters.

In the following excerpt from a student story, the land is the only real character. The narrative begins to fail with its long beginning which is no more than a static picture of a farm as morning arrives. Here, the very monotony of scene tends to put the reader into a doze.

A soft light had started in the east, and the birds were beginning their early morning chatter when the door of the house opened. The figure of a man stood on the porch drinking in the early morning peaceful stillness and the dampness. A dog barked some-where in the distance and then settled down again to sleep. The man walked across the wet lawn slowly, looking at the dark sky overhead, and then at the water beads on the grass that would dis-appear with the hot sun.

As he crossed the lawn, crickets stopped their chirp and some birds flew prematurely out of the dark shadow of a magnolia tree. The man did not stop to look at these daily occurrences, just as he would not see the deer, caught at its early morning feed, in its mad retreat to the darkness and safety of the woods. He would not see the deer stop at the edge of the woods to watch as he walked to the barn, and then slowly return for some more grass before the world became cognizant that this was another day. Finally, when all was awake, the deer would return to the forest, and to seclusion.

The day quickly matured as the sun rose above the horizon. The crickets quieted and the deer returned to the forest. The mist that had been hovering above the lake lost itself in the sunlight and became part of the lightening sky. The cool dampness of the night was lost with the hot frenzy of another day. A slow monotonous buzz of hidden peepers was the only accompaniment for the rise of the sun.

The lay of the land was now visible, and the sky had emerged from streaks of light, to a deep red glow and then finally to the gray-blue of day. Green-yellow fields gave way to a great forest which grew into a mountain that loomed behind the farm. In front of the house were a few well placed trees which outlined large fields, and crops which were turning yellow from the lack of rain. The forest had not lost the splendor of green leaves but they too were turned down dejectedly, starting to wilt. The lake had lost several feet of water and would lose more unless nature helped the underground springs which fed the house and barn.

The day was fully matured.

D. E.

In a novel or a short story where the conflict with the land is at the core, this introduction might not be too long if the farmer were brought strongly into our vision and if his actions were offered as a contrast to nature. But in the passage just quoted, and in the final part of the story, the student included more and more nature description and no movement at all. The story is too well located. The following dialogue, written by another student, not only is awkward in itself but is not located at all.

"Jon, let's don't go anyplace special tonight; my head is splitting."

"Open the glove compartment, Kath, I always keep a couple of APC's in there."

"Oh, aspirin? I just had four."

"At one time?"

"Yes," she answered holding her head in her hands. "I've had so many they don't seem to do any good anymore."

"Kath, you're going to be my best patient—my own hypochondriac."

"How can you say that? Your head's not hurting!" Big tears came into her eyes. "I am not a 'hypo'. My head hurts like hell and I don't feel like arguing."

Jon placed a protective arm around her. "Go ahead and cry." And Kathy did.

D. L. H.

One way to show setting is to intersperse details of place in a character's responses, focusing them according to the point of view of one person. For instance, you may have chosen a ship as the setting for an episode, as the student writer, C. H., chose a blue apartment façade in the snow. In the following selection, the narrator's reactions to the cabin in which a party is being held are an attempt to make the reader share the distaste for the party felt by the person who is giving it.

The sun burned into every corner of the city, and everyone thought it couldn't be any hotter than it was in his particular location. As we drove through the port of Buenos Aires past the big warehouses, the white concrete glared, and I felt like an egg in a giant oven. Even in the light cotton suit I was wearing I sweated freely, and the hair on my body prickled and burned maddeningly against my skin. It was hard to concentrate on the fact of my leaving.

There was going to be a farewell party on the ship, and I had invited nearly everyone to come. I wondered how many would be there . . . feared the heat would be warmer than the friends I had and they would stay away. Mother was talking incessantly about what to do and not do on the ship . . . whom to see when I got to New York . . . be sure to call Uncle Ed . . . and Dad was checking with the chauffeur to be sure we hadn't forgotten anything. And I was thinking about leaving.

"Back to the States," Ralph and Andy and the rest of them had said. "You lucky dog!" "Send us some of the latest records," the girls had said, Mona, Gaby, and Susie, and tried to give me the money, but I refused it.

"Sure, we'll be there," they had all reassured me when I gave them passes to get on board for the party. "Wouldn't miss a last beer blast with you for anything," Harlan had said.

There was a big crowd of people on the dock where the ship was tied up. Black smoke issued from its twin funnels and I felt the urgency again to see and talk to as many of them as I could, to keep them till the last minute. We got out of the car and Rudolfo carried the bags on to my room. Dad squared away my allowance with the purser, Mother fanning and trying to forget about not seeing me for the next six months.

Nobody was there yet . . . we had come early to check on the party and everything. When I stepped into the small room which the ship had fixed up for us, I was at first dismayed, then angry, then frustrated. It was Christmas, and they had a little Christmas tree, kiddie stools and tables, cookies and ice cream and punch. There was a quick consultation with the stewards . . . they thought it was for a younger boy . . . no, it was too late for cocktails or beer. "To hell with it," I said. "The ice cream will be nice on a hot day like this," said Mother. But I knew it would happen. Something always did . . . like the night Mona and I were sitting on the gate outside her house and I leaned and tried to kiss her and the gate had moved and we both fell backwards on the lawn.

So I sat there on a kid's stool with a glass of cherry punch in my hand until Ralph and Harlan and Gaby showed up and I gestured helplessly and then it was all right because it was a big joke but to me it wasn't all right, nothing ever had been the whole time I was there because I had fallen in love with the people and the way we lived together in sin and innocence and youth. And because of their easy, relaxed ways of letting things come to them and because I tried too hard I would never be a part of them, though they liked and accepted me.

More of them came, and I was trying again to tell them I didn't want to leave and needed their friendship and I never could really tell them. And Mona and Terry came and gave me a bowl with two goldfish and I groaned and thought what the hell am I going to do with two goldfish and they said, "Tell us which one dies first," and I nearly broke down then and there.

And the time passed and passed and they had to get off and I had to stay. So I led them to the gangplank and something happened I shall never forget. The girls all kissed me good bye and cried, and Andy and Harlan shook my hand and talked of when we would meet and then Mother and Dad and then they were gone.

I went up to the rail where I could see them and they waved and shouted and I shouted back till I couldn't trust myself anymore.

The ship pulled away and they sang the hymno nacional and I couldn't laugh or cry but did both. Then I went down to the hot cabin to sit alone for a long time and thought "I will see them again. I will!"

C. H.

The four preceding excerpts show how three students tried to give scene its proper role in a story. It appears as climate, color, nature, an object, an apartment, a ship's cabin, and as various carefully selected items in the cabin, including kiddie stools, ice cream, and punch—which tell us something about a character.

How are you attempting to use scene in your own present story?

## GIVING SCENE ITS PROPER ROLE: Assignment 21

Answer the following questions and hand them in to your instructor.

1. What is my intention and purpose in using the scene I have chosen for my second story?

2. Should I use only one place in the story, so as to keep my narrative compact, or do I need a variety of settings?

3. Am I giving the proper emphasis to scene? How dominant a role can I allow it to play in the life of my characters?

4. Am I being careful to use sensory impressions to evoke my characters' responses to scene?

5. After I select and arrange the right details for my scene, how can I project them concretely for the effect I want?

6. Does my scene come through as deliberate exposition or have I merged it effectively into the structure of the story?

7. Can I justify my choice of scene in terms of the environmental pattern in which I am working?

You can work on a one-set scene—a room, a café, a car, or a train. Or you can bring in environment by using a particular setting to represent the conditions and influences that overcast your work as a whole. Some writers use a generic setting at the start and later employ particular scenes to illustrate it.

A ONE-SPOT SETTING IN WHICH ACTION TAKES PLACE

So the fight was to take place at seven o'clock. This was known to everyone, not by announcement or words, but understood in the unquestioning way that rain is understood, or an evil odor from the swamp. So before seven o'clock everyone gathered gravely around the property of Miss Amelia. The cleverest got into the café itself and stood lining the walls of the room. Others crowded onto the front porch, or took a stand in the yard.

Miss Amelia and Marvin Macy had not yet shown themselves. Miss Amelia, after resting all afternoon on the office bench, had gone upstairs. On the other hand Cousin Lymon was at your elbow every minute, threading his way through the crowd, snapping his fingers nervously, and batting his eyes. At one minute to seven o'clock he squirmed his way into the café and climbed up on the counter. All was very quiet.

It must have been arranged in some manner beforehand. For just at the stroke of seven Miss Amelia showed herself at the head of the stairs. At the same instant Marvin Macy appeared in front of the café and the crowd made way for him silently. They walked toward each other with no haste, their fists already gripped, and their eyes like the eyes of dreamers. Miss Amelia had changed her red dress for her old overalls, and they were rolled up to the knees. She was barefooted and she had an iron strengthband around her right wrist. Marvin Macy had also rolled his trouser legs—he was naked to the waist and heavily greased; he wore the heavy shoes that had been issued him when he left the penitentiary. Stumpy MacPhail stepped forward from the crowd and slapped their hip pockets with the palm of his right hand to make sure there would be no sudden knives. Then they were alone in the cleared center of the bright café.

There was no signal, but they both struck out simultaneously. Both blows landed on the chin, so that the heads of Miss Amelia and Marvin Macy bobbed back and they were left a little groggy. For a few seconds after the first blows they merely shuffled their feet around on the bare floor, experimenting with various positions, and making mock fists. Then, like wildcats, they were suddenly on each other. There was the sound of knocks, panting, and thumpings on the floor. They were so fast that it was hard to take in what was going on—but once Miss Amelia was hurled backward so that she staggered and almost fell, and another time Marvin Macy caught a knock on the shoulder that spun him around like a top. So the fight went on in this wild violent way with no sign of weakening on either side.

During a struggle like this, when the enemies are as quick and strong as these two, it is worth-while to turn from the confusion of the fight itself and observe the spectators. The people had flattened back as close as possible against the walls. Stumpy MacPhail was in a corner, crouched over and with his fists tight in sympathy, making strange noises. Poor Merlie Ryan had his mouth so wide open that a fly buzzed into it, and was swallowed before Merlie realized what had happened. And Cousin Lymon—he was worth watching. The hunchback still stood on the counter, so that he was raised up above everyone else in the café. He had his hands on his hips, his big head thrust forward, and his little legs bent so that the knees jutted outward. The excitement had made him break out in a rash, and his pale mouth shivered.

Perhaps it was half an hour before the course of the fight shifted. Hundreds of blows had been exchanged, and there was still a deadlock. Then suddenly Marvin Macy managed to catch hold of Miss Amelia's left arm and pinion it behind her back. She struggled and got a grasp around his waist; the real fight was now begun. Wrestling is the natural way of fighting in this country—as boxing is too quick and requires much thinking and concentration. And now that Miss Amelia and Marvin were locked in a hold together the crowd came out of its daze and pressed in closer. For a while the fighters grappled muscle to muscle, their hipbones braced against each other. Backward and forward, from side to side, they swayed in this way. Marvin Macy still had not sweated, but Miss Amelia's overalls were drenched and so much sweat had trickled down her legs that she left wet footprints on the floor. Now the test had come, and in these moments of terrible effort, it was Miss Amelia who was the stronger. Marvin Macy was greased and slippery, tricky to grasp, but she was stronger. Gradually she bent him over backward, and inch by inch she forced him to the floor. It was a terrible thing to watch and their deep hoarse breaths were the only sound in the café. At last she had him down, and straddled; her strong big hands were on his throat.

But at that instant, just as the fight was won, a cry sounded in the café that caused a shrill bright shiver to run down the spine. And what took place has been a mystery ever since. The whole town was there to testify what happened, but there were those who doubted their own eyesight. For the counter on which Cousin Lymon stood was at least twelve feet from the fighters in the center of the café. Yet at the instant Miss Amelia grasped the throat of Marvin Macy the hunchback sprang forward and sailed through the air as though he had grown hawk wings. He landed on the broad strong back of Miss Amelia and clutched at her neck with his clawed little fingers.

The rest is confusion. Miss Amelia was beaten before the crowd could come to their senses. Because of the hunchback the fight was won by Marvin Macy, and at the end Miss Amelia lay sprawled on the floor, her arms flung outward and motionless. Marvin Macy stood over her, his face somewhat popeyed, but smiling his old half-mouthed smile. And the hunchback, he had suddenly disappeared. Perhaps he was frightened about what he had done, or maybe he was so delighted that he wanted to glory with himself alone—at any rate he slipped out of the café and crawled under the back steps. Someone poured water on Miss Amelia, and after a time she got up slowly and dragged herself into her office. Through the open door the crowd could see her sitting at her desk, her head in the crook of her arm, and she was sobbing with the last of her grating, winded breath. Once she gathered her right fist together and knocked it three times on the top of her office desk, then her hand opened feebly and lay palm upward and still. Stumpy Mac-Phail stepped forward and closed the door.

The crowd was quiet, and one by one the people left the café.

From "The Ballad of the Sad Café," by Carson McCullers

We spent hours, about three, going up that long, long valley. In that time it grew to late afternoon and the light was growing amber and shadows were falling ominously in the valley of dry boulders and instead, though, of making you feel scared it gave you that immortal feeling again. The ducks were all laid out easy to see: on top of a boulder you'd stand, and look ahead, and spot a duck (usually only two flat rocks on top of each other maybe with one round one on top for decoration) and you aimed in that general direction. The purpose of these ducks, as laid out by all previous climbers, was to save a mile or two of wandering around in the immense valley. Meanwhile our roaring creek was still at it, but thinner and more quiet now, running from the cliff face itself a mile up the valley in a big black stain I could see in the gray rock.

Jumping from boulder to boulder and never falling, with a heavy pack, is easier than it sounds; you just can't fall when you get into the rhythm of the dance. I looked back down the valley sometimes and was surprised to see how high we'd come, and to see farther horizons of mountains now back there. Our beautiful trail-top park was like a little glen of the Forest of Arden. Then the climbing got steeper, the sun got redder, and pretty soon I began to see patches of snow in the shade of some rocks. We got up to where the cliff face seemed to loom over us. At one point I saw Japhy throw down his pack and danced my way up to him.

"Well, this is where we'll drop our gear and climb those few hundred feet up the side of that cliff, where you see there it's shallower, and find that camp. I remember it. In fact you can sit here and rest or beat your bishop while I go ramblin around there, I like to ramble by myself."

Okay. So I sat down and changed my wet socks and changed soaking undershirt for dry one and crossed my legs and rested and whistled for about a half-hour, a very pleasant occupation, and Japhy got back and said he'd found the camp. I thought it would be a little jaunt to our resting place but it took almost another hour to jump by the steep boulders, climb around some, get to the level of the cliff-face plateau, and there, on flat grass more or less, hike about two hundred yards to where a huge gray rock towered among pines. Here now the earth was a splendorous thing—snow on the ground, in melting patches in the grass, and gurgling creeks, and the huge silent rock mountains on both sides, and a wind blowing, and the smell of heather. We forded a lovely little creek, shallow as your hand, pearl pure lucid water, and got to the huge rock.

Here were old charred logs where other mountainclimbers had camped.

"And where's Matterhorn mountain?"

"You can't see it from here, but"—pointing up the farther long plateau and a scree gorge twisting to the right—"around that draw and up two miles or so and then we'll be at the foot of it."

"Wow, heck, whoo, that'll take us a whole other day!"

From *The Dharma Bums*, by Jack Kerouac

A SPECIFIC SETTING THAT PROJECTS THE ENVIRONMENT IN A NARRATIVE

The valley of ashes is bounded on one side by a small foul river, and, when the drawbridge is up to let barges through, the passengers on waiting trains can stare at the dismal scene for as long as half an hour. There is always a halt there of at least a minute, and it was because of this that I first met Tom Buchanan's mistress.

From *The Great Gatsby*, by F. Scott Fitzgerald

A GENERIC SETTING ILLUSTRATIVE OF THE ENVIRONMENT OF THE NARRATIVE

. . . the unseen lights of the Loop were reflected in the sky like light from some gigantic forge beating in the pit of the city's enormous heart. A heart seeming now to beat in suppressed panic. A panic lying in wait, each midnight hour, at his own heart's forge.

Night of the All Nite restaurants, the yellow-windowed machineshop night where daylight was being prepared on lathes. Night of the thunderous anvils preparing the city's iron heart for tomorrow's iron traffic. Night of the city lovers, the Saturday Night till Sunday Morning lovers, making love on rented beds with the rent not due till Monday.

Night of iron and lovers' laughter: night without mercy. Into a morning without tears.

From where the narrow alley ran a child's cry, high-pitched, brief and cut off sharply, came up to him like the cry of a child run down in the dark by a drunken driver. A cry that held no hope of help at all, a cry that pitched the very darkness down. Tautly, as he himself had pitched his tent that winter on the Meuse, with the stakes driven through the cloth like the cloth of the heart, the way darkness pinned any child down between tavern and trolley and tenement.

The darkness through which all such children of the broken

sky line moved, their small white faces guided only by a swinging
arc lamp's gleam and the swift-changing neon guide lights of the
city's thousand bars. Till the difference between daylight and darkness seemed to them only the difference between the light of the
alleyways under the El and the light down any gin-mill basement.

From *The Man with the Golden Arm*, by Nelson Algren

In the last two examples, the novelists use a social background
rather than scene in a restricted sense. Place here embraces the
conditions that affect the characters, including the hovering
shadow of time. Scene, setting, environment, milieu, the climate
of any fiction, are terms intimately connected with time, and
in choosing a narrative site, you should, as Conrad suggested,
try to create not only the atmosphere of place but also of time.


## LINKING PLACE WITH TIME:   Assignment 22

1. Write out as fully as you can a description of the particular
setting or settings in your second story.

2. Link these settings to the *time* you expect your second story to
cover. Explain your reasons for the time limits you have chosen for
your present work.


In actual life, although time is always passing for us, the present time does exist. In the finished work of fiction, or in any
portion of it, we catch time and hold it out of motion in a
created world. But even as we write, the moment in which we
are recording becomes part of the other moments that have
gone before; and so a finished narrative always has a calendar
in which time exists only in the past.

You can manipulate time freely in fiction once you have restricted it in formal borders that mark the beginning and ending of your work. You can schedule a story in a region where
apparently no clock ticks. You can write in the supposed present, using the past tense but presenting the events as if they
are happening to your character at the moment of being written
down. You can even draw on your own observations of the
moment, apart from those of your characters. One novelist

interpolated into her narrative the sounds of her dog lapping up milk which she heard as she wrote. But again, when she got them into the manuscript they were already part of the past. So the real-life movement she wanted to simulate had gone by.

Her fiction had a calendar of its own. Actually, any piece of fiction has several calendars. Your characters, if they exist at all, are moving through time and space. Say that you are using a time pattern of a day. That day covers a crucial moment in the life of your main character and the events that led him to his crisis. That is one calendar. The author's own calendar of work, on the other hand, may extend over a period of months. When he is done, he still has on paper only a day or part of one.

Further, a fictional day may include much more than the surface action taking place during that day. The one day covered in James Joyce's *Ulysses* includes a montage of past days and of many moments superimposed on other moments through the conscious and subconscious memory of the characters. When that is true, you may write of a single day but the reader assimilates a much longer segment of the characters' lives.

Again, in *The Ledge*, by Lawrence Sargent Hall, the last lingering hours in the life of a fisherman trapped by a rising tide contract for the person who is reading the story. Yet, if the time pattern is handled well, a person who needs only an hour to read the story can apprehend esthetically the entire day or any time span in which a writer may be working.

Time has a differing significance, then, for the reader, the story itself, and also for the writer. For some writers, the hours are an agony which drag each word from them slowly. For others the words flow well and the work seems done before the writing schedule has begun. Joseph Conrad reports a much more halting progress than does Ernest Hemingway.

I am at it day after day, and I want all day, every minute of a day, to produce a beggarly tale of words or perhaps to produce nothing at all. And when that is finished (I thought it would be so on the first of this month,—but no fear!) I must go on, even go on at once and drag out of myself another 20,000 words, if the boy is to have his milk and I my beer (this is a figure of speech,—I don't drink beer, I drink weak tea, yearn after dry champagne) and if the world is not absolutely to come to an end. And after I have written and have been paid, I shall have the satisfaction of knowing that I can't allow myself the relaxation of being ill more than three days under the penalty of starvation. . . .

From a letter to E. L. Sanderson

Hemingway's use of writing time is described in the following excerpt from an interview:

*Interviewer:* Are these hours during the actual process of writing pleasurable?

*Hemingway:* Very.

*Interviewer:* Could you say something of this process? When do you work? Do you keep to a strict schedule?

*Hemingway:* When I am working on a book or a story I write every morning as soon after first light as possible. There is no one to disturb you and it is cool or cold and you come to your work and warm as you write. You read what you have written and, as you always stop when you know what is going to happen next, you go on from there. You write until you come to a place where you still have your juice and know what will happen next and you stop and try to live through until the next day when you hit it again. You have started at six in the morning, say, and may go on until noon or be through before that. When you stop you are as empty, and at the same time never empty but filling, as when you have made love to someone you love. Nothing can hurt you, nothing can happen, nothing means anything until the next day when you do it again. It is the wait until the next day that is hard to get through.

From *The Paris Review*

Establishing a writing time is hard for most writers, especially in the beginning, and some of them work only when they have the "inspiration." But many professionals will tell you that they make a time for work each day. The problem for the beginner is to schedule himself. If you can work four hours each morning or evening, you will be off to an excellent start.

Your actual time pattern for any story, including the beginning, the ending and all of the events between, comes out of the process of giving a form to multiple moments, dark or luminous, that lie in your past and are the raw material of art. Often the forming of a time pattern is a long process. Sometimes a story will lie waiting in your mind and then seem to bring itself to light after an interval of years, perhaps in a calendar of its own choosing.

In beginning to schedule a story, even in using "time in flow," which means forming a sensory chain of remembrance that has no obvious time links, you will not really be including everything. Thomas Wolfe said nobody could write about the inside of a telephone booth without selecting, nor could you write about a minute inside the booth without selecting, for we do not have total recall even though some bores might make us wonder. The creative process is always a selective one, and the time element, like other elements, must be controlled.

Fiction, even at its most shapeless, is bounded like every art by a limiting frame that gives it its form; the writer must devise techniques so to modulate that form that it will most adequately convey his intentions to the reader. A novel, even at its longest, must come to an end; the writer must plan his beginning and ending, and his whole work must provide within itself the reason why these should fall where they do and not elsewhere. He must exploit different devices to urge the reader's attention forward and prompt his unposed question: "and next?"; "what then?" He must consider how to relate or link one part to another. He will experiment with suspense and tempos, with rhythm and climax and plotting. And time is a central feature of them all.

From *Time and the Novel*, by A. A. Mendilow

Time has always been a formal element in literature for the novelists who have wanted to conquer its passing, and *when* always has a major place in the constellation of features that make up the form and substance of a narrative.

But in treating time formally, we often find ourselves in difficulty, since it may well escape from the schedule we prescribe for it. The calendar for the story may, when you begin to apply it, take on a protean form, since time limits are only fictional hourglasses and a story is a living thing with a movement of its own. Time has a habit of overflowing, of changing as we attempt to arrest it, of slipping its boundaries even in the simplest narrative. It is an element that, in a story as in life, may be designated in any number of ways and yet goes its own way. On the other hand, in life we do try to control it with calendars and clocks, and in fiction, too, it must be regulated and bracketed by the start and finish of our story.

Suppose we start with a "Once upon a time," a magic, still-unworn phrase brought to us from long ago, from fables and fairy tales. In our own day, even though a story may not open with precisely this phrase, a writer can nevertheless work within a span that seems to go from once-upon-a-time to forever-after. The action in a story of this sort may seem to take place in the present or the past, but it actually represents a time not on any clock. James Thurber writes a fable of a moth who "once" desired a star and lived to a great age in attempting to fulfill his desire. For all we know the moth might still be in the sky, flying happily ever after.

## THE MOTH AND THE STAR*

A young and impressionable moth once set his heart on a certain star. He told his mother about this and she counseled him to set his heart on a bridge lamp instead. "Stars aren't the thing to hang around," she said; "lamps are the thing to hang around." "You get somewhere that way," said the moth's father. "You don't get anywhere chasing stars." But the moth would not heed the words of either parent. Every evening at dusk when the star came out he would start flying toward it and every morning at dawn he would crawl back home worn out with his vain endeavor. One day his father said to him: "You haven't burned a wing in months, boy, and it looks to me as if you were never going to. All your brothers have been badly burned flying around street lamps and all your sisters have been terribly singed flying around house lamps. Come on, now, get out of here and get yourself scorched! A big strapping moth like you without a mark on him!"

The moth left his father's house, but he would not fly around street lamps and he would not fly around house lamps. He went right on trying to reach the star, which was four and one-third light years, or twenty-five trillion miles away. The moth thought it was just caught in the top branches of an elm. He never did reach the star, but he went right on trying, night after night, and when he was a very, very old moth he began to think that he really

* Permission the author; © 1939 The New Yorker Magazine, Inc.

had reached the star and he went around saying so. This gave him a deep and lasting pleasure, and he lived to a great old age. His parents and his brothers and his sisters had all been burned to death when they were quite young.

*Moral: Who flies afar from the sphere of our sorrow is here today and here tomorrow.*

From *Fables for our Time,* by James Thurber

The other type of timeless story is the one in the *supposed, continuous,* or *prolonged present.* This is a method of writing about past time as if it were now, of keeping close to the emotion, avoiding abstractions. You give the past tense a vibrant immediacy by bringing it into the present time of your reader, recreating the sensations of the past so strongly that you close the gap between *now* and the *then* of the events.

This supposed present functions superbly in Ernest Hemingway's *A Farewell to Arms.* The novel takes place in a time span of almost three years but it keeps the reader so close to the main character's emotional responses to each situation that the reader and the hero always seem to be experiencing the events at the very instant they are happening.

The starting point of the novel is a summer when World War I is still unreal for the characters. The ending is long after the hero has deserted the big guns and made a separate peace. But Hemingway, choosing moments that are taut with emotion, keeps us in a now-time until the very end, after the heroine's death, when the hero walks out into the rain-sodden street.

In the following passage, the hero of *A Farewell to Arms* has been thinking of spending his furlough in the high country of the Abruzzi, where it is clear, cold, dry, and where God is not a dirty name. Instead, he goes to the city. Hemingway recreates that furlough of many years ago for us as if it were taking place now.

I had gone to no place where the roads were frozen and hard as iron, where it was clear cold and dry and the snow was dry and powdery and hare-tracks in the snow and the peasants took off their hats and called you Lord and there was good hunting. I had gone to no such place but to the smoke of cafés and nights when the room whirled and you needed to look at the wall to make it stop, nights in bed, drunk, when you knew that that was all there was, and the strange excitement of waking and not knowing who it was with you, and the world all unreal in the dark and so exciting that you must resume again unknowing and not caring in the night, sure that this was all and all and all and not caring. Suddenly to care very much and to sleep to wake with it sometimes morning and all that had been there gone and everything sharp and hard and clear and sometimes a dispute about the cost. Sometimes still pleasant and fond and warm and breakfast and lunch. Sometimes all niceness gone and glad to get out on the street but always another day starting and then another night. I tried to tell about the night and the difference between the night and the day and how the night was better unless the day was very clean and cold and I could not tell it; as I cannot tell it now. But if you have had it you know.

From *A Farewell to Arms*, by Ernest Hemingway

Hemingway has used straight narration in time, starting with late summer in 1915 and moving in a direct chronological line to his final scene in the spring of 1918. He displays his chain of events as they would move in actual time over periods of hours, days, years. He draws only infrequently on his characters' remembrances of the events that happened to them before the main action of the book began.

This scheduling of occurrences in their proper sequence helps keep a story in the fictional present and also it gives a logical beginning, middle and end. You can bulwark the sense of present time by linking the seasons and the weather to the emotions of your characters but this can easily be overdone. Your main concern is to keep to a straight time sequence. Remember again that in the supposed present, you are usually working close to the *now* of your characters without much emphasis on events in their far past.

In the *definite past*, which, on the other hand, ranges from yesterday to any date gone by, many writers work out an exact time span and use it as an axis for their narrative. Or maybe we should say that they work so accurately a time plan can be made from the story. This definite time schedule is presented as a calendar by Thomas Hardy in *Far from the Madding Crowd*.

## CALENDAR OF EVENTS

|  |  |  |  |
|---|---|---|---|
|  |  | 1841: | birth of Gabriel Oak. (Hardy was born in 1840.) |
|  |  | 1845: | birth of Troy. |
|  |  | 1849: | birth of Bathsheba. |
|  |  | 1850: | birth of Fanny. |
|  | December | 20, 1869: | the story begins. |
|  | December | 21, 1869: | Oak's first words with Bathsheba. |
|  | December | 26, 1869: | Bathsheba is of service to Oak. |
|  | January, | 1870: | Oak proposes. |
|  | February, | 1870: | Oak arrives at Weatherbury. |
| Sat., | Feb. | 12, 1870: | Bathsheba goes to market. |
| Sun., | Feb. | 13, 1870: | a valentine is sent. |
| Mon., | Feb. | 14, 1870: | a valentine is received. |
| Tue., | Feb. | 15, 1870: | Oak receives a letter. |
| Sat., | Feb. | 19, 1870: | another trip to market. |
| Fri., | May | 27, 1870: | Boldwood speaks. |
| Sat., | May | 28, 1870: | Gabriel is dismissed. |
| Sun., | May | 29, 1870: | Gabriel is recalled. |
| Wed., | June | 1, 1870: | Troy appears. |
|  | July, | 1870: | Bathsheba sets out for Bath. |
| Wed., | Aug. | 17, 1870: | Bathsheba is married. |
| Sat., | Oct. | 8, 1870: | Bathsheba meets Fanny. |
| Sun., | Oct. | 9, 1870: | the end of Fanny's walk. |
| Mon., | Oct. | 10, 1870: | the news reaches Weatherbury. |
| Tue., | Oct. | 11, 1870: | a swimming event. |
| Sat., | Oct. | 15, 1870: | Bathsheba faints. |
|  | July, | 1871: | a circus hires a new actor. |
|  | September, | 1871: | the circus goes to Greenhill. |
| Sun., | Dec. | 24, 1871: | a Christmas Eve party. |
|  | March, | 1872: | royal clemency. |
|  | August, | 1872: | Bathsheba visits the cemetery. |
|  | Dec. | 26, 1872: | Oak tries to resign. |
|  | January, | ?, 1873: | the Weatherbury band performs. |
|  | July, | 1873: | Hardy begins to write the story of it all. |

From *Far from the Madding Crowd,* by Thomas Hardy

Hardy does not date his chapters, but he keeps to his calendar through the internal events of the novel. The definite past can also be used in a very short story, as we see in the following

frightening tale where the action takes place in a day and con-
cludes that same night when Death claims the man who is trying
to escape her. The storyteller lets us find out for ourselves that
one single day in the past marks the boundary of the story.

There was a merchant in Bagdad who sent his servant to market
to buy provisions and in a little while the servant came back, white
and trembling, and said, Master, just now when I was in the market-
place I was jostled by a woman in the crowd and when I turned I
saw it was Death that jostled me. She looked at me and made a
threatening gesture; now, lend me your horse, and I will ride away
from this city and avoid my fate. I will go to Samarra and there
Death will not find me. The merchant lent him his horse, and the
servant mounted it, and he dug his spurs in its flanks and as fast as
the horse could gallop he went. Then the merchant went down to
the market-place and he saw Death standing in the crowd and he
came to Death and said, Why did you make a threatening gesture
to my servant when you saw him this morning? That was not a
threatening gesture, Death said, it was a start of surprise. I was
astonished to see him in Bagdad, for I had an appointment with
him tonight in Samarra.

W. Somerset Maugham

Once you have set your story in its temporal limits, you may
want to move about in the past, skipping from one moment to
another, to establish a mood, to show a passage of years, or
to give us a close acquaintance with what is happening to a
character. Thomas Wolfe approached the problem of time ob-
jectively in a passage from *Look Homeward, Angel*. The ital-
icized time-words give a framework for his character's changing
response to his environment.

Eugene was loose *now* in the limitless meadows of sensation: his
sensory equipment was so complete that *at the moment* of perception of a single thing, the whole background of color, warmth,
odor, sound, taste established itself, so that *later*, the breath of hot
dandelion brought back the grass-warm banks of *Spring, a day*,
a place, the rustling of young leaves, or the page of a book, the
thin exotic smell of tangerine, the wintry bite of great apples; or, as
with GULLIVER'S TRAVELS, a bright windy *day* in *March*. . . .

From *Look Homeward, Angel*, by Thomas Wolfe

To get into the past, you may want to use a *flashback*, a

device by which you can show events that have taken place prior to the opening scene of your work. In Emily Brontë's *Wuthering Heights* a man moves into a house and is told by his housekeeper the events of the tragedy that took place on the Heights before his time. We then see the events for ourselves. At the end of the novel we return to the houseowner walking through a graveyard where the actors of the main tale are buried. A flashback acts as an envelope of past time out of which you can take the prior action of your story and then show it directly.

The characters themselves may begin to remember what happened to them and then report it. They may tell a story someone else has told them, or have a reverie, or use a dream as a device for getting into the past. One of the most terrifying dreams in all fiction is presented as straight action in a flashback by Feodor Dostoyevsky when the student Raskolnikov, about to become a murderer, dreams of watching a poor little horse being flogged to death.

Raskolnikov dreamed a terrible dream. He dreamed of the time when he was a child. It was a holiday, late in the afternoon, and he was out for a walk in the country with his father. . . . A particular circumstance attracted his attention . . . some peasant's small, lean, greyish-brown mare was harnessed to one of those huge carts, the sort of poor old nag which he had seen so often. . . . there was a shout, "Gee-up!" and the poor mare started pulling away with all her might. . . . she was gasping for breath, standing still, pulling at the cart again, and almost collapsing in the road.

"Flog her to Death!" shouted Mikolka. "I don't mind. I'm going to flog her to death myself! . . .

Raskolnikov ran beside the old mare, he ran in front of her, he saw her being whipped across her eyes, across her very eyes! . . .

"Finish her off!" Mikolka shouted, jumping down from the cart, blind with rage.

A few young men, also red-faced and drunk, seized whatever they could lay their hands on—whips, sticks, and shaft—and ran to the dying mare. Mikolka stood on one side and started raining blows across her back with the iron bar without bothering to see where the blows were falling. The mare stretched out her head, heaved a deep sigh, and died.

Raskolnikov woke up in a cold sweat, his hair wet with perspiration, gasping for breath, and he raised himself in terror.

In this shortened version of the dream, we see a past incident in a flashback and then come into the main story again. In another story of a murder, William Faulkner's "That Evening Sun," the narrator starts by recalling Jefferson, Mississippi, as it was fifteen years earlier during the main action of the story. After a few paragraphs of exposition, the central situation is brought into the foreground—the three Compson children and a Negro woman who is waiting for Death.

. . . fifteen years ago, on Monday morning the quiet, dusty, shady streets would be full of Negro women with, balanced on their steady, turbaned heads, bundles of clothes tied up in sheets, almost as large as cotton bales, carried so without touch of hand between the kitchen door of the white house and the blackened washpot beside a cabin door in Negro Hollow.

Nancy would set her bundle on the top of her head, then upon the bundle in turn she would set the black straw sailor hat which she wore winter and summer. She was tall, with a high, sad face sunken a little where her teeth were missing. Sometimes we would go a part of the way down the lane and across the pasture with her, to watch the balanced bundle and the hat that never bobbed nor wavered, even when she walked down into the ditch and up the other side and stooped through the fence. She would go down on her hands and knees and crawl through the gap, her head rigid, uptilted, the bundle steady as a rock or a balloon, and rise to her feet again and go on.

Sometimes the husbands of the washing women would fetch and deliver the clothes, but Jesus never did that for Nancy, even before Father told him to stay away from our house, even when Dilsey was sick and Nancy would come to cook for us.

And then about half the time we'd have to go down the lane to Nancy's cabin and tell her to come on and cook breakfast. We would stop at the ditch, because Father told us to not have anything to do with Jesus—he was a short black man, with a razor scar down his face—and we would throw rocks at Nancy's house until she came to the door, leaning her head around it without any clothes on.

"What yawl mean, chunking my house?" Nancy said.

From "That Evening Sun," by William Faulkner

Following "Nancy said," the story swings into the more remote past and begins to cover the main action. Once he starts those events, Faulkner keeps a straight time progression; although he never does come up to the Monday morning with which he began.

In Faulkner's *The Sound and the Fury*, which is again centered in Jefferson and also deals with the Compson family, the episodes take place on four days of an Easter week. But the long time-span of the book is from 1910 to 1928 and in the minds of many of the characters time is not fixed but flowing.

In the fiction you write you may also want to use *flowing time*, for a subjective presentation of your characters, showing them through their own thoughts. You can go directly into your characters' minds, using the stream-of-consciousness technique, giving the underlying flow of memories and sensibilities in any time sequence you like.

Flowing time is always shown subjectively. In the Compson novel, Faulkner moves freely through the minds of the characters. Benjy, who opens the book, has a time pattern in which one word is associated with another and the associated words shift us through the years. In another section, dealing with Quentin, we have a much more complex time arrangement.

*The Sound and the Fury* is the story of the Compsons through each of the three brothers in turn. First, we see time as it flows through the idiot, Benjy, for whom yesterday and today merge in watery wastes of sensation. The passage of years is shown in the pattern of associative words representing the images that make up Benjy's life. He responds to perfume, to rain, to a flower, and to the sound of his sister's name.

We are working with the total range of awareness of Benjy as a character. In the following passage, he is caught in a broken place in a fence. Luster, the colored boy, starts to unhook the snagged clothes. In Benjy's mind, the moment flows back in time to a day when his sister, Caddy, was with him. Then we go into still another time sequence with a Negro named Versh, our only linking words being *cold* and *froze*. One cold time takes Benjy into another.

"Wait a minute," Luster said. "You snagged on that nail again. Cant you never crawl through here without snagging on that nail?"
*Caddy uncaught me and we crawled through. Uncle Maury said to not let anybody see us, so we better stoop over, Caddy said. Stoop over, Benjy. Like this, see. We stooped over and crossed the garden, where the flowers rasped and rattled against us. The*

*ground was hard. We climbed the fence, where the pigs were*
*grunting and snuffing. I expect they're sorry because one of them got*
*killed today, Caddy said. The ground was hard, churned and knotted.*

    *Keep your hands in your pockets, Caddy said. Or they'll get*
*froze. You don't want your hands froze off Christmas, do you.*

    "It's too cold out there," Versh said. "You don't want to go out
doors."

    "What is it now." Mother said.

    "He want to go out doors." Versh said.

    "Let him go." Uncle Maury said.

    "It's too cold." Mother said.

                From *The Sound and the Fury*, by William Faulkner

James Joyce used time in flow as it stretches to infinity, not
only defying fixed temporal boundaries but defying the logic
of grammar and emphasizing a nonverbal level of thought. As
Judge Woolsey commented in 1933 in his famous decision
which removed the ban on *Ulysses* in the United States:

    Joyce has attempted—it seems to me, with astonishing success—
to show how the screen of consciousness with its ever-shifting
kaleidoscopic impressions carries, as it were on a plastic palimpsest,
not only what is in the focus of each man's observation of the
actual things about him, but also in a penumbral zone residua of
past impressions, some recent and some drawn up by association
from the domain of the subconscious. He shows how each of these
impressions affects the life and behavior of the character which
he is describing.

    What he seeks to get is not unlike the result of a double or, if
that is possible, a multiple exposure on a cinema film which would
give a clear foreground with a background visible but somewhat
blurred and out of focus in varying degrees.

    In the sirens episode of *Ulysses*, we partake of a timelessness
like that which comes when we are deep in dreams or going
under anesthesia and perhaps into eternity.

He seehears lipspeech. One and nine. Penny for yourself. Here.
Give him twopence tip. Deaf, bothered. But perhaps he has wife
and family waiting, waiting Patty come home. Hee hee hee hee.
Deaf wait while they wait.

    But wait. But hear. Chordsdark. Luguguubrious. Low. In a
cave of the dark middle earth. Embedded ore. Lumpmusic.

    The voice of dark age, of unlove, earth's fatigue made grave
approach, and painful, come from afar, from hoary mountains,

called on good men and true. The priest he sought, with him would
he speak a word.

Tap.

From Ulysses, by James Joyce

But Joyce, although he ranged freely through many levels
of consciousness, and drew his characters from any time, had
a schedule just as strict as Thomas Hardy's. He tells of events
happening simultaneously, showing, for instance, two episodes
taking place at 10 o'clock. But all of *Ulysses* happens on a single
day in Dublin, June 16, 1904. Following is an abbreviated schedule of the timing of the novel.

| | |
|---|---|
| 8 A.M. | Stephen Dedalus, who has just returned from a year in Paris, is discovered living in an abandoned tower overlooking Dublin Bay. |
| 10 A.M. | Stephen is giving a lesson in ancient history at Mr. Deasy's School for Boys. |
| 11 A.M. | Stephen, having finished with his class is walking restlessly along the beach watching the rising tide which symbolizes the uprushing current of his own thoughts. |
| 8 A.M. | Mr. Leopold Bloom prepares breakfast for his wife, Molly, at their home. He knows of an intrigue in which his wife is engaged but takes no action against her. |
| 10 A.M. | Mr. Leopold Bloom, who will become Stephen's spiritual father, starts off on his day's work. |
| 11 A.M. | Mr. Bloom, in company with Stephen Dedalus's real father and some other sedate-appearing Dubliners, attends a funeral. |
| Noon | Mr. Bloom visits a newspaper office to arrange for an advertisement. |
| 1 P.M. | Mr. Bloom looks into a popular eating place, withdraws, wanders through the streets, and finally satisfies his hunger with a sandwich and some wine at a pub. |
| 2 P.M. | Stephen Dedalus stands in a library talking with friends. Bloom passes by them on his way to look up an advertisement in a newspaper file but does not actually speak to Stephen. |
| 3 P.M. | A street scene in Dublin. Mr. Bloom, Stephen Dedalus, and countless others, take part in this symphony of the sights and sounds of the city. |
| 4 P.M. | In the Ormond Hotel, Mr. Bloom finds Stephen Dedalus' father who is dedicating his existence to wine, |

women and song. At the same time Mr. Bloom's wife is being unfaithful to him at their home.

5 P.M.       Mr. Bloom in a tavern meets a citizen who is antagonistic to Jews. Mr. Bloom retreats and begins to walk about the city.

8 P.M.       Mr. Bloom goes down to the beach for some cool air. He is attracted by a girl on the beach and is mentally unfaithful to his wife.

10 P.M.      Mr. Bloom meets Stephen by chance in a hospital where the older man is visiting a friend. The two men go together to a brothel.

Midnight     In the brothel, the two men watch their secret thoughts and innermost desires materialize before them in a Witches' Sabbath.

1 A.M.       Stephen does not want to return to his tower so he decides to go home with Mr. Bloom. They stop for coffee in a cabman's shelter on the way.

2 A.M.       Finally, in Mr. Bloom's kitchen, the father and his spiritual son recall together certain events giving them meaning by analyzing Bloom's personality and antecedents.

That night   Bloom lies in bed beside his wife who is expressing her thoughts of "unrefined femininity." The novel ends with Molly thinking yes, yes, to a lover, asserting the eternal female principle of life in the flowing remembrance of accepting him.

How well Joyce has succeeded in controlling his time pattern in the pages of his novel is a matter you must decide by investigating his method, which is a difficult one, and trying to understand it. How well you yourself can restrict time effectively in any story you are writing, is a matter of working in various temporal patterns and finding the one that will work best for you.

## A CALENDAR FOR YOUR STORY:   Assignment 23

Write a brief comment on your reasons for choosing the time pattern you are using in your second story.

Specifically, at what moment does your narrative start? At what moment does it end?

Explain the way you will link your time pattern to your narrative point of view in your second story.

## 10

# The Importance of Plot

One young writer, in analyzing his own work, calls a story "a reconstruction of the world of experience and self," and asks that every fiction-maker agree with him. Another student claims that "Jesus wept" is the greatest of short stories because it acquaints us with an important event—he says a story is an incident with an implied meaning. Still another, as you may remember, insisted that a story was "between you and me." He once wrote a tale of how he was going to leave his girl's house and do a swan dive right off the Empire State Building: "Yeh. Then I'll be splattered all over the sidewalk. She'll really be sorry then." This last sentence tells *why*, and so has the shadowy beginning of a plot.

In *Aspects of the Novel*, E. M. Forster defines a story as a narrative of events in their time sequence, then separates *story* from *plot* by saying that in the latter the emphasis falls on causality. In a story we ask, "And then?" But in a plot we concentrate on the *why* that lies behind an event and the events linked to it. We want to know what makes an event happen at least as much as we want to know what is going to happen next.

Do you know the "Pardoner's Tale," Chaucer's ironic story about the three thieves of Flanders? It is a plot story in which the central motive of greed locks the events together. As the men sit drinking in a tavern, they learn that one of their companions has died and they set out to kill Death himself. Hunting for Death, they find a hoard of gold and now each of the three schemes to kill the others. All succeed. Two of the men bludgeon the third and, afterwards, waiting for an opportunity to kill each other, they drink the poisoned wine the dead man had previously prepared for them. In interlocking the events of the tale, Chaucer satisfied our desire for action and also our curiosity.

The desire to witness action has always been inherent in those who want to hear a story. Their command to the writer is not, "Tell me how you felt. Tell me what you thought." Rather, it is, "Tell me what they did and why. Keep me in suspense." For in a story, if not in life, we want conflict, we want to be led on through the moments of suspense like a donkey following a carrot dangled before him. And most of us prefer to know that something is going to happen and to be kept wondering when and why rather than to be hit by a surprise.

Surprise comes when an unexpected event is flung at the reader without preparation. Suspense comes when we tease, give hints, and at the same time withhold information from the reader. Suspense is an emotional reaction generated by the reader's ignorance of whether a character will get what he wants or go down in defeat. At the end of the story, although the character's fate may come as a surprise, it should have been so well prepared for by the writer that in retrospect the final action seems inevitable. At the end of a story we are done with suspense—we want the satisfaction of catching up with the carrot.

But suspense and surprise do not make a plot. To understand what a plot really is we must go back to Aristotle's *Poetics*, in which he analyzes Greek tragedy. Aristotle points out that while a plot must deal with a whole action—or, more precisely, with an "imitation" of an action—a writer cannot use all that happens but includes only those incidents that have been made probable or inevitable by other incidents lying within the framework of the tragedy. Every work of art should have a beginning, after which something naturally comes, and an ending which itself naturally follows what has preceded. Moreover, the different parts of the action, "must be so related to each other that if any part is changed or taken away the whole will be altered or disturbed."

An action that seems contrary to expectation must still be

brought about by the action that precedes it. In other words, plot, as it was defined for the Greeks, has a design that arises from the internal structure of the play. If we take the viewpoint of D. H. Lawrence, who felt that plot in fiction was simply a flow and that reversals were brought about by psychic maladjustments in people, then Aristotle's demands may seem mechanical. But Greek tragedy, at its best, gives importance to both the mechanics and to the character in conflict, meshing them as partners.

Aristotle says that plots are either simple or complex. The latter includes a reversal (or a veering around of the action) and a recognition scene, which sometimes involves a messenger bringing news that causes a man to know the truth about himself. A recognition scene shows a character, who is marked for good or bad fortune, coming to understand what has happened to him. This understanding affects his attitude toward those around him. A simple plot is a single, continuous action in which the change of fortune comes about without a reversal or recognition scene. The following description of the attributes of plot as action and necessity is Aristotelian.

In a plot, the interplay of one force on another may show the protagonist in conflict against his fellow man or against himself, or he may be in conflict against a personalized idea of God or against a force in nature. These divisions of conflict may overlap, as in a Hamlet who is fighting his own procrastination in revenging his father and, simultaneously, the opposition of his uncle, the king. The divisions are seldom as clear-cut as they appear to be here, but they can act as a background against which to test the validity of the conflict in your own story.

Probably any conflict you choose for your narrative will have its roots in a real life situation colored by your imagination and fitted into an invented plot. You may show someone like yourself in the related events of a created pattern. You may take people you know and put them into the situations they seem to deserve. In this sense, every plot rests on a foundation of personal experience. But any invented interrelationship of action must mean as much to other people as the impetus for creating it meant to you.

. . . [I]t is perhaps more helpful to describe plot than to define it with generalities. The incidents which are part of a plot are, it has been said, (1) *planned;* they are preconceived by the author; they spring from his conscious thought; they are not simply taken over from life. No matter how realistic an author may be, he must arrange and select his incidents according to a plot purpose since life itself only rarely, if ever, unfolds according to the plans of a fiction plot. Plot is, too, (2) a *series of actions* moving from a beginning through a logically related sequence to a logical and natural outcome. One incident—an afternoon's cruise—does not make a plot, no matter how interesting the afternoon may have been. Several incidents—if the story is one of action—are essential. There must at least be a beginning, a middle, and an end in the interplay of the opposing forces and, most frequently, this means three or more episodes. And these incidents grow one upon another; incident two following by a causal relationship from incident one, and incident three following, by this same relationship, from two. The difference between a simple narrative and a story of plot is the difference between a calendar and a knitted scarf. In the calendar the pages follow one another logically, but in the scarf the texture is the result of weaving one thread over and under another. In a story with closely knit plot the removal of one incident would bring the whole structure down upon one's head much as though he had removed an important prop from the scaffolding for a building. In a story of mere unrelated incidents, the removal of one incident would leave, simply, a gap. (3) This interrelationship of action is the result, as has been said, of the *interplay of one force upon another.* . . . Plot is, in this sense, an artificial rather than a natural ordering of events. Its function is to simplify life by imposing order upon it. It would be possible, though most tedious, to recite *all* incidents, *all* events, *all* thoughts which pass through the minds of one or more characters during a period of, say, a week. And somewhere in this recital might be buried a story. But the demands of plot stipulate that the author *select* from this welter of event and reflection those items which have a certain unity, which point to a certain end, which have a common interrelationship, which represent not more than two or three threads of interest and activity.

> From *A Handbook to Literature,* by William Flint
> Thrall and Addison Hibbard, revised and enlarged
> by C. Hugh Holman

The student who wrote, "Yeh . . . I'll be splattered all over the sidewalk. She'll really be sorry then," may never have actually wanted to take a swan dive off a tall building because his girl turned away from him. But part of the character's actions reside in the writer, and part of every writer resides in the struggles of his characters. Robert Penn Warren has pointed out that Shakespeare did not live *Hamlet*, but from his own inner responses to life he did understand the impact of that rottenness in Denmark on the son of the dead king.

Perhaps a writer is a person, talented in words, through whom the semblance of a conflict usable in fiction must filter before he can externalize it on the printed page. For plot may be defended as externalization of action through interlocked events. For some of us it is not an easy externalization. Many writers who have a facility for creating character or a setting get into difficulty when they try to "think up" a plot to *show* a reader what happens and why. Aldous Huxley confesses that he is one of them.

I have great difficulty in inventing plots. Some people are born with an amazing gift for story-telling; it's a gift which I've never had at all. One reads, for example, Stevenson's accounts of how all the plots for his stories were provided in dreams by his subconscious mind (what he calls the "Brownies" working for him), and that all he had to do was to work up the material they had provided. I've never had any Brownies. The great difficulty for me has always been creating situations.

From *The Paris Review*

The following student sketch is no more than an exercise in writing out an invented situation. In reading it, we see at once that the action so necessary in a plot is still unformulated. Any real conflict in this sketch of a chance meeting with an intruder—as does any result which the conflict might bring—lies outside the incident the author presents.

There were two of us standing on the corner that afternoon directing the church group down to the lodge and picnic grounds. I was twelve and somewhat aware of the consequences of talking to a stranger, but that afternoon was nice and warm and pleasant.

It was a big Saturday for all of us. As we were playing around with our direction flags, one strange car passed by us and slowed down. I can't describe any strong feelings either way about the guy's passing by and looking at us, but I do remember that among ourselves we wondered what he wanted.

Mother had always warned us about strangers, especially people who were overly friendly to youngsters. Hitch hiking had never bothered me; it made my life seem much easier because I didn't have to walk everywhere I went. Sure, Mother always gave good advice—at least that's what Dad said. But I knew different. The world was a bundle of roses, all covered with niceties and good. No one would hurt a kind, an innocent little brat like me. After all, the worst thing I had done to anybody was when I broke Mr. Clark's window glasses in the old garage. And he didn't hurt me, either.

The car turned around and came back up the street. It was about dark by then. As the guy rolled his window down and stopped the car, all of us stopped what we were doing and went over to see if we could help him. Maybe we could help him. There are lots of twelve-year-olds who know what they're talking about. After all, I had started to smoke occasionally, and if I could smoke, I could give directions—and I might be able to help this man—this stranger, as Mother would have said.

"Hi'ya mister. What can we do for ya?"

The stranger seemed pretty young, about 24 or 25. He smiled and inquiringly asked, "What are you boys doing on the street this late?"

"Just directing traffic for our party. You know, the one down at the picnic grounds. We're having a wiener roast and a hay ride down there."

"Then why don't you let me take you down there, so you won't have to walk. Maybe we can stop at a store and get you fellahs some ice cream or something."

Don, my next door neighbor and buddy, walked away and told me to come on with him. He was 14 and tried to boss people around who were younger than he, but he was still my buddy.

"Sorry, mister, but I've got to stay here and direct traffic for the rest of the people. What are you doing around here, anyway? I never saw you before."

"Don't worry about that, kid. Are you coming or ain't you? If you're not, I'm going down the street and take some other kids down town and buy them all the things they want at the dime store."

"I still can't go with you, cause I might miss some of the people, and then I'd miss the party too."

As the guy pulled away, Don said that he was just trying to be friends with us. But I knew a little different. Don was older than I was, but what I had never believed about strangers I began to believe. Dad had once told me about a neighbor of ours who had a son killed by some strange man and he had warned me about those people. But never had I really taken him or Mom serious before.

I did that Saturday afternoon.

We have seen that nothing really happens between the boy and the stranger, that there is no necessity of action, no succession of incidents related to each other by a causal factor. The narrator feels a vague fear and from his uneasiness draws the conclusion that his parents gave him good advice. As an exercise in plot, the student later listed the following possible linked events:

## THE GREEN CAR
### Outline by L. B.

1. A boy who lives with his widowed mother in an isolated part of a town hears a newscast that a dangerously insane inmate has escaped from a state institution. The boy is warned by his mother to "stay away from strangers," but does not take her warning seriously.
2. At a wooded corner of the road, just off the main highway, the boy gets a ride with a stranger in a green Chevrolet who talks to him genially and learns that the boy lives just back there in the house near the pond, and learns, too, about the picnic.
3. Obligingly, the stranger stops at a meat shop where the boy is to pick up the wieners that will be his contribution to the picnic. When others of the church group happen along just as the boy is leaving the shop the stranger pulls away in a hurry. Now the boy begins to wonder how wise he was in talking so much.
4. At the picnic, when one of the other boys does not appear, someone jokingly suggests that he has been taken away by the escaped criminal. It turns out that one of the group has learned from a late broadcast that the wanted man is thought to have stolen a green Chevrolet that belonged to a shopkeeper.
5. The boy, frightened now, and silent, rides toward home with the others in the station wagon the church sends to the picnic

ground, wishing he had not talked so freely. Since it is late, he is dropped off at the corner near his house where he first waited for a ride. As he starts for home on foot, he sees a green Chevrolet parked not far from his house. Running fast, he pushes open his front door, calls wildly for his mother, and finds the stranger waiting for him.

This outline gives us a progression of events and a causal factor that relates the first incident to those that follow. The incidents fall into a pattern in which the conflict is made apparent and in which we see the results of the conflict. The student now has the elements of a plot.

Any story that employs plot as action and necessity has an ending in which the hero succeeds or fails, or finds a solution of sorts to recompense him for apparent failure. We are defining plot as an organic one in which the incidents seem not to be artificially introduced. The results of the conflict then rise naturally from the preceding action and the story is able to flow rather than march forward, whatever its level of action may be.

Although it should flow, four stages (or four basic incidents) can be distinguished in a workable plot. In the plot outline of the boy's meeting with the stranger in the green car, we have an opening *situation* in which the youth disregards his mother's warning. It is followed by a *complication* of sorts when the stranger, fearing to be recognized by one of the church group, drives away taking with him the knowledge of the boy's home address. The boy's discovery that a green Chevrolet has been stolen is an incident in the rising action. The *key scene* or *climax* comes at the door when the boy again meets the stranger he has been warned to avoid. But we never have a real *resolution* or decisive ending in which we actually know the fate of the main character.

Many "plot writers" are able to keep a story going by presenting a trap and then making us want to know how the main character is going to get out of the trap. The artist suggests from the start, perhaps through some character trait, the way the action is going to result, and gives hints all along the way not only about what is going to happen but why. Where plot rises naturally from the picture of the character involved in the initial situation we care deeply for the person in the trap, taking sides either for him or against him.

In the following story, Guy de Maupassant is not particularly interested in having us sympathize with the peasant who picks up the piece of string. But we do know why he picks it up and that *why* is organic to his fate. "The String" is an example of the way a plot works when it is used by an artist who fulfills the classic plot necessities. From the first, we feel the shadow of what must eventually be the fate of the peasant.

Along all the roads around Goderville the peasants and their wives were coming toward the little town, for it was market-day. The men walked with plodding steps, their bodies bent forward at each thrust of their long bowed legs. They were deformed by hard work, by the pull of the heavy plough which raises the left shoulder and twists the torso, by the reaping of the wheat which forces the knees apart to get a firm stand, by all the slow and strenuous labors of life on the farm. Their blue smocks, starched, shining as if varnished, ornamented with a little design in white at the neck and wrists, puffed about their bony bodies, seemed like balloons ready to carry them off. From each smock a head, two arms, and two feet protruded.

Some led a cow or a calf at the end of a rope, and their wives, walking behind the animal, whipped its haunches with a leafy branch to hasten its progress. They carried on their arms large wicker-baskets, out of which here a chicken and there a duck thrust forth its head. The women walked with a quicker, livelier step than their husbands. Their spare, straight figures were wrapped in a scanty little shawl, pinned over their flat bosoms, and their heads were enveloped in a piece of white linen tightly pressed on the hair and surmounted by a cap.

Then a wagon passed, its nag's jerky trot shaking up and down two men seated side by side and a woman in the bottom of the vehicle, the latter holding on to the sides to lessen the stiff jolts.

The square of Goderville was filled with a milling throng of human beings and animals. The horns of the cattle, the rough-napped top-hats of the rich peasants, and the headgear of the peasant women stood out in the crowd. And the clamorous, shrill, shouting voices made a continuous and savage din dominated now and again by the robust lungs of some countryman's laugh, or the long lowing of a cow tied to the wall of a house.

The scene smacked of the stable, the dairy and the dung-heap, of hay and sweat, and gave forth that sharp, unpleasant odor, human and animal, peculiar to the people of the fields.

Maître Hauchecorne, of Bréauté, had just arrived at Goderville. He was directing his steps toward the square, when he perceived upon the ground a little piece of string. Maître Hauchecorne, economical like a true Norman, thought that everything useful ought to be picked up, and he stooped painfully, for he suffered from rheumatism. He took up the bit of string from the ground and was beginning to roll it carefully when he noticed Maître Malandain, the harness-maker, on the threshold of his door, looking at him. They had once had a quarrel on the subject of a halter, and they had remained on bad terms, being both good haters. Maître Hauchecorne was seized with a sort of shame to be seen thus by his enemy, picking a bit of string out of the dirt. He hid his find quickly under his smock, and slipped it into his trouser pocket; then he pretended to be still looking on the ground for something which he did not find, and he went towards the market, his head thrust forward, bent double by his pain.

He was soon lost in the noisy and slowly moving crowd, which was busy with interminable bargainings. The peasants looked at cows, went away, came back, perplexed, always in fear of being cheated, not daring to decide, watching the vendor's eye, ever trying to find the trick in the man and the flaw in the beast.

The women, having placed their great baskets at their feet, had taken out the poultry, which lay upon the ground, tied together by the feet, with terrified eyes and scarlet crests.

They listened to offers, stated their prices with a dry air and impassive face, or perhaps, suddenly deciding on some proposed reduction, shouted to the customer who was slowly going away: "All right, Maître Anthime, I'll let you have it for that."

Then little by little the square was deserted, the church bell rang out the hour of noon, and those who lived too far away went to the different inns.

At Jourdain's the great room was full of people eating, and the big yard was full of vehicles of all kinds, gigs, wagons, nondescript carts, yellow with dirt, mended and patched, some with their shafts rising to the sky like two arms, others with their shafts on the ground and their backs in the air.

Behind the diners seated at table, the immense fireplace, filled with bright flames, cast a lively heat on the backs of the row on the right. Three spits were turning on which were chickens, pigeons, and legs of mutton; and an appetizing odor of roast meat and gravy dripping over the nicely browned skin rose from the fireplace, lightening all hearts and making the mouth water.

All the aristocracy of the plough ate there, at Maître Jourdain's, tavern keeper and horse dealer, a clever fellow and well off.

The dishes were passed and emptied, as were the jugs of yellow cider. Everyone told his affairs, his purchases, and sales. They discussed the crops. The weather was favorable for the greens but rather damp for the wheat.

Suddenly the drum began to beat in the yard, before the house. Everyone rose, except a few indifferent persons, and ran to the door, or to the windows, their mouths still full, their napkins in their hands.

After the public crier had stopped beating his drum, he called out in a jerky voice, speaking his phrases irregularly:

"It is hereby made known to the inhabitants of Goderville, and in general to all persons present at the market, that there was lost this morning, on the road to Benzeville, between nine and ten o'clock, a black leather pocketbook containing five hundred francs and some business papers. The finder is requested to return same to the Mayor's office or to Maître Fortuné Houlbrèque of Manneville. There will be twenty francs' reward."

Then the man went away. The heavy roll of the drum and the crier's voice were again heard at a distance.

Then they began to talk of this event discussing the chances that Maître Houlebrèque had of finding or not finding his pocketbook.

And the meal concluded. They were finishing their coffee when the chief of the gendarmes appeared upon the threshold.

He inquired:

"Is Maître Hauchecorne, of Bréauté, here?"

Maître Hauchecorne, seated at the other end of the table, replied: "Here I am."

And the officer resumed:

"Maître Hauchecorne, will you have the goodness to accompany me to the Mayor's office? The Mayor would like to talk to you."

The peasant, surprised and disturbed, swallowed at a draught his tiny glass of brandy, rose, even more bent than in the morning, for the first steps after each rest were specially difficult, and set out, repeating: "Here I am, here I am."

The Mayor was waiting for him, seated in an armchair. He was the local lawyer, a stout, solemn man, fond of pompous phrases.

"Maître Hauchecorne," said he, "you were seen this morning picking up, on the road to Benzeville, the pocketbook lost by Maître Houlbrèque, of Manneville."

The countryman looked at the Mayor in astonishment, already terrified by this suspicion resting on him without his knowing why.

"Me? Me? I picked up the pocketbook?"

"Yes, you, yourself."

"On my word of honor, I never heard of it."

"But you were seen."

"I was seen, me? Who says he saw me?"

Monsieur Malandain, the harness-maker."

The old man remembered, understood, and flushed with anger.

"Oh, he saw me, the clodhopper, he saw me pick up this string, here, Mayor." And rummaging in his pocket he drew out the little piece of string.

But the Mayor, incredulous, shook his head.

"You will not make me believe, Maître Hauchecorne, that Monsieur Malandain, who is a man we can believe, mistook this string for a pocketbook."

The peasant, furious, lifted his hand, spat at one side to attest his honor, repeating:

"It is nevertheless God's own truth, the sacred truth. I repeat it on my soul and my salvation."

The Mayor resumed:

"After picking up the object, you went on staring, looking a long while in the mud to see if any piece of money had fallen out."

The old fellow choked with indignation and fear.

"How anyone can tell—how anyone can tell—such lies to take away an honest man's reputation! How can anyone—"—

There was no use in his protesting, nobody believed him. He was confronted with Monsieur Malandain, who repeated and maintained his affirmation. They abused each other for an hour. At his own request, Maître Hauchecorne was searched. Nothing was found on him.

Finally the Mayor, very much perplexed, discharged him with the warning that he would consult the Public Prosecutor and ask for further orders.

The news had spread. As he left the Mayor's office, the old man was surrounded and questioned with a serious or bantering curiosity, in which there was no indignation. He began to tell the story of the string. No one believed him. They laughed at him.

He went along, stopping his friends, beginning endlessly his statement and his protestations, showing his pockets turned inside out, to prove that he had nothing.

They said:

"Ah, you old rascal!"

And he grew angry, becoming exasperated, hot and distressed at not being believed, not knowing what to do and endlessly repeating himself.

Night came. He had to leave. He started on his way with three neighbors to whom he pointed out the place where he had picked up the bit of string; and all along the road he spoke of his adventure.

In the evening he took a turn in the village of Bréauté, in order to tell it to everybody. He only met with incredulity.

It made him ill all night.

The next day about one o'clock in the afternoon, Parius Paumelle, a hired man in the employ of Maître Breton, husbandman at Ymauville, returned the pocketbook and its contents to Maître Houlbrèque of Manneville.

This man claimed to have found the object in the road; but not knowing how to read, he had carried it to the house and given it to his employer.

The news spread through the neighborhood. Maître Hauchecorne was informed of it. He immediately went the circuit and began to recount his story completed by the happy climax. He triumphed.

"What grieved me so much was not the thing itself, as the lying. There is nothing so shameful as to be placed under a cloud on account of a lie."

He talked of his adventure all day long, he told it on the highway to people who were passing by, in the inn to people who were drinking there, and to persons coming out of church the following Sunday. He stopped strangers to tell them about it. He was calm now, and yet something disturbed him without his knowing exactly what it was. People seemed to wink at him while they listened. They did not seem convinced. He had the feeling that remarks were being made behind his back.

On Tuesday of the next week he went to the market at Goderville, urged solely by the necessity he felt of discussing the case.

Malandain, standing at his door, began to laugh, on seeing him pass. Why?

He approached a farmer from Criquetot, who did not let him finish, and giving him a poke in the stomach said to his face:

"You clever rogue."

Then he turned his back on him.

Maître Hauchecorne was confused, why was he called a clever rogue?

When he was seated at the table, in Jourdain's tavern he commenced to explain "the affair."

A horse-dealer from Monvilliers called to him:

"Come, come, old sharper, that's an old trick; I know all about your piece of string!"

Hauchecorne stammered:

"But the pocketbook was found."

But the other man replied:

"That'll do to tell, pop. One man finds a thing, and another man brings it back. No one is any the wiser, so you get out of it."

The peasant stood choking. He understood. They accused him of having had the pocketbook returned by a confederate, by an accomplice.

He tried to protest. All the table began to laugh.

He could not finish his dinner and went away in the midst of jeers.

He went home ashamed and indignant, choking with anger and confusion, the more dejected for the fact that he with his Norman cunning was capable of doing what they had accused him of, and even of boasting of it as a good trick. His innocence seemed to him, in a confused way, impossible to prove, for his sharpness was well known. And he was stricken to the heart by the injustice of the suspicion.

Then he began to recount the adventure again, enlarging his story every day, adding each time new reasons, more energetic protestations, more solemn oaths which he formulated and prepared in his hours of solitude, his whole mind given up to the story of the string. The more complicated his defense and the more subtle his argument, the less he was believed.

"Those are lying excuses," people said behind his back.

He felt it, ate his heart out over it, and wore himself out with useless efforts. He was visibly wasting away.

The wags now made him tell about the string to amuse them, as they make a soldier who has been on a campaign tell about his battles. His mind, seriously affected, began to weaken.

Towards the end of December he took to his bed.

He died early in January, and in the delirium of his death struggles he continued to protest his innocence, and to repeat his story:

"A piece of string, a piece of string—look—here it is."

"The String," by Guy de Maupassant

## RECOGNIZING THE ELEMENTS OF A PLOT:
Assignment 24

Using the pattern suggested by the plot outline of "The Green Car," list the incidents that represent the following successive plot stages in "The String": (1) opening situation, (2) complication, (3) key scene or climax, (4) resolution or falling action.

Relate your second story to as many of the above plot terms as fit into the pattern of your present work. Show your complication, your moments of crisis, your climax, and your falling action, if you have worked them out.

De Maupassant lets Destiny play his trick for him. If we fill in the story for ourselves we see that the irony of the peasant's fate lies in a trait of his own character, in being niggardly. His greed for saving led him into the initial action of picking up the string on his way to town and his reversal of status among his fellow men came naturally from that first movement. Unlike a writer who is concerned with showing the inner life of his character, de Maupassant concentrates on an objective action.

In any story that is based primarily on the revelation of the inner life of a character, you may have very little plot in Aristotle's sense of the word. James Joyce, for instance, in a story like "Eveline" writes what could be called a monologue in the third person, simply showing how a person of ordinary circumstances is caught in an emotional trap and fails to break away. There is no trick, as there is in a tale that depends on surprise for its real effect.

I am sure you have heard the capsule story that has been given as an example of the trick plot to many beginning writers. Two men are walking along a dark road at midnight and one of them says to the other, "Do you believe in ghosts?" "Of course not," the second man replies. "I do," says the first and disappears. Here the trick is used on the level of the supernatural. In the following story, Scott Griffith has written a variation of the trick story and given it an overcast of symbols.


## THE GUARDIAN

SCOTT GRIFFITH

When he heard the car pull away from in front of the big house Paul turned and went upstairs to his room. He lay back on the bed and thought about the dog. It was really only a puppy, just a few months old and wiggly, cute the way all little cocker spaniel puppies are. And as he thought of it, the feeling came to him again.

"Your father and I will be gone for a few days," his mother had informed him, the first time the feeling had come, "and we'll have to leave Cleo with you." She had gone on to explain about feeding and how it was such a good dog and all but that they couldn't possibly think of taking it with them, ending with something about how he couldn't imagine what a big help it would be.

No, he didn't guess he could imagine, Paul thought. She was standing at the door with the animal in her arms. "Be sure to take extra special care of her now," she said. "If anything were to happen to poor Cleo, I'd just die." His father had called to her from the car and she put the dog on the floor, blew it a tender kiss, and left.

Lying there on the bed Paul knew what she'd do if something were to happen. She'd probably weep loudly and cry, "I can't understand how you could be so thoughtless!" She'd sob some more and then scream, "After all I told you!" Those would be her very words.

Paul turned over on his stomach, pressing his face against the bedspread, his teeth clenched tightly together, not wanting to speak but having the words come as if of their own accord. He was mumbling aloud, mockingly to the empty room. "No, we can't risk poor Cleo's catching cold or exposing her to lord knows what kind of other dogs, can we? We'll have to leave Cleo with you." He groaned once and then lay there quietly for a long while before letting himself fall asleep. Asleep, he dreamed.

It was very late at night and he was being pursued by two crazy killers. Cleo was there and he was running as fast as he could but Cleo scampered playfully along at his heels, getting in his way. It was very dark, he was getting more and more tired and out of breath, but the crazy killers were slowly gaining on him, getting closer and closer with each step. He stopped briefly at the mouth of a black alley and then ran in, but the killers saw Cleo run in after him and kept coming. He couldn't see where he was going, stumbling over crates he couldn't keep running much longer. Finally, he came to a hiding place that appeared before him and Cleo ran in after him and he was just able to pull a garbage can in front of the opening before the killers ran up. He cowered there in the blackness, completely exhausted and breathing hard as quietly as he could but still it sounded as loud as thunder and he was afraid the crazy men would hear him. For what seemed like years they stood there foaming at the mouth and looking wild-eyed before they finally began to move off. Suddenly Cleo started barking and he tried to grab her but it was too late. The garbage can was kicked away and the killers yanked him out and raised their clubs high over their heads in the moonlight.

Paul screamed and sat up in bed, his face and body wet with sweat. There was a loud clamoring nearby. The puppy was beside his bed yapping. He clamped his hands to his temples yelling, "Stop it, you bitch!" at the top of his lungs. The little animal danced out into the center of the room and began barking even more loudly.

Then Paul turned his head and looked at it, letting his hands drop to his lap. After a moment of staring at the noisy dog he swung his feet onto the floor and called softly, "Cleo." Then in a very sweet tone, "Come here, little dog."

The puppy pranced over to him and raised up to be petted, putting its forepaws on the edge of the bed between Paul's legs. Paul reached out slowly, first with one hand and then the other, scratching it behind the ears. Then he moved his hands down to the throat where he'd often seen his mother caress the little animal. He looked into its eyes and suddenly tightened his grip. He had it around the throat tightly, slowly squeezing tighter and tighter. Fear came to the animal's eyes and he could feel the muscles in its neck contract as he squeezed harder. Now the animal's eyes were wild and it started to struggle but Paul had too good a grip. Harder and harder he squeezed with all his strength, the muscles in his jaw working out, the animal wriggling desperately to break loose, its hind legs off the floor. Squeeze harder, tighter, longer, squeeze. The puppy gave one last violent jerk and then went limp, its eyes lifeless.

Paul carried the dead dog to his mother's room, placed the limp body on her bed and went downstairs and out of the house.

"The Guardian" involves the use of symbols, or having an object stand for something else. For the psychotic boy, the dog is a symbol of injustice, acting both as a love object and as a representation of the boy's hatred for the mother. The symbolism is developed in a series of four incidents:

1. The initial incident with the mother, in which the dog is left in the son's care.
2. The dream incident, which is a device for forecasting the action that will take place after the dream.
3. The killing of the dog, which is the key action.
4. The placing of the dead dog on the mother's bed, which is a deliberate effort by the son to make her aware of his hatred.

I have called this a trick story that resembles in plot the one of the two men walking along the road in the dark. But on looking deeper we see that the ending is not really a surprise for—despite the fact that there is no compelling sense of character in the story—everything in "The Guardian" leads us to an ending that on second look is the logical one. The reader looks back and says to himself that he did not know what was going to happen and yet should have known.

Closely resembling the story in which plot depends on symbolism is the psychological tale in which the emphasis is not so much on the objective action as on the force that drives a character. The following outline of "The Rocking Horse Winner" shows how a boy reacts to his mother's desire for money. Paul's attempts to supply the needs of his mother's "house" take him into a realm of the psychic, but the initiating force remains a woman's greed and her son's emotional response to it.

1. A boy, Paul, lives with his careless parents and has an obsessive love for a mother who gives him splendid and expensive toys.
2. In the very moment of receiving one of them, a shining modern rocking horse, Paul is aware of his mother's desperate need for money.
3. When Paul asks his mother why they don't keep a car, although they live in a fashionable house, she tells him that it is because his father has no luck, and adds that luck is what causes you to have money.
4. Deciding that he must find luck for himself and hoping to aid his mother by his luckiness, Paul begins to ride his new rocking horse, beating the horse as if it were in a home stretch. He rides his glassy-eyed animal through a barrier of time and place to win a race at Ascot.
5. When his uncle and the gardener, Bassett, talk to Paul about the horse and tell him he is too old for such sport, he answers that his horse is known by many names but that last week he was called Sansovino. As Bassett knows, Sansovino was an Ascot winner.
6. Paul's Uncle Oscar, at first delighted that his nephew keeps up with racing events, finds out from the gardener that the boy, and the gardener too, are making money (up to three hundred pounds) betting on horses the boy rides as winners on his wooden nursery horse.
7. When the Uncle questions him about his winnings, after a race they have attended and from which they have won a small fortune, Paul confesses that he started the nursery racing for his mother's sake, hoping that money would make her happy and make the house stop whispering and laughing behind his mother's back in its need for money.
8. The Uncle, noticing the terrible stress and emotion under which Paul labors whenever his mother's debts are mentioned, suggests that she be given some of the money Paul has made riding his

rocking horse, and the boy agrees, but only on the condition
that the mother must never learn the source of the income.

9. As the mother gets more money she spends more, and the house
   whispers more loudly than ever. While his mother apparently
   blossoms in luxury, Paul grows more intense, more harassed,
   and finally begins to lose his gift of riding his horse through the
   barrier of time and finding a sure winner.

10. In one last tremendous effort just before the Derby, Paul rides
    once more, urging the steed ahead. His mother, who has been
    worried about his increasingly strange behavior, returns from a
    party to find him shouting the name of the winner *Malabar* . . .
    *Malabar* before he falls unconscious to the floor.

11. The sick boy regains consciousness long enough to find out that
    he has won over seventy thousand pounds for his mother on
    Malabar. Turning to her, he whispers that he is lucky, then dies
    leaving her with the money the house has whispered for from
    the first moment in the story.

"The Rocking Horse Winner" is not a surface action story,
although, basically, it is an account of a child who tries to get
something—in this case money—does succeed in getting it, and
through the effort meets his death. It is interesting to notice
how Lawrence's narrative faintly echoes the plot we referred
to at the beginning of these comments—Chaucer's story of
greed and the fate it brings.

A variation on the greed plot is the story of the man who
wants to give to others rather than take for himself. In the
parable of the good Samaritan, we have very little action in the
sense of a complex plot, but we do have a man who is motivated
by the desire to do good. Here we have a so-called happy
ending in that the man who fell among thieves is rescued. When
Jesus adds, "Go thou and do likewise," he is drawing us into
the action, using it for teaching, and taking the story out of
the category of fiction.

The oldest of the many "happy ending" plots is the Cinderella tale which is as good an example of an action plot as
you are likely to find. It has survived through the years and
has many versions, including that of the "patient Griselda" in
which a girl is placed in a series of difficult situations by her
husband but through fortitude survives all trials. A Cinderella

plot works well for many people who like a heroine who gets what she wants.

## OUTLINE OF CINDERELLA

### GRIMM'S FAIRY TALES

1. When her father remarries, the young, beautiful daughter of a rich man is reduced to the state of a servant girl by her new stepmother. Also in the household are two stepsisters, scheming and cruel but fair of face. These wicked women exile Cinderella to the kitchen where she sleeps before the hearth and is grimy with ashes.

2. One day, when the father is going to a Fair, he asks the three girls what he shall bring them. The two stepsisters ask for pearls and fine clothes but Cinderella wants her father to break for her the first branch that knocks against his head as he rides toward home. He brings her a hazel branch, which Cinderella plants on her dead mother's grave and waters with her tears until it grows to be a fine tree. A little white dove always comes to the tree and whatever Cinderella wishes for he throws down to her.

3. The king of the country orders a feast which is to last three days and to which all the girls in the country are invited in order that the King's son may choose himself a bride. Cinderella has no clothes but after managing with the help of her friend the dove to finish the task of picking the lentils, which has been foisted on her by her stepmother, she goes to her mother's grave, wishes for a gown, and is thrown a gold and silver dress and slippers embroidered with gold and silver. She goes with all speed to the feast where the Prince becomes entranced with her.

4. The next night of the feast Cinderella appears in newer and finer clothes given by the bird, and evades her family and the Prince who is seeking her by taking the clothes back to the grave and resuming her place in the ashes. On the third night, the Prince who is intent upon following her has the palace stairway smeared with pitch. On the stairway, Cinderella loses her slipper which is small and dainty and all golden. The Prince vows that his wife will be no one but the girl whose foot the golden slipper fits.

5. The next morning the Prince goes to Cinderella's father and tells him his vow. The two stepsisters, who have pretty feet, think that surely one of them will be chosen as the bride. The eldest goes into the bedroom and tries on the shoe. When the shoe is too small she cuts off her toes. The Prince takes her on his horse and

rides away but, as they pass the grave under the hazel tree, the dove calls out that there is blood on the shoe. The Prince takes the false bride home and gives the shoe to the younger sister who finds her heel will not fit into the slipper and so cuts off a bit of her heel. Again, the Prince starts out with his bride and again the dove cries out that there is blood in the shoe.

6. The Prince takes the younger sister home and asks the father if he has another daughter. Only Cinderella is left and the stepmother says the girl is much too dirty to show herself. But when the Prince insists, Cinderella is called. She washes her hands and face clean, bows to the Prince and tries on the slipper which fits like a glove. "This is the true bride," the Prince cries. And as they pass by the hazel tree the dove cries to him, "The true bride rides with you."

7. At the wedding ceremony, the sisters want to share in the good fortune. One stepsister stands at the right side of the church, the other at the left. The dove that has been Cinderella's guardian picks out the eyes of the cruel sisters so that all their days the sisters are blind. But Cinderella and her Prince live in the happiness that good people deserve.

In other versions of this story, the slipper is a glass one, the dove becomes a fairy godmother, and the two sisters live happily with the forgiving Cinderella. In a recent tale built on this plot the girl was a model in New York who won a contract in the movies against the scheming of other models and her Prince was a visitor from a Mediterranean country much in arrears in its finances. The model and the Prince of course lived happily ever after.

At the opposite pole from the action tale is what we are going to call a "mood story," which is one that may have a trace of plot as we have defined it here but always subordinates action to atmosphere or to a character in an atmosphere. In any mood story, the tenor of the world immediate to the character, and his emotional responses to his environment, are far stronger elements than the line of action you employ.

A mood story may have dramatic elements. Poe's "Fall of the House of Usher" has all the ingredients of melodrama. If it were not for the genius of the writer in evoking atmosphere we would have no more than a girl shrieking in her tomb, a house falling into a pond, a man running away—and a reader running from the story itself. But Poe makes for us a superb mood piece that carries a certain objectivity.

In the "inner-life" or subjective mood story, the writer often concentrates on a moment of emotion and tries to make that moment represent a life revelation for character. James Joyce has called this revelation an epiphany or "showing forth" of the true identity of the person involved in the story. In the following student sketch, C. R. tries to show a moment in which the coming death of a man is displayed for us in the moment of the man's departure from a bus.

## THE DEATH OF A MAN

C. R.

In a voice too loud for ordinary conversation the old man suddenly turned and said, "Hey, hey, what's the matter there?" The infant who had been crying in his mother's arms suddenly stopped and slowly turned to inspect the face that had addressed him so. Just as abruptly a twinkling appeared in the old man's eyes, a gentleness, and he began to smile and play an amusing game with the child. There were whispers among the others as many heads turned to watch the old man, who bursting from behind the mask of his wrinkled hands, would raise his thick white eyebrows and grin at the infant. Together they would burst into laughter unmindful of the serious world and the staring faces. Then the old man would mask his face again behind the wrinkled hands and the child would grow still and sad. Often amid the cries of laughter, holding his mother's blouse tightly in one hand, the babe would lean toward the old man and wave his hand in the air, seemingly to brush away the comic image. Again the old man would quickly hide his face amid great shrieks of laughter from the babe. This wonderful playfulness continued for several minutes until the two seemed transformed into one, and carried far away from reality and the many solemn faces that watched their game. All seemed bewitched by these two and their private world of joy and the old man kept his bewitchment even after the infant and his mother left the bus.

Alone, the old man's face grew pensive and intent with worry. Having returned once again to reality he turned with taut face glancing nervously at his watch. Several times he arose painfully from his seat to look out into the darkness at the street signs rushing by, "No, not quite yet, but four more blocks and then I shall have to . . ." Suddenly a wonderful smile burst over his face, and as before with the child he seemed a different person, looking nowhere he saw nothing, enveloped in the past.

When the four blocks had gone he jumped to the door and leaped into the darkness, so that it seemed that the Darkness had literally sucked him from the vehicle and in his place had suddenly thrown another, thrust there by the angry world to replace the old man.

Here is a look at the life of any old man, not at one of the heroes whom Aristotle demanded for a tragedy. Aristotle wanted a man of greatness who stood out from a crowd like a tree from other trees in a forest and who was struck down because of some flaw in himself. The heroes of our own mood pieces are often decidedly little people whose great characteristic is the particular way they share the fate of all men, living or dying.

A classic example of a mood story is "Miss Brill" by Katherine Mansfield. In it, we come to know Miss Brill through a series of luminous little scenes, never causally connected in the action sense, that show her as having grown apart from the people in the park around her. You can call this a symbol story, for the park is life, and Miss Brill is as dead as her fur piece, but primarily it is a tale in which a writer asks the reader to share the feeling, the perception, and small sorrow, of the character she has created.

## MISS BRILL

### KATHERINE MANSFIELD

Although it was so brilliantly fine—the blue sky powdered with gold and great spots of white like white wine splashed over the Jardins Publiques—Miss Brill was glad that she had decided on her fur. The air was motionless, but when you opened your mouth there was just a faint chill, like a chill from a glass of iced water before you sip, and now and again a leaf came drifting—from nowhere, from the sky. Miss Brill put up her hand and touched her fur. Dear little thing! It was nice to feel it again. She had taken it out of its box that afternoon, shaken out the moth-powder, given it a good brush, and rubbed the life back into the dim little eyes. "What has been happening to me?" said the sad little eyes. Oh, how sweet it was to see them snap at her again from the red eiderdown! . . . But the nose, which was of some black composition, wasn't at all firm. It must have had a knock, somehow. Never mind—a little dab of black sealing-wax when the time came—when it was absolutely necessary. . . . Little rogue! Yes, she really felt like that about it. Little rogue biting its tail just by her left ear. She could have taken it off and laid it on her lap and stroked it. She felt a tingling in her hands and arms, but that came from walking, she supposed. And when she breathed, something light and sad—no, not sad, exactly—something gentle seemed to move in her bosom.

There were a number of people out this afternoon, far more than last Sunday. And the band sounded louder and gayer. That was because the Season had begun. For although the band played all the year round on Sundays, out of season it was never the same. It was like some one playing with only the family to listen; it didn't care how it played if there weren't any strangers present. Wasn't the conductor wearing a new coat, too? She was sure it was new. He scraped with his foot and flapped his arms like a rooster about to crow, and the bandsmen sitting in the green rotunda blew out their cheeks and glared at the music. Now there came a little "flutey" bit —very pretty!—a little chain of bright drops. She was sure it would be repeated. It was; she lifted her head and smiled.

Only two people shared her "special" seat: a fine old man in a velvet coat, his hands clasped over a huge carved walking-stick, and a big old woman, sitting upright, with a roll of knitting on her embroidered apron. They did not speak. This was disappointing, for Miss Brill always looked forward to the conversation. She had become really quite expert, she thought, at listening as though she didn't listen, at sitting in other people's lives just for a minute while they talked around her.

She glanced, sideways, at the old couple. Perhaps they would go soon. Last Sunday, too, hadn't been as interesting as usual. An Englishman and his wife, he wearing a dreadful Panama hat and she button boots. And she'd gone on the whole time about how she ought to wear spectacles; she knew she needed them; but that it was no good getting any; they'd be sure to break and they'd never keep on. And he'd been so patient. He'd suggested everything—gold rims, the kind that curved round your ears, little pads inside the bridge. No, nothing would please her. "They'll always be sliding down my nose!" Miss Brill had wanted to shake her.

The old people sat on the bench, still as statues. Never mind, there was always the crowd to watch. To and fro, in front of the flower-beds and the band rotunda, the couples and groups paraded, stopped to talk, to greet, to buy a handful of flowers from the old beggar who had his tray fixed to the railings. Little children ran among them, swooping and laughing; little boys with big white silk bows under their chins, little girls, little French dolls, dressed up in velvet and lace. And sometimes a tiny staggerer came suddenly rocking into the open from under the trees, stopped, stared, as suddenly sat down "flop," until its small high-stepping mother, like a young hen, rushed scolding to its rescue. Other people sat on the benches and green chairs, but they were nearly always the same. Sunday after Sunday, and—Miss Brill had often noticed—there was something funny about nearly all of them. They were odd, silent, nearly all old, and from the way they stared they looked as though they'd just come from dark little rooms or even—even cupboards!

Behind the rotunda the slender trees with yellow leaves down drooping, and through them just a line of sea, and beyond the blue sky with gold-veined clouds.

Tum-tum-tum tiddle-um! tiddle-um! tum tiddley-um tum ta! blew the band.

Two young girls in red came by and two young soldiers in blue met them, and they laughed and paired and went off arm-in-arm. Two peasant women with funny straw hats passed, gravely, leading beautiful smoke-colored donkeys. A cold, pale nun hurried by. A beautiful woman came along and dropped her bunch of violets, and a little boy ran after to hand them to her, and she took them and threw them away as if they'd been poisoned. Dear me! Miss Brill didn't know whether to admire that or not! And now an ermine toque and a gentleman in gray met just in front of her. He was tall, stiff, dignified, and she was wearing the ermine toque she'd bought when her hair was yellow. Now everything, her hair, her face, even her eyes, was the same color as the shabby ermine, and her hand, in its cleaned glove, lifted to dab her lips, was a tiny yellowish paw. Oh, she was so pleased to see him—delighted! She rather thought they were going to meet that afternoon. She described where she'd been —everywhere, here, there, along by the sea. The day was so charm-ing—didn't he agree? And wouldn't he, perhaps? . . . But he shook his head, lighted a cigarette, slowly breathed a great deep puff into her face, and, even while she was still talking and laughing, flicked the match away and walked on. The ermine toque was alone; she smiled more brightly than ever. But even the band seemed to know what she was feeling and played more softly, played tenderly, and the drum beat, "The Brute! The Brute!" over and over. What would she do? What was going to happen now? But as Miss Brill wondered, the ermine toque turned, raised her hand as though she'd seen some one else, much nicer, just over there, and pattered away. And the band changed again and played more quickly, more gayly than ever, and the old couple on Miss Brill's seat got up and

marched away, and such a funny old man with long whiskers hob-
bled along in time to the music and was nearly knocked over by
four girls walking abreast.

Oh, how fascinating it was! How she enjoyed it! How she loved
sitting here, watching it all! It was like a play. It was exactly like a
play. Who could believe the sky at the back wasn't painted? But it
wasn't till a little brown dog trotted on solemn and then slowly
trotted off, like a little "theatre" dog, a little dog that had been
drugged, that Miss Brill discovered what it was that made it so exciting. They were all on the stage. They weren't only the audience,
not only looking on; they were acting. Even she had a part and
came every Sunday. No doubt somebody would have noticed if she
hadn't been there; she was part of the performance after all. How
strange she'd never thought of it like that before! And yet it explained why she made such a point of starting from home at just the
same time each week—so as not to be late for the performance—and
it also explained why she had quite a queer, shy feeling at telling her
English pupils how she spent her Sunday afternoons. No wonder!
Miss Brill nearly laughed out loud. She was on the stage. She
thought of the old invalid gentleman to whom she read the newspaper four afternoons a week while he slept in the garden. She had
got quite used to the frail head on the cotton pillow, the hollowed
eyes, the open mouth and the high pinched nose. If he'd been dead
she mightn't have noticed for weeks; she wouldn't have minded.
But suddenly he knew he was having the paper read to him by an
actress! "An actress!" The old head lifted; two points of light quivered in the old eyes. "An actress—are ye?" And Miss Brill smoothed
the newspaper as though it were the manuscript of her part and said
gently: "Yes, I have been an actress for a long time."

The band had been having a rest. Now they started again. And
what they played was warm, sunny, yet there was just a faint chill—
a something, what was it?—not sadness—no, not sadness—a something
that made you want to sing. The tune lifted, lifted, the light shone;
and it seemed to Miss Brill that in another moment all of them, all
the whole company, would begin singing. The young ones, the
laughing ones who were moving together, they would begin, and
the men's voices, very resolute and brave, would join them. And
then she too, she too, and the others on the benches—they would
come in with a kind of accompaniment—something low, that
scarcely rose or fell, something so beautiful—moving. . . . And Miss
Brill's eyes filled with tears and she looked smiling at all the other
members of the company. Yes, we understand, we understand, she
thought—though what they understood she didn't know.

Just at that moment a boy and a girl came and sat down where
the old couple had been. They were beautifully dressed; they were

in love. The hero and heroine, of course, just arrived from his father's yacht. And still soundlessly singing, still with that trembling smile, Miss Brill prepared to listen.

"No, not now," said the girl. "Not here, I can't."

"But why? Because of that stupid old thing at the end there? asked the boy. "Why does she come here at all—who wants her? Why doesn't she keep her silly old mug at home?"

"It's her fu-fur which is so funny," giggled the girl. "It's exactly like a fried whiting."

"Ah, be off with you!" said the boy in an angry whisper. Then: "Tell me, ma petite chere—"

"No, not here," said the girl. "Not *yet*."

.    .    .    .    .    .    .    .    .

On her way home she usually bought a slice of honey-cake at the baker's. It was her Sunday treat. Sometimes there was an almond in her slice, sometimes not. It made a great difference. If there was an almond it was like carrying home a tiny present—a surprise—something that might very well not have been there. She hurried on the almond Sundays and struck the match for the kettle in quite a dashing way.

But to-day she passed the baker's by, climbed the stairs, went into the little dark room—her room like a cupboard—and sat down on the red eiderdown. She sat there for a long time. The box that the fur came out of was on the bed. She unclasped the necklet quickly; quickly, without looking, laid it inside. But when she put the lid on she thought she heard something crying.

The mood of Miss Brill is evoked (1) through the old couple who share Miss Brill's separation from the life in the park; (2) through the music played by the band, which gives her the illusion that she is part of the performance; (3) through the turning point, which comes when the boy and the girl sit down where the old people have been and ask each other why Miss Brill is allowed to be in the park at all; (4) through the fur-piece, which was introduced in the first paragraph of the story, and which becomes Miss Brill herself crying in the box.


## THE ELEMENTS OF A MOOD STORY:   Assignment 25

Taking the student's sketch, "The Death of an Old Man," as a

model, write an incident that shows a reversal of mood on the part
of one character. Concentrate on creating the atmosphere in which
this change of emotional attitude takes place.

If you are a writer who believes that a story should first of
all have a definite line of action based on a situation and its re-
sulting conflict then you are likely to think that the mood story
as we have been discussing it here consists of no more than an
over-projection of a moment in the life of a mediocre person.
You may agree with W. Somerset Maugham when he says of
Katherine Mansfield and her method:

The writer of fiction, in order to tell the truth as he sees it, must
play his part in the hurly-burly of life. If what the dictionary tells
us is correct, that a story is a narrative of events that have happened
or might have happened, it must be admitted that Katherine Mansfield had no outstanding gifts for telling one. Her gifts lay elsewhere. She could take a situation and wring from it all the irony,
bitterness, pathos and unhappiness that were inherent in it . . . her
most characteristic stories are those that are commonly known as
stories of atmosphere. I have asked various of my literary friends
what in this connection is the meaning of the word atmosphere; but
they either could not, or would not, give me an answer that quite
satisfied me. The Oxford Dictionary does not help. After the obvious definition it gives, "figuratively, surrounding mental or moral
element, environment." In practice it seems to mean the trimmings
with which you decorate a story so thin that without them it would
not exist.
                    From *Points of View*, by W. Somerset Maugham

In commenting on the power of invention that is so intimately connected with plot, Maugham adds of Mansfield's
stories:

Their form she owed to Chekhov. The pattern of the short story as
it was written in the past is simple. It consists of A, the setting, B, the
introduction of the characters, C, what they do and what is done to
them, and D, the outcome. This was a leisurely way of telling a
story and the author could make it as long as he liked; but when
newspapers began to publish stories their length was rigidly deter-
mined. In order to satisfy this requirement the author had to adopt
a suitable technique; he had to leave out of his story everything that
was not essential. The use of A, the setting, is to put the reader in a
suitable state of mind to enjoy the story or to add verisimilitude to

it; it can conveniently be omitted, and today generally is. To leave D, outcome, to the imagination of the reader is a risk. He has been interested in the circumstances described, and if he is not told what they result in he may feel cheated, but when it is evident, to omit it is intriguing and effective. . . . This pattern well suited the nature of Katherine Mansfield's temperament and capacity.

From *Points of View*

But we try to judge each writer in terms of his intention in writing a story. For the attitude a writer has toward his material is often as important as the way he treats the fictional situation. As you can see from Miss Mansfield's comments which follow here, she simply was not interested in plot as Maugham knows it. She wanted to use details that would fit Miss Brill on that day and in the moment we come to know her in the park.

It's a very queer thing how *craft* comes into writing. I mean down to details. *Par example.* In *Miss Brill* I choose not only the length of every sentence, but even the sound of every sentence. I choose the rise and fall of every paragraph to fit her, and to fit her on that day at that very moment. After I'd written it I read it aloud—numbers of times—just as one would *play over* a musical composition—trying to get it nearer and nearer to the expression of Miss Brill—until it fitted her.

Don't think I'm vain about the little sketch. It's only the method I wanted to explain. I often wonder whether other writers do the same—if a thing has really come off it seems to me there mustn't be one single word out of place, or one word that could be taken out. That's how I AIM at writing.

From *The Letters of Katherine Mansfield*, edited by J. Middleton Murry

Katherine Mansfield's intention was to create a mood for a particular character on a day that passes with the quickness of a moment. At the other extreme, a writer like W. Somerset Maugham uses conflict, crisis, climax, to produce an integrated action. Any plot based on action or any created mood has as its true function the revealing of character.

We are back where we began, with the boy who wanted to take a swan dive from the Empire State, with the three thieves who found death because of their greed, and with the person whom you are in the process of creating and putting into the action of a story or a novel. Your plot may be simple or complex. It may conform to D. H. Lawrence's idea of flow in a story, or it may have as many twists as the plot Thomas Hardy used over and over again in his novels. Remember always that the primary function of plot is to translate character into action.

## PLOT ELEMENTS IN YOUR SECOND STORY:
Assignment 26

1. Is your plot an organic one, rising naturally from the nature and the acts of your main character, or does it consist primarily of an imposed line of action?

2. Relate your choice of type of plot, action, symbol, mood—or whatever you consider the dominant element—to the main point you are trying to make in your story.

## 11

# Revealing through Theme

Must a story have a theme at all? Isn't it possible simply to try to entertain a reader? What of the detective story and its many admirers? Are they hunting for a moral tag? And in a novel does the character have to wear a badge saying he is *good* or *bad* to get across the point that an evil man comes to an evil end? What is theme anyway? These are the questions one young writer asked only yesterday.

Today, a student wrote a sketch portraying the world as an elevator with a character caught between floors in a car that had lost its power of movement. He got angry when I suggested that he might be beginning to work with a theme. He did not want that word to be related to any story he wrote. You might agree with him that it is best to put what you believe into a story and attach no label. But in spite of your protest against emphasis on meaning, and of my own which I make now and then, *theme* in serious fiction would exist and keep on existing.

Theme is the point you want to give your tale. You may make the point shyly or hammer it home every inch along the way. Tolstoi did this last in his parable about the peasant who was so greedy for land that he ran himself to death trying to add another acre to those he had already won. Tolstoi's point, whether we agree with him or not, was that all we can really own is the space that is our grave. He drove it home so hard that the theme almost obliterates the story.

There are as many ways of displaying theme as there are writers, yet each way has a resemblance to the others just as each writer is a brother to the next one. How, then, do you make a point in a story? For the moment, nobody questions any belief you may hold. You may think that the "loud world" is no place for anyone, or that it is a wonderful tumbling ground for us all. If your belief is significant for you, how do you present it in fiction?

Suppose we start with *The Scarlet Letter* by Hawthorne, in which the writer began by displaying theme through the symbol of a rose growing at a prison door. The story that follows is about the consequences of adultery. Its theme is a plea for understanding sin as it exists in the world and in our own inner selves. The power of the book rises from Hawthorne's own conviction of guilt and grace. Within the novel's framework of setting, plot, and character, lies the indubitable inner image of the writer.

Hawthorne was able to lift up his narrative and make it an illumination for many, because he had a theme that was true for him. He could say to his characters, and to his readers, "Be true! Be true! Show freely to the world, if not your worst, yet some trait whereby the worst may be inferred." The rose, the prison, and the many other symbols integral to the book, enhance the revelation of theme for the reader.

This is not to say you must pick a theme like "Be true!" and try to write a story around it, making a pattern of events particularize an abstraction for you. Theme is not so deliberately chosen as that. At its best, it grows up in a story and never appears to be imposed from the outside. Like Hawthorne's prison flower, it springs out of necessity and brings its own significance. As the novelist Daphne Athas points out below, it is always a discovery.

I take theme to be the significance of a work.

.    .    .    .    .    .    .    .    .    .    .

For most people and most writers life and writing are an exploration. If one recognizes it, one may plunge with joy into the fray. The name of the fray is of no moment. Given two or more far and boundless poles staring with challenge, you get action. Out of action something results. The implication of that result must be discovered. When you discover that, you have found your theme.

This is the divinity of significance, and the reason one writes.

Hawthorne almost always wrote out of a theme that clarified itself for him somewhere in the process of creating his story. Often he started by putting into his notebooks a hint for a narrative and then, years later perhaps, picking up his own hint and incorporating it into fiction. In making his point he used a black flower, or a jeweled heart with a poisonous odor, or a veil that became the veil every human being wears. Sometimes, finding symbolism not enough, he announced his theme directly.

The cloak that his Lady Eleanore Rochcliffe wore in "Lady Eleanore's Mantle," is a symbol of a spirit that "held itself too high to participate in the enjoyment of other human souls." In the end, the mantle brings the plague to the people of Massachusetts and to Lady Eleanore herself. Hawthorne spells out his moral by having the main character say, "I wrapped myself in PRIDE as in a MANTLE, and scorned the sympathies of nature; and therefore has nature made this wretched body the medium of a dreadful sympathy." Here, he snatches away from us the meaning we want to find for ourselves.

Such an explicit statement of theme is not fashionable in the writing of our own time, but at least we can see that, through the announcement, Hawthorne was anxious for the reader to get the point. He was more successful aesthetically in *The Scarlet Letter*, where the sermon is in the rose and also in the mouths of the characters. In the novel, the statements of theme seem to be discovered by the characters and not put on them as a tag or a garment.

In your second story, begin to analyze your own presentation of point or theme.

## THEME THROUGH SYMBOL AND STATEMENT:
Assignment 27

Choose one symbol from your second story and explain it as a particularization of theme. If the narrative is in no way symbolic indicate a statement you used to underscore and particularize your point.

Revealing theme through symbol or statement will obviously be only one aspect of the aesthetics of your story. A primary use of symbols is to heighten the emotional effect of your narrative and the mood it is intended to create. The mood, or feeling, which permeates your story and projects itself to your reader is only one part of your total intention. In *The Scarlet Letter*, symbols combine with other fictional elements, including statement, to project theme.

To his symbols and the mood they generated, Hawthorne added a perfectly good triangle plot. He used, too, his setting of Puritan New England in which his characters move from crisis to climax. He never gets far away from the rose by the prison door: the flower is there at the beginning of the book and also at the end. Nor does the author get away from the action to which the symbols are intimately related.


## REVEALING THEME THROUGH ACTION: Assignment 28

Using the line of action that you have planned for your second story as a point of departure, comment on your key scene as an illustration of the point of your story.

After symbol, statement, mood, and action, we come to theme as it reveals itself through character. But we have never been far away from the fact that people do carry the burden of a story and that the fictional world cannot exist without them. In a serious story, what does a character reveal about theme? And how can he himself be the point of the narrative? How can you project him so that he becomes the representation of the significant thing you are trying to say?

Primarily through the presentation of a character, the following student story, "The Day After Tomorrow," points out that a college education does not always prepare a man for life. The portrait is apparently one of Harry Meggs, but the true focus of the tale is on the narrator who comes to realize that he, like Harry, must face his own "day after tomorrow." The story shows us two faces, one of them reflected in the other.

The discovery of the point of the story comes for the reader, and for Pete Stevens, through a gradual recognition of the inadequacy of Harry Meggs. The tale has no plot in the ordinary sense of the word, but many signs lead us to the truth about Harry that foreshadows a possible-truth-to-be about Pete. For the narrator is presented as a shadow-likeness of the man he comes to know during the summer at the fraternity house.

# THE DAY AFTER TOMORROW

CHARLES NISBET

It was during summer school, after I had graduated, that I got to know Harry Meggs. I had met him a little earlier, because he came to the house several days before graduation. I was very busy then, getting ready to graduate, so I didn't have time or take time to talk to him. Apparently, neither did anyone else. He came in quietly, settled himself in an already vacated room and watched the confusion. School was over, and the only boys left were waiting for graduation. We were pretty accustomed to seeing old alumni drop into the house from time to time. They usually came in droves on the big dance weekends. Some young, some even middle-aged, all trying to get a glimpse of something they had lost sight of after college. If anyone had stopped to think about it, they might have thought it a little strange that anyone would want to visit just before graduation. But no one ever did, so Harry went unquestioned.

The first thing I remembered about Harry, even before I met him, was his suitcase. It was a new, brown, expensive-looking suitcase with the initials H.A.M. stamped on it in gold letters. At the time I thought it was mildly funny. Later I thought it was just pitiful.

The first time I met Harry, I was hurrying to the cleaners with my graduation robe. My room was at the end of the hall, and I had to pass the one he had camped in on the way out. I was just beyond his room when he spoke. All he said was "Hello!" His voice was deep, without resonance, and for some reason sounded a little artificial. Later I figured out that he was pushing his voice back in his throat, trying to make it deeper, and that was what gave it the artificial sound.

I backed up and stuck my head in his room. He was sprawled comfortably on a straight-backed chair. From his skin and his hairline he looked to be around thirty. But the rest of him looked ten years younger. His hair was crewcut and very black, and he was comfortably overweight without being fat. He was smoking a cigarette, holding it between his thumb and forefinger and constantly tapping it with his middle finger as though it were a cigar. This irritated me, and I began to mildly dislike Harry from the first. He stood up and stuck out his hand. "I'm Harry Meggs. Harry Alexander Meggs. Some people call me 'Ham'." He laughed. "I was a Gamma here. Graduated in fifty-two." He laughed again. "Seven long years ago." He drew out the "long", and this irritated me also.

"Pete Stevens. Glad to meet you."

He finally stopped shaking hands with me. "Who could I see about renting a room for the summer? You see, I'm thinking about entering law school—"

"You can see me. I'm the house manager for the summer. Make yourself comfortable, and we'll talk about it later. I've got to get this robe to the cleaners now."

"What! Why, they're shafting you boys. What's happening to this place? When I was here nobody ever got a gown that wasn't already cleaned and pressed!" He waved his stub of a cigarette through the air like it was a foot long.

"Yes, things are getting bad all over. I'll see you later." I left, glad to get away. I hadn't cared to tell him that the robe was in perfect shape when I got it, and that several of us had gotten very drunk the night before and had our own graduation rehearsal in the back yard. I knew he would have slapped me on the back and laughed his damn throaty-condescending laugh and said that "the boys" hadn't changed so much since his time after all.

My parents came up for graduation—all of it. Mother bustled as usual, and Dad looked a little bewildered which was not at all usual. I was glad to see them. We live five hundred miles from school, and I hadn't been home since Christmas. Yet their coming had its disadvantages. I had to go to the Baccalaureate sermon with them for one thing. And for another, they added to the confusion. But I was still glad to see them. The afternoon of the day they arrived we sat on the back porch of the almost deserted fraternity house and drank gin and tonic. It was very hot and the drinks were dry and cooling and tasted so good that I had too many of them and got tipsy and tried not to act that way for my parents. Mother asked me if I felt different now that I was a college graduate, and I told her no. Then Dad talked about summer school and my plans for the future. It made me a little uncomfortable to talk about it, because in going to summer school I was admitting that I had made a mistake earlier.

When I first came to college, Dad and I had planned for me to go into the business school. By the end of my Freshman year I had discovered how hard the accounting course was and how many people had flunked it and had consequently flunked out of business school. By the middle of my Sophomore year I had come to the conclusion that the business school was for people who couldn't get along in the world on their own initiative. So, at the end of my Sophomore year I registered for the school of English and for the next two years got a very liberal education.

Toward the end of my Senior year I began to get scared. It was largely just a fear of having to strike out on my own, but it took the form of wondering just what kind of job I could get with a solid background in English literature. After much emotional fumbling and a little thinking, I decided to go to summer school and take all the business courses I could cram in. This, I felt, should give me some good preparation. And it would very conveniently postpone severing the long-attached cord for at least three more months.

Graduation was a nuisance. There was a lot of standing, a lot of sitting and a lot of ignoring of speakers. I kept telling myself that it would mean a lot to me later and so managed to get through.

My parents left the day after graduation, and since summer school was only two days off, I didn't have time to go home. The house was empty except for Harry, myself, and Gene Birch, who, like myself, lived too far away from school to go home. Gene had a girl friend who was also staying for summer school, so I didn't see much of him. There was no one left for me to associate with but Harry.

We started eating out together, Harry and I, not because I particularly liked the idea of eating with Harry Meggs, but because the campus was practically deserted, and eating with Harry was better than eating alone.

Walking downtown with him was even worse than listening to him talk at mealtime. I think Harry was absolutely the slowest walking man I'd ever seen. Sometimes I wondered how he kept going. But he always managed to get one foot in front of the other, keeping his shoulders hunched over and his head dangling on the end of his neck.

The first time we went out, he talked to me about rooming at the fraternity house. "Like I started to tell you the other day, I'm thinking about going to law school." He settled himself down into the diner booth, stationed his elbows on the table and looked across his folded hands at me. "You see, Pete, I'm in insurance. I've been in the business for, oh, six or seven years now. And I guess I've made some pretty good money in my time." He smiled at me with all of his face but his mouth, which was turned down at the corners. It was the silent expression of his condescending laugh. He went on. "In the last three years I've averaged five hundred dollars a month," he paused, "on commissions!" He paused again to let the "commissions" sink in. "But I've been thinking about it. It's hard work. Awfully hard work. If I kept this up much longer I'd have a good case of ulcers. Besides, I'm not the type of man to be satisfied with six thousand a year. There are things I want out of this life that can't be had on that kind of money.

"Well, I've just about decided that law school would be the best thing for me. With my business experience and a law degree, I could go into either law or business and make a killing. A real killing. And then there's a certain amount of prestige attached to a professional man."

"So you're going to start back to school this summer?"

"Not on your life! Not at this school. Harvard, Pete, Harvard. The best in the country. So you ask why I'm here now. I'll tell you. Living high is a weakness of mine. I was renting a house back home that ran one fifty per month, eating all my meals out, and spending one hell of a lot of money on fine liquor and beautiful women." He winked at me and I ignored him. "Now, I'm going to need money for school, and I figured I could live cheaper here than just about anywhere else. And, believe me, boy, there's a lot of insurance to be sold in this territory. And one other thing, I may pick up a law course or two while I'm here. Just to get started, you know. I'm a little rusty on this school business. Well, now, can you give me a room?"

"For fifteen a month."

"Fine, fine. Oh, and do you think I could have a single? I'll be using it as an office, sort of, and have stuff spread out all over the place. It would probably get in anyone else's way and—you know."

"I know. Just keep the one you're in. You can have it to yourself."

By this time I had finished eating, so I pretended to be in a hurry and left him with half his meal to go.

That night I couldn't go to sleep for a while so I thought about Harry. I decided that I didn't really dislike him after all. He was too simple for that. I just thought he was a little contemptible. But in spite of that I couldn't help admiring him for what he was doing. To give up everything at thirty and start all over again took a certain amount of courage. I seriously doubted I could have done it.

It wasn't long before I got fed up with Harry. I got to the point where I was even willing to eat alone to avoid him. But the choice was no longer mine. Harry would always find me just before mealtime and ask me to join him. And when we ate, he always managed to dominate the conversation. I didn't particularly care to talk to him, so I let him talk without saying much myself. His conversation was remarkably monotonous. He talked about money. At first I felt that I should make an effort to be interested. Since I was going to be sitting through business courses for the summer, I knew I'd have to get used to it sooner or later. But Harry was so damned obnoxious about it.

One thing he loved to talk about was the financial statistics on ex-Gammas. "Do you realize that the average income of the man who graduated from this chapter is twenty thousand a year? Now that doesn't mean that being a Gamma will make you successful. But it does seem to indicate that the Gammas only take potentially successful men. At least that's the way I look at it."

Or he would get out a pencil, begin scratching figures on a napkin and tell me how he could accumulate five hundred thousand in the next ten years.

"All I need is ten thousand to start with. You've got to have capital, boy. Capital. That's the key word in the business world.

"Now you take my graduating class. I could sit down right now and give you no less than five boys, five of them, in that class, who made good because of capital. And I can tell you, I think without bragging, that none of them had any more brains *or* a better business head than I do. Now I'm not saying this to build myself up. I'm just trying to let you see how important capital is."

"I see."

He smiled at me with his mouth turned down, and for a moment he looked almost sad. "But those fellows had rich fathers who were willing to set them up. My Dad could have done it, but he didn't. He wanted to see me make it on my own. From scratch. Now I'm glad he did, you know. I've had to work hard, but I've done well for myself. And if I go back into insurance after law school, I'll make a real killing."

He never did say what he would have done with all that capital he didn't have.

For the next few days I managed to avoid Harry. School started, and I was busy going to class, buying books, and getting used to summer school. I wanted to get off to a good start, so I kept myself on the go right at first.

One night just after classes had begun, I sat down and made out an elaborate set of books so I could keep my house-managing duties straight. As it turned out, this was a farce. I lost the books three days later and never did bother to make up new ones. I decided that, after all, I was intelligent enough to keep that little bit of math in my head. But I did start out with good intentions.

Business school was barely tolerable, but there were compensations. It was good to see new faces, especially new female faces. There weren't many girls in business classes, but those on campus were easy to meet. And most of them were there for a good time. Summer school was a wonderful combination of education and vacation.

It wasn't long before I was drinking beer in the afternoons and dating almost every night. I am sure that the Gamma house witnessed some of the best parties of its career that summer.

Harry would usually come to the parties. But he would just stand and look. He never had a date and he never drank. Usually he would go to bed early. I felt a little sorry for him in spite of myself. He was an obnoxious character, there was no doubt about that. But he couldn't be too happy at this point. The life he was leading was almost debasing, living in a small, single room, having to save every penny he could, and having no one his own age to associate with. For a while I wondered why he hadn't married and settled down. But then I decided he probably couldn't find anyone who would have him.

After I got settled down into the routine of summer school, I began to notice something about Harry that hadn't struck me before. He rarely left his room unless it was for meals. His door was usually closed and his radio going.

Harry had a car that sat behind the Gamma house all the time. He never drove it, probably because he never went anywhere. It was a new black and cream Chevrolet with five thousand miles on it. Harry had told me that he didn't particularly like it. He said he would have bought a Jaguar, but it wouldn't do for an insurance man. An insurance man's car, he said, had to present a picture of financial respectability, but couldn't be flashy. The prospects would think he was crooked or something.

One day toward the end of June I looked out my window and saw a big Cadillac parked in the back yard. Two older men and Harry were standing around Harry's Chevy. One of the men was throwing stuff out of the car. The other was talking to Harry. After a few minutes one of them got in Harry's car, the other got in the Cadillac and they drove off. Then Harry ambled back toward the house. Just before he got to the house, I yelled down to him. "Couldn't you keep up the payments?" I tried to make it sound like a big joke, but I was really curious.

He laughed and said, "Not at all. Not at all. I sold it. I wasn't using it much anyway. I can do most of my business here on foot. And I needed the money for school next year, you know."

Later he told me he thought he'd buy a second hand car with part of the money, but he never did.

It wasn't too long after he sold the car that the typewriter business came up. One afternoon I was sitting in my room writing my parents for money when this strange guy knocked on my open door and asked me where he could find Harry Maggs.

"His name is Harry Meggs and he lives down the hall." I went with him to show him Harry's room. When he pushed the door open we saw that Harry wasn't there. I was flabbergasted.

"Do you know anything about his typewriter?" this guy said.

"No. I didn't know he had one."

"He had a 'for sale' ad for it in the paper. Fifty dollars."

So we looked around and found the typewriter under the bed, and the guy left a check on Harry's desk.

I asked Harry about it later, and he said it was for his school fund. It seemed kind of stupid to me. I should think he'd need the typewriter more than the fifty dollars, but I didn't say anything.

Harry certainly was a strange character. I spent a lot of my free time trying to figure him out. He was still hibernating in his room. I would only see him every now and then walking downtown. I could spot him every time from at least a hundred yards. Nobody else walked like that. And he always wore the same clothes, khaki pants and a white shirt rolled up to the elbows.

One night toward the end of June I dropped into Gene Birch's room for a talk. I liked Gene, but because he was so busy studying and seeing his girl I never got a chance to have a real talk with him. I wanted to see what he thought about Harry. By this time he was a complete mystery to me. Gene was studying psychology, and he usually had one or two theories about everybody. I figured a weird guy like Harry would be just his dish. Gene was finishing up school this summer. He had the army behind him and, ahead of him, a nice woman and a very good job with some advertising company. He was a fairly nice looking guy in spite of the fact that he was tall, rather thin and had red hair. When I pushed open his door, he was leaning back in his chair with his bare, size twelve feet propped up on the desk.

"You studying?" I asked.

"I'm through now. Come on in, Pete. I was just sitting here trying to figure something out. Do you think it's better to rent a house or apartment, or go on and make a down payment on your own? That is, assuming you have a steady income."

"Are you asking me?"

"I just want an opinion. You're in business school. Your mind should be adapted to this sort of thing."

I laughed. "You've got the wrong man, my friend. The only time I think about business is when I'm in class. I'm not even a decent house manager."

He smiled at me and lit a cigarette. "All right. What do you think about?"

I lit a cigarette too. He was primed for a conversation now. "Sex and beer. And one other thing. This idiot who lives down the hall here."

"Which one?"

"Harry. Harry A. Meggs. Some people call him Ham. I can't figure that guy out. What the devil is he doing here? Do you ever see him?"

"He comes in here and talks to me just about every night."

"Has he told you anything about himself?"

"Just that he's going to law school and is selling insurance."

"But he's not selling anything as far as I can see."

"Neither is he going to law school."

"He told you that?"

"No. That's my own idea." Gene puffed on his cigarette and thought for a moment. "Now this is just my theory, of course, but look at it this way. If you were getting ready to go to school for two or three years, would you quit working three months before school started?"

"Not unless I was rich."

"Exactly. And Harry is not rich. He says he can live more cheaply here. I guess he's told you the same story. That part of it is true. But he surely can't put away any money if he's not working. No matter how cheaply he's living. I think Harry was fired. Or he was doing such a poor job of selling insurance, assuming that he really was doing that, that he just quit."

"But why would he come here?"

"Where could he go?"

"I'd go home. At least until I got another job."

"If you were thirty years old? That would be even more embarrassing than coming here. Can you imagine going home to Daddy after all this time? He would be admitting complete defeat then. Besides, his parents wouldn't believe the stories he's been telling us. And whether we believe them or not, he must think we do."

"It makes sense. I wonder what he's going to do?"

"I doubt that he knows any more than we do. The first thing he has to do is face reality. I wouldn't be at all surprised if he believes a lot of these lies that he's been telling us. He probably thinks that he really is going to law school. Harry is one of these people who can't face his own limitations. When he graduated here seven years ago he must have thought of himself as a financial genius. The world owed him a living. Then he got out into the world and everything didn't follow according to his little plan. To some extent this happens to almost everyone. And most people adjust their aspirations to their capabilities. But apparently, Harry hasn't been able to do that. He still thinks he's a genius. And because the world around him won't admit it, he lives in a world of his own making. He talks about law school and amassing fortunes when he hasn't got enough money to eat on. Do you know, he had to borrow some money from me to eat on? Two days ago I saw him in the drugstore drinking a nickel coke. I'm sure that was his lunch. That night he came in and asked if he could borrow ten dollars. He said he'd pay it back when the money from his car came in. But I know that's ten dollars down the drain."

"You don't think he'll get any money for the car?"

"He didn't sell that car. It was taken from him. Probably by the finance company."

"I kind of figured the same thing myself. Why did you lend him the money then?"

"Because he was hungry. I can't stand to see a man go hungry when I'm eating. I feel sorry for Harry. He's worthless and he's an inveterate liar, but I still feel sorry for him. He must be going through a little hell now. Because it's come to the point where he's going to have to face reality or become a bum. And you can believe that the reality he'll have to face will be a very unpleasant one. I'm curious to see whether he'll do it or not."

That night I tried to piece together what Gene had said with what I had seen of Harry. It all made sense. But I wondered how a man who had been a Gamma and graduated from this school could turn out to be so worthless. It was a little like finding out there was no Santa Claus. For a while it made me a little uncomfortable. But not for long. I decided that Harry was just an unusual case. I didn't know any other Gamma alums who weren't at least moderately successful.

From then on I began to watch Harry with interest. I was dying for a good chance to talk to him and several times I even asked him to join me for a meal. But he had always just finished or wasn't hungry then or something. Once when I was trying to find him I looked in his room. He wasn't there so I went in and looked around a little. The first thing I noticed was a half-empty loaf of bread on his desk. I looked around to see if I could find any more food, but there was nothing. Only some bits of cheese on the floor that were being carried off by ants.

While I was looking, I noticed a rough draft of a letter in his desk drawer. It was an application for a job as a sporting goods salesman. In his list of qualifications he stated that his last job had been as a salesman with a sporting goods firm that had gone out of business. He said nothing about ever having been an insurance salesman. I didn't know what to think.

The only other thing I saw that interested me was a pile of dirty clothes on his closet floor. I remembered then how Harry had been wearing the same clothes for so long.

I was really beginning to feel like a detective. The next day I dug up all the old fraternity records and looked up Harry. I found out that he lived in a small town in the Eastern part of the state and that his father was manager of a textile factory there. At the bottom of the page, added in a later hand was. "Occupation—Insurance salesman for State Life."

For the first time that summer I began to think about collecting the rent from Harry. I must admit, I hadn't been much of a house manager. As a matter of fact, Gene Birch was the only person I had collected the rent from. And that was only because he walked in my room with the money one night.

By this time there were several bills overdue, so I decided I'd better get busy and collect some rent to pay them.

I found Harry in his room late one night. The lights were on and he was lying on his unmade bed, fully clothed, staring up at the ceiling. The window was closed, it was hot, and I was sure I could smell some kind of cheese.

As soon as I came in he turned his head in my direction and shot a frown-grin at me. The whole time we talked he never got off the bed or even sat up. He just lay there.

"Come in, Pete old boy. Come in. What can I do for you?"

I fell into his armchair and lit a cigarette. "I've got to collect the rent. Need the money to pay the bills. If I don't pay soon, we won't have any water and electricity around here."

"Well, Pete." He cleared his throat for a while. "I phoned about my car money last night. It should be here by tomorrow, so I can pay you then."

I was feeling pretty mean so I said, "Don't you have any money with you?"

He laughed. "Flat broke, Pete."

"What's happened to the money you made selling insurance in this red-hot territory?"

He never batted an eye. "Didn't you know? I haven't been selling insurance for several weeks. I made some good money, but it's all in my college fund."

"Why did you quit?" I knew perfectly well he never had started.

"Well, I decided the time could be better spent studying. It wouldn't do me a bit of good to make a million dollars if I couldn't get into law school. And stay there. So I've started studying. You know, I haven't been in school for seven years. I've been spending five or six hours a day in the law library, reading."

That night I had a good laugh to myself over that. The idea of Harry reading for five or six hours a day was ridiculous.

The next day after classes I noticed that Harry wasn't in his room. I didn't have anything to do that afternoon, so I decided to go down to the law library just to prove to myself what a big joke it really was.

But he was there. His back was to the entrance so he didn't see me. He was reading one book, and there were three or four more stacked up in front of him. I didn't speak to him. I just went out and walked and tried to figure it out. Maybe we had been wrong about Harry all along. Maybe he really was going to law school and had been straight with us the whole time. On the other hand, maybe he had a hunch I would check on his story.

I told Gene about it that night. He didn't seem at all surprised. He just sat for a while and thought. I lit a cigarette.

"I still doubt that he's really going to law school," he said. "But that doesn't mean he's been lying to us. If a person believes something is true and tells someone else, he isn't lying is he? At least not intentionally. I think this fits with the other things we've figured out. Harry no doubt thinks he's going to law school. But I doubt it. If he has enough money to go to school for three years, he surely has enough to eat three square meals a day. Doesn't it seem that way to you?"

"I guess so. The guy's really sick isn't he?"

"I think he is."

"I wonder how a guy like that ever got to be a Gamma?"

"I doubt seriously that he's the only Gamma who turned out this way."

"It makes you a little uncomfortable, doesn't it? You hear so many statistics proving how successful Gammas are. It's always given me a nice secure feeling."

I was being serious, but Gene laughed. "You had better watch your step. Harry probably felt the same way."

For about a week I worried so much about myself that I almost forgot about Harry. Exams weren't too far off so I started studying furiously trying to make up for all the loafing I had done that summer. I made up a new set of books for the house and tried to collect some rent money. And I spent a lot of time wondering what I'd be doing in seven years. Once I looked in the mirror and smiled with my mouth turned down. It was amazing how that one little expression could make anyone look like Harry.

But after a while I stopped worrying so much about it all. Things had always taken care of themselves before, and I guessed they still would.

I got curious about Harry again and started checking by the law library every day. He was always there, reading with a stack of books in front of him. I was always careful not to let him see me.

The law library was the only place I ever saw Harry. He left the house before I got up and came in after I went to bed. One time I did see him on the campus. He was sitting on a bench with his head drooping down on his chest. I think he was asleep.

About a week and a half before school was over, Harry stopped going to the library and took to his room again. Sometimes he wouldn't close the door, and I could see him lying on his bed, dressed, staring at the ceiling.

One day I decided to make a final effort to collect his rent. As usual, he was lying on the bed, staring at the ceiling. For the first time, I noticed how much Harry had changed over the summer. When he first came to the Gamma house he was sunburned and a little chubby. I guess he had lost twenty pounds. And his skin was a sickly pale color. When he produced his frown-smile he seemed to be the ghost of Harry Meggs I had met at the first of the summer.

It was useless to ask him for the rent. He made some feeble excuse about the people not paying him for his car yet.

"How long you planning to stay?" I said.

"Well, I'd like to go directly to law school from here. Could I stay until September the seventh?"

"Afraid not. The house will be locked up between the end of summer school and the beginning of fall semester."

"You couldn't leave me a key? I could lock it up when I'm not here."

"I can't do that, Harry."

"Well," he stared up at the ceiling, "I guess I'll just go home for a while."

The upstairs telephone in the Gamma house was next to my room. Two days after my last conversation with Harry, I was sitting at my desk reading a paperback western. It was about nine o'clock when I heard him on the phone. I recognized his voice right away and stopped reading to listen. As soon as his call got through he started shouting over the phone.

"Sorry to call collect, Dad, but I'm using a friend's phone—

"I've decided to take you up on your offer—

"No. I think I'll thumb home. I'll give you a ring if I can't get to the house—

"I know, Dad, I'm willing to start out in the mill. But I learn fast. You know that."

The next morning Harry was gone, and that was the end of it.

I've been out of school for a year now. You wouldn't believe this, but I'm working for an insurance company. I have a pretty nice apartment and date some nice girls without having to worry about being trapped.

I never did see or hear of Harry again. But now and then I think about him. I try not to do that too much though, because it scares me a little.

I'm thinking about changing jobs now, and sometimes I think that the same thing could happen to me that happened to Harry. But the fear doesn't last long. After all, Harry was pretty sick. And he was just one in a million.


## REVEALING THEME THROUGH CHARACTER:
Assignment 29

1. How does the first line of "The Day After Tomorrow" indicate that the narrator is about to undergo an initiation through the contact he is to have with Harry?

2. Why does Pete Stevens indicate a dislike for Harry so early in the story? What function does this feeling of dislike serve as the narrative progresses?

3. What advantage does the author gain for himself in choosing summer school as the setting for his story?

4. Comment on four specific areas in which Harry seems to be a success and then emerges as a failure.

5. Comment on four objects that are used to point up Harry's inadequacy in learning to get along in life.

6. Show four similar areas in which Pete himself seems to be uncertain of his own ability.

7. Does the author justify himself for devoting so much attention to the delineation of a mediocre character?

8. What final point or truth does the narrator perceive through Harry and exactly when in the story does he relate this truth to himself and his own future?

9. Comment on the point or theme your own second story conveys through the delineation of the main character.

10. Hand in your second story to your instructor who will return it to you with comments for revision.

"The Day After Tomorrow" is a quiet story. It never grabs the reader by the shoulder or shouts what it has to say. Such effect as it may have is gained by beckoning the reader along, asking him to regard Harry Meggs through the days of a slow summer and by implication know him in all his summers. It was written out of Charles Nisbet's own belief that by looking at others you can find out something about yourself and the world around you.

Nisbet is not writing from a theme but into one. He knows just as well as you do that a morality tale is not good fiction. But when it is serious, good fiction does come out of what you believe or what you are finding out about belief. Your theme may rise from a new, passionate idea or from a long process of discovery. In the end, it must say for you, through symbol, statement, characterization, or a fusion of many devices, what you have come to believe about others and about the world.

## PART THREE

# A WRITER PRODUCES

# 12

# Hints for Revision

Your urge to create has forced you into the work of writing a story. From the deep well of memory, through the power of the imagination and some understanding of the writing process, you have attempted to project a fictional world containing people in action. The idea or point in your narrative is supported by a style that suits your material. In handing your work to your instructor, you have already begun to test its appeal to a reader.

When your instructor gives you his comments, you may agree with them, reject them, or incorporate them in setting up critical opinions of your own. You may decide to test your story by reading it to a friend. Whatever you decide, you will probably need a few suggestions for revision.

Suppose you begin by taking a second look at your title.

What of this title? How well does it stand up in relation to the material of the narrative itself? Titles can work for a story in many ways. They also have many sources. Sometimes a title stays in hiding and then appears out of the context of the narrative almost at the moment of completion. At other times an editor may reject the author's label and insist on one of his own choice. A title can even be suggested by a writer in irony and then fix itself to a narrative never to be detached. This happened to Ford Madox's Ford's best novel, *The Good Soldier.* Ford says, in dedicating the novel:

This book was originally called by me *The Saddest Story* but since it did not appear till the darkest days of the war were upon us, Mr. Lane importuned me with letters and telegrams—I was by that time engaged in other pursuits!—to change the title, which he said would at that date render the book unsaleable. One day, when I was on parade, I received a final wire of appeal from Mr. Lane, and the telegraph being reply-paid I seized the reply-form and wrote in hasty irony: "Dear Lane, Why not *The Good Soldier*?" To my horror six months later the book appeared under that title.

An editor said to me recently in discussing a manuscript, "The only thing wrong with the title is that it has been used before." In all your work, the title should be original with you, and not resemble too closely any used in the past. Ask yourself whether your title fits your material. Does it have the quality of intriguing your reader? Specifically, what is its relationship to the whole intention of your story?

In reinforcing a point or theme, a title that may at first appear commonplace can gain a power of its own. Shirley Jackson's "The Lottery" is a shocking parable about the survival of the scapegoat superstition in our own day. The rite of drawing lots to see who will be chastized for the village in a ritual of atonement results in the stoning of a woman on what first appears to be any ordinary day in any ordinary town. Because "The Lottery" is a cruel story, the title comes to carry a stone of its own.

A title that at first appears to have one meaning may take on multiple meanings for a reader as he absorbs the idea of a narrative. This is true of Flannery O'Connor's title, "A Good Man Is Hard to Find." In the context of the tale—whose final pages are quoted later in this chapter—the word *good* might at first mean a provider. But then we begin to see that *good* is related in a special way to the necessity for recognizing the presence of evil in the world. And so, the person to whom the title is given—for a title is a gift to the reader—senses that further significance.

A title may reflect the subject matter of the story, and if the narrative is a powerful one, an old word will gain new strength by association with the approach of a writer to his material. "The Dead," by James Joyce, gives us again a word we use more than we realize, whether we like to use it or not. Nobody can read through the last tremendous lines of this story without gaining an entirely new conception of the word *dead*.

Again, a title may be a capsule account of the action you are presenting. Ernest Hemingway's "The Short Happy Life of Francis Macomber" describes a situation in which a man, having redeemed himself after a cowardly action, is granted only a short time to live happily in a world where fear has no part. When Francis Macomber's wife shoots him, she puts a period after his life and after the title of the tale.

At the other pole is Faulkner's *The Sound and the Fury*, which suggests the atmosphere and emotional tone of the Compson novel. This title comes from the passage in *Macbeth* beginning, "Tomorrow, and tomorrow, and tomorrow, creeps in this petty pace from day to day, to the last syllable of recorded time"—which has been combed through by many writers.

Think of your title as a lure to attract your reader. It may be elusive or symbolic. It may fascinate in a way a reader finds repulsive but cannot resist. It may invite, demanding to be investigated. A good title is a hint, a suggestion, or a declaration that leads a reader into the beginning of your story and propels him toward the end.

## TESTING YOUR TITLE: Assignment 30

As a final check, ask yourself the following questions. Is my title misleading in that it suggests a story unlike the one I am writing? Is my title too obscure? Is it pretentious? Is it in sympathy with the style I am using and with the point I want my story to make?

In opening your narrative you have probably made one of the following choices: (1) You have taken a straight chronological line from your first incident to the last; (2) You have used a flashback at the start to draw your reader into prior action; (3) You have started at some off-balance point, as if taking it for granted that the reader had knowledge of the story before. Your true opening, wherever your starting point in the time-pattern, and wherever the physical location of the beginning, lies in that moment when the problem with which you are dealing becomes apparent.

The simplest beginning is probably with the moment that initiates the action. Do you remember the student plot-outline of the boy who met the man in the car and found out that the stranger who offered him a ride was a murderer? The meeting of those two characters does not follow anything that came before, but it does demand that something should result from it. Here the problem is apparent right at the start of the action.

On the other hand, some straight-line chronological stories concern themselves almost entirely with the result of an action. *The Scarlet Letter*, for instance, is a study of the consequences of adultery. Hawthorne's logical beginning is in the moment in the prison when the unfaithful wife meets her husband after a long absence and recognizes him. The husband's cry for revenge makes the problem of the story apparent.

Hawthorne writes a leisurely opening, too leisurely, many people say. We read through a rambling introduction, a symbolic sequence at the prison door, and are forced to witness a crowd scene before we arrive at the true start. But since the adultery itself is over, Hawthorne has excellent reasons for taking his time in getting underway. He wants us to see why his characters are what they are before he plunges us into the story. In the aesthetic structure of his book, the beginning has its right, true place.

"A Good Man Is Hard to Find" has its own starting place when the maniac who murders an entire family first makes contact with the grandmother, through the newspaper account of him. Flannery O'Connor then writes the narrative in two parts that are almost like the two halves of an apple, showing an action and then showing its results, going through chronologically without any break in time. The fast pace of the beginning and the violence of the ending complement each other perfectly in the pattern of the story. Again, it is in the opening paragraph that the problem becomes apparent.

The grandmother didn't want to go to Florida. She wanted to visit some of her connections in east Tennessee and she was seizing at every chance to change Bailey's mind. Bailey was the son she lived with, her only boy. He was sitting on the edge of his chair at the table, bent over the orange sports section of the *Journal*. "Now look here, Bailey," she said, "see here, read this," and she stood with one hand on her thin hip and the other rattling the newspaper at his bald head. "Here this fellow that calls himself The Misfit is aloose from the Federal Pen and headed toward Florida and you read what it says he did to these people. Just you read it. I wouldn't take my children in any direction with a criminal like that aloose in it. I couldn't answer my conscience if I did."

No word in this passage is there by chance. The family does go to Florida, does meet the criminal, and does die. The grandmother is the last victim of The Misfit. The story is as simple and as terrible as that, with the ending prepared for right at the beginning. Make sure the starting point of your own story foreshadows the results that will appear at the end.

One of Ernest Hemingway's finest stories begins, "It was now lunch time and they were all sitting under the double green fly of the dining tent pretending that nothing had happened." This is a superb lead into a flashback, or dramatic presentation of what has gone on before the main event of the narrative. Who are they? Where are they and what are they pretending? Not many people could read these opening words without being driven to find out where they lead.

If you start off casually, almost as if your reader knows the story already, you may run into the danger of taking too much knowledge on his part for granted. It is all right to take a confiding tone but dangerous to confuse the reader by expecting him to know as much at the start as you do. If he does, you have no reason for making him your confidant. In the very first sentence of your story, give him a hint of what lies ahead.

Charles Nisbet's "The Day After Tomorrow" hints in the first line at what the summer school interval will bring, but the story has its roots in the fear of failure that has existed during the entire college life of the narrator. When Pete Stevens says, "It was during summer school, after I had graduated, that I got to know Harry Meggs," the narrator's doubt about his own future is foreshadowed.

"The Day After Tomorrow" follows Edgar Allan Poe's advice that the very first sentence of a narrative should directly or indirectly tend to bring about the preconceived effect for which the writer is striving. Look at your own first sentence and your own first scene. Remember that your beginning has to pull your reader into a story. A beginning must say, "Stay with me! Hear me, I have a thing to tell you!"

## TESTING YOUR BEGINNING:   Assignment 31

In checking your story, ask yourself whether you have started too early by writing an opening scene or paragraph that is superfluous, uninteresting, misleading. Or have you started too late, cutting your reader into the story, failing to orient him into the scene? Have you made it clear from the start who your people are and where they are? Is your reader straightway given a hint of the problem they are facing?

Repetition can be used effectively in many ways. A word, or phrase, for instance, may be reiterated to underscore its importance in the narrative pattern. In "A Good Man Is Hard to Find," the key word echoes and re-echoes through the climactic scene in which the grandmother is killed. "I know you're a good man," the old lady says to The Misfit just before he shoots her. This is only one of the many times she insists on the lie she wants so desperately to believe.

"You shouldn't call yourself The Misfit because I know you're a good man at heart. I can just look at you and tell."

"I just know you're a good man," she said desperately. "You're not a bit common."
"Nome, I ain't a good man."

"Jesus," the old lady cried. "You've got good blood."

After shooting her, The Misfit says, "She would of been a good woman if it had been somebody there to shoot her every minute of her life."

"Haircut," a famous Ring Lardner story of a small-town

sadist is narrated by a barber who has a tremendous admiration for his deceased customer. To the barber, Jim Kendall is a fine figure of a joker, but the author, through the use of repetitive irony, makes us hate the dead man. One of the most effective reiterations is that of the phrase, "He certainly was a card," which is threaded into the story more than a dozen times.

A repeated word can intensify the atmosphere of your story. The dull, dark tone of "The Fall of the House of Usher" is heightened by the constant references to the tarn into which the house itself finally falls. Poe's genius draws us in spite of ourselves to the house with its eye-like windows and to the tarn that serves as a motif for the theme of decay.

> the lurid tarn that lay in unruffled lustre
> looking down within the tarn
> the dim tarn into which they all looked down
> the still waters of the tarn
> and the deep and dank tarn at my feet closed sullenly and silently

## THE USES OF REPETITION:   Assignment 32

Make certain that every word, phrase or sentence which echoes through your story directs the reader toward the meaning rather than promises him a revelation he will not receive and so becomes an aimless or obstructive element in the narrative pattern.

A transition is the period, place, or passage in which a change is effected. In a story, this change may be gradual or sudden, a long bridge or a short one. Usually, it is best to make your transitions as brief and as unobtrusive as possible, using them as "lead strings" to bridge time and place so gracefully that your reader is unaware of being led at all.

Before me is a story that is no more than a calendar. "For five nights . . . the first week of March . . . it took quite a while . . . it took several days. . . ." The monotony of reiterated time sequences detracts from such small power as the narrative possesses. The writer simply does not understand that a passage in time, or a movement in place, is important only when it defines the action. Transitional elements that are threaded through a narrative just for their own sake should be struck out at once.

Sometimes a short transition can be used to give the reader a hint of what comes next. The Flannery O'Connor story contains such transitions as "The next morning the grandmother was the first one in the car, ready to go." This suggests what the character is like and also moves her forward in time and place, but you never feel that the writer is deliberately shoving the grandmother forward while you read the story. Transitions are most effective when the reader is not aware of them at all.

O'Connor knows how to change pace. Now she moves the action quickly, now she slows down the narrative by introducing a quiet interval as a prelude to violence. The story of the grandmother and The Misfit also gives us an ending which inevitably follows the beginning. Paradoxically, this inevitable ending appears to emerge spontaneously.

Alone with The Misfit, the grandmother found that she had lost her voice. There was not a cloud in the sky nor any sun. There was nothing around her but woods. She wanted to tell him that he must pray. She opened and closed her mouth several times before anything came out. Finally she found herself saying, "Jesus, Jesus," meaning, Jesus will help you, but the way she was saying it, it sounded as if she might be cursing.

"Yes'm," The Misfit said as if he agreed. "Jesus thrown everything off balance. It was the same case with Him as with me except He hadn't committed any crime and they could prove I had committed one because they had the paper on me. Of course," he said, "they never shown me my papers. That's why I sign myself now. I said long ago, you get you a signature and sign everything you do and keep a copy of it. Then you'll know what you done and you can hold up the crime to the punishment and see do they match and in the end you'll have something to prove you ain't been treated right. I call myself The Misfit," he said, "because I can't make what all I done wrong fit what all I gone through in punishment."

There was a piercing scream from the woods, followed closely by a pistol report. "Does it seem right to you, lady, that one is punished a heap and another ain't punished at all?"

"Jesus!" the old lady cried. "You've got good blood! I know you wouldn't shoot a lady! I know you come from nice people! Pray! Jesus, you ought not to shoot a lady. I'll give you all the money I've got!"

"Lady," The Misfit said, looking beyond her far into the woods, "there never was a body that give the undertaker a tip."

There were two more pistol reports and the grandmother raised her head like a parched old turkey hen crying for water and called, "Bailey Boy, Bailey Boy!" as if her heart would break.

"Jesus was the only One that ever raised the dead," The Misfit continued, "and He shouldn't have done it. He thrown everything off balance. If He did what He said, then it's nothing for you to do but throw away everything and follow Him, and if He didn't, then it's nothing for you to do but enjoy the few minutes you got left the best way you can—by killing somebody or burning down his house or doing some other meanness to him. No pleasure but meanness," he said and his voice had become almost a snarl.

"Maybe He didn't raise the dead," the old lady mumbled, not knowing what she was saying and feeling so dizzy that she sank down in the ditch with her legs twisted under her.

"I wasn't there so I can't say He didn't," The Misfit said. "I wisht I had of been there," he said, hitting the ground with his fist. "It ain't right I wasn't there because if I had been there I would of known. Listen lady," he said in a high voice, "if I had of been there I would of known and I wouldn't be like I am now." His voice seemed about to crack and the grandmother's head cleared for an instant. She saw the man's face twisted close to her own as if he were going to cry and she murmured, "Why you're one of my babies. You're one of my own children!" She reached out and touched him on the shoulder. The Misfit sprang back as if a snake had bitten him and shot her three times through the chest. Then he put his gun down on the ground and took off his glasses and began to clean them.

Hiram and Bobby Lee returned from the woods and stood over the ditch, looking down at the grandmother who half sat and half lay in a puddle of blood with her legs crossed under her like a child's and her face smiling up at the cloudless sky.

Without his glasses, The Misfit's eyes were red-rimmed and pale and defenseless-looking. "Take her off and throw her where you thrown the others," he said, picking up the cat that was rubbing itself against his leg.

"She was a talker, wasn't she?" Bobby Lee said, sliding down the ditch with a yodel.

"She would of been a good woman," The Misfit said, "if it had been somebody there to shoot her every minute of her life."

"Some fun!" Bobby Lee said.

"Shut up, Bobby Lee," The Misfit said. "It's no real pleasure in life."

The story pauses after The Misfit kills the grandmother, puts his gun down on the ground, then takes off his glasses and begins to clean them. It pauses again when he tells Bobby Lee that the old lady would have been a good woman if there had been someone there to shoot her every minute of her life. The true ending comes when The Misfit announces that there is no real pleasure in life.

Aristotle says that an ending must, of necessity, follow something else but that nothing, of necessity, follows the ending. A terminal point of "A Good Man Is Hard to Find" is the death of the grandmother, which was prepared for from the start. The twist is The Misfit's admission—after having said earlier, "No pleasure but meanness"—that the multiple murders have not brought him pleasure either, that there is, in fact, no pleasure at all. The admission gives added depth to the story.

Every story can have a legitimate twist at the ending. Or even a surprise. But after the surprise the reader should think, "I ought to have known."

Just as in the beginning a problem is made apparent, so in the ending the problem is resolved, or at the very least a resolution is hinted at. But again, an ending should emerge through the characters and their situation rather than be thrown at the reader by the author. Only then will the ending be a discovery for the person who has gone with you from the first word of your story to the last.

## TESTING THE ENDING:   Assignment 33

Since the beginning and the ending of your story should act reciprocally on each other, look once more at your final scene, asking yourself the following questions. Does the ending of my story go into areas that are not foreshadowed from the start of my narrative? Is the final scene a resolution of my characters' problem, or at least a hint of the resolution? Is the surprise element in my ending legitimate? Will my reader look back and say, "The final twist has cheated me," or will he say instead, "I should have known"?

Throughout the process of rewriting, you will of course be doing much more than testing the beginning, the transitions, the repetitions, and the ending of a story. The truth is that knowing when to stop working on a story is a discovery each person has to make for himself. You can get all kinds of advice, but your problem will be learning how much of it to take seriously.

One novelist, for instance, thinks it good to rewrite endlessly, endlessly, endlessly, and keep on rewriting after a narrative is finished. Another says that he refuses to look at a story once he has gone through the ending, but this attitude can be just as dangerous as the one that forces an author to keep on picking at a piece of work long after the life has gone out of it. Still, how does one make a revision of a story before sending it out on its own?

Hemingway said, when asked how much rewriting he does,

"It depends. I re-wrote the ending of *Farewell to Arms*, the last page of it, thirty-nine times before I was satisfied."
*Interviewer:* "Was there some technical problem there? What was it that had stumped you?"
*Hemingway:* "Getting the words right."

Try to get your words right, whether you are cutting, expanding, or changing some underlying current of your story. Only then will you fulfill what Hemingway goes on to say is the artist's function.

. . . you make something through your invention that is not a representation but a whole new thing truer than anything true and alive, and you make it alive, and if you make it well enough, you give it immortality. That is why you write and for no other reason that you know of. But what about all the reasons that no one knows?
From "The Art of Fiction," by Ernest Hemingway
in *The Paris Review*

## 13

# The Finished Story

The idea for the story which follows came to its author after a visit to a state prison near the southern town in which she was born. Her purpose in the visit was to bring comfort to men who had broken the law and to give them hope, but at the camp she felt so virtuous she began to question her own motives. Afterward, she wrote this story for a class in creative writing.

The author did not sit down and say, "Through a style of my own, I intend to create a character, reveal through action the subconscious motives she never understands, and leave her in a moment of frustration." A writer does not work that way. But in creating the story, the author did use techniques of expression that are common to all writers and that had been discussed in her class.

## THE PROUD AND VIRTUOUS

DORIS BETTS

She could see the row of them working, their backs turned sullenly to the sun, the arms rising and falling almost languidly in the August heat. Things glinted sometimes in their hands; picks or shovels or spattered buckets caught the sun and held it as brightly as little distant mirrors. Occasionally some of them shouted back and forth, for a head would come up, and down the road a second head to listen; and then the second man would do something by reply, nod or wipe his neck with a bandanna or go for fresh air. She couldn't hear them, of course; they were too far away for that. She could just move the edge of blue ruffled curtain in the living room and look down the long brown field to the highway where they had worked all that morning since the school bus passed.

Their soundlessness made her think of ants moving; she knew they must live and communicate and move toward a purpose (completion of the highway), but they remained to her some distant, strange and very tiny species. Some kind of bug, she thought with distaste, and her white flesh crawled at the thought.

Mildred Stuart dropped the curtain and glanced toward the clock that had belonged to her grandmother. Half-past ten and no one for lunch today but herself. The major work was done too—dishes and bedmaking and sweeping and dusting. It was one of those days that left time for extra things: the back windows, or trying out a new recipe, or the bathroom fixtures. She supposed she really ought to do the bathroom fixtures.

She had started upstairs when the telephone rang and she recognized the anxious voice of her neighbor, Carrie Nash. Carrie was always anxious; she lived in a world where the catastrophe was always just about to happen—blizzard or accident or heart attack. Perhaps it was having eight children that made her feel that way, as if one were more divided up, susceptible.

"Are you all right, Millie?"

"Of course I'm all right!" She sat at the telephone table touching her crisp hair daintily, a little pleased with Carrie for calling. "You're a worry wart, for goodness' sake! You're worse than George." (Much worse, some honest corner of her mind put in. George didn't worry at all, except about the poor Oriental farming methods, which weren't any of his business really.)

"Well, I just wish George were home today, that's all. Where'd you say he'd gone?" Carrie Nash had already called twice that morning but she had a terrible memory for things. It was probably because her mind was always extended in front of her, groping for tragedy.

"Into town to price some stock," said Mildred patiently. "There's a sale on hogs at the market." As she said it she could picture George leaning halfway into the pen, his eyes wide with pleasure as the hogs came by. That was George all right; a good ham interested him far more than any human female curve. Her own, for instance.

"I sure would feel better if George was there with you," Carrie said. "And none of your kids getting home till the late bus. Looks like those men are going to be there most of the day."

"Carrie, they're *not* going to bother me." While she talked Mildred ran one palm around the other forearm, smoothing the pale hairs evenly, a habit she had acquired when she was a young girl. She had nice arms, slender and tapering, she thought, and the hairs like down on the breasts of birds. "They're way down at the highway, Carrie. None of them will be up here."

"Thieves and murderers and the good Lord knows what all," sighed Mrs. Nash. "It'll be a mercy if George doesn't come home and find you cold and dead on the floor!"

Mildred could not help but laugh at this, the picture of herself chilling delicately on the kitchen linoleum, her trim feet pointing mutely at the ceiling. It would serve him right, she thought. It would make him wonder what she had been like inside. Aloud she said: "You've no faith in human beings. There's some good in everybody, Carrie. You've got to depend on the goodness of people."

"Somebody's depended on it once too often with that crew or they wouldn't be where they are," snapped Carrie. "Any of them got a ball and chain? Or striped suits?"

Feeling ridiculous, Mildred peeked beyond the blue curtain again but it was too far and the sun was too bright to be sure. She thought there was one striped suit among them but it was hard to tell in the glare.

"What would it matter if there was?" she said.

"Those are the bad ones. The lifers. You watch out none of them breaks loose down there, Millie. They don't have anything to lose, those lifers."

"I've got a gun," said Mildred. "Now quit worrying." She didn't really know where George kept the gun or how it worked but it sounded good. It sounded important, like the things women said in movies.

But after she had hung up the telephone she went to the front doorway and stood there, shading her eyes to see if any of them were wearing the striped suits like Carrie said. It seemed to her now there were at least four of them, and perhaps another, almost out of sight. When she went inside her eyes were full of sun so that there were yellow splotches all across the room. I wish Carrie Nash had left well enough alone, she thought irritably. I've been doing fine all morning.

Mildred Stuart always said nobody had ever done her a real harm in her life—she'd never been robbed, for instance, and the time she'd lost her glasses in the store a clerk had kept them for her. It was all in the attitude you took toward people; if you naturally expected a man to stab you in the back, why, the knife was as good as in your ribs, she always said. That's what she taught Margaret and Peter too, though George said it wasn't fair to them.

"What kids ought to learn in this world is to purely mind their own business," George was always saying. That was one thing you had to say for George; he was the greatest Own Business Minder in the world.

But that was typical of the way George was in everything. She'd read a sentence in a history book once that described George perfectly. "After the crisis is over," it said, "the farmer or peasant is the first to revert to conservatism." That was the kind of sentence Mildred liked, the kind that rolled richly off the tongue and sounded important by itself; that was the way she wanted to talk, so people would notice. Sometimes movie heroines talked that way when they were involved in great international movements. There were some of those sentences in the Psalms and in Isaiah and in a little book called *Famous Speeches* she had bought for Margaret. The Gettysburg Address had them, and Winston Churchill and some of the radio talks of Franklin Roosevelt. She certainly did miss Franklin Roosevelt; the others sounded like mandolins beside him.

But all this wasn't getting the day's work done and Mildred put it out of her mind. It was just that she got bored sometimes.

Upstairs Mildred cleaned the bathroom fixtures with her usual grimaces of disgust, leaving the room whitely sterile and smelling like an operating chamber. Sometimes she stopped and looked on tiptoe out the small high window. The men were still working on the road; it seemed they had not moved an inch. She wondered if now and then one of them glanced calculatingly up the hill to where her trim house sat, measured the distance and took into account the honeysuckle mat between and the remnant of old stone wall that might have served as cover. This thought tugged at her mind until she kept going back to stare out nervously, half expecting to see a striped suit sprinting up the hill, the bullets kicking puffs of dust about the running feet.

I could kill Carrie Nash, thought Mildred impatiently. She's made me nervous.

She kept the radio going while she ate lunch, although this was no comfort to her. She kept leaving the table to glance out a front window, half afraid the broadcast might have covered the excitement of an escape so that the renegade might be already standing in her living room.

Lunch was tasteless; the toasted sandwiches sandpapered her gums, the cheese seemed rubbery, the coffee lingered on her tongue with a peculiar bitterness. When the telephone rang she clattered her coffee cup into the saucer and caught at her throat. Then she realized it must be Carrie again and composed herself to speak coolly. I won't have you frightening me, Carrie, she would say. I simply won't have it.

But when she lifted and spoke into the mouthpiece it was George's voice on the other end.

"Mildred? Is that you, Mildred?" George always opened his conversations this way, irritating her beyond endurance and tempting her to say no, it was Lana Turner or Amelia Earhart or Helen of Troy.

"Yes," she snapped impatiently. "It's me, George." Sometimes she had the feeling that if she should squat in the hall of an evening

George would come through and drop his coat upon her without noticing. This thought made her especially angry with him and she sat at the phone with her face set.

"Look, I thought I'd get home early in the afternoon but Pat Walkins wants me to go by the county agent's office. They're giving away some experimental wheat to see if this section can make a crop."

Mildred experienced complete and overwhelming boredom, the way she nearly always did at George's progressive farming. "Oh," she said almost contemptuously. "New wheat."

"You need anything from town?"

An armed guard, she thought irritably. The state militia. But aloud she said without much interest: "A box of aspirin. Oh, and buy me a magazine, will you?"

There was a silence that was calculated to give her time to take back this unreasonable request. George hated to buy magazines; drugstores were so cluttered, he said, that you were always expecting to knock things over. George was a fairly awkward man, with hands and feet that always seemed to be going out in all directions, and he generally did manage to upset something, looking woebegone about the whole business.

Finally, seeing she would not give in, he grunted: "What kind of magazine?"

She felt a glow of triumph. "Oh, movies, I guess. Or one of the fashion magazines."

George did not exactly snort but Mildred was sure if he had not been at a public telephone he would surely have snorted. He was an expert at this noise; it always sounded like a mule drinking, having suddenly got water up his nostrils. It was, thought Mildred now, an exceedingly irritating sound and she waited for him to make it. As it was, she heard a faint and unmistakable sniffle.

"On second thought, bring both magazines," she said vengefully, and was about to hang up when she remembered the other thing. "They've got a chain gang working down on the road today," she said.

"That so? Needs it bad on that curve. Putting on shoulders, I expect."

"I expect so," said Mildred, and waited.

"Well, anything else?"

She could have throttled him with the telephone wire. "Nothing," she said dryly. "Not a thing, George. Enjoy your wheat seed." It sounded rather as if she were speaking to an out-of-sorts canary.

When they had hung up Mildred sat for a few minutes eyeing the phone and reflecting on Carrie's suggestion that George might come home to find her cold and dead on the kitchen linoleum. He might, too, she thought with some satisfaction. How like him not to consider it, never to worry about her, always to take her for granted! She felt like a competent electrical system that warmed up his bath water, toasted his bread, kept the beer cold. He might open the fuse box if anything ceased to work, but normally he would bathe and munch toast and slurp beer and never notice it.

When she got back to the kitchen the coffee had gotten cold and she saw there were bread crumbs scattered all about her chair. I'll let it alone, she thought tiredly, until suppertime. The kids will be back here after school anyway.

It was the picture of Margaret and Peter tracking in dust and banging the breadbox and rattling through the refrigerator that suggested to her the magnanimous gesture. The minute she thought of it Mildred was amazed it had taken her so long. It was the kind of thing Carrie Nash would say was typical of her ("Absolutely typical, my dear")—the complete vindication of her whole philosophy that no one would harm a person who had trusted him. (Here she recalled angrily that George was forever comparing this attitude to the old theory of staring a wild animal in the eye to avoid being bitten; and how this was probably all right if the animal had read the same book you had. She could remember George comparing the two completely unrelated things, just as he had that horrible afternoon to the vacuum cleaner salesman. And the salesman such a gentleman, too, and so complimentary . . . something George would never think of being . . .)

Mildred broke off her thoughts and went back to the original inspiration. She would walk down to the highway herself (it was a public highway; there was nothing wrong in that) and she would nod and smile distantly the way she always did to working people, grocery boys and things. She might even, for good measure, seek out with her eyes the striped-suit men, looking at them compassionately and with understanding. It's all right, her eyes would tell them. I'm not afraid, you see.

She could almost picture the scene in the cell block (that was what they called them, wasn't it, cell blocks?) late that evening, the men nodding thoughtfully to one another and talking about the rather attractive mature woman who had passed them on the highway. "A real lady, she was," some of them would say respectfully, by their very tone making of her a symbol, a symbol of mercy and decency—all the values of a world they had by some lone act renounced. Perhaps then one of the men would begin to play some haunting tune on his harmonica and the prisoners would fall silent in their cells, lost in the thoughts that the unknown woman had called forth in them all. And there would be perhaps one sensitive-eyed young man who looked like Montgomery Clift; he would think of her long after that day had passed, he would be released, "go straight," build a whole new life around that momentary inspiration she had given him on a summer's day. When he was old he would say nostalgically to his children: "Once there was a lovely lady who believed in me . . ." and then he would let the sentence trail off, full of mystery and time and the faintest of perfumes . . .

Mildred woke from her reverie with abruptness as she thought of still a further act of kindness she might do, something more she could give these men. She would speak to the foreman; she would tell him what a hot day it was; she would suggest that later in the afternoon he bring the men to her back porch for cold water. No, not just that, real ice water (she thought happily), with real ice floating in the tall glasses and tinkling from side to side in their grimy, respectful hands. How they would look at her then! As if she were an angel condescending from some better world.

She was so excited that her hands were trembling while she dressed—the crisp green skirt, the fresh blouse, a string of pearls clasped chastely at the neck. As an afterthought she added a white rose to her hair. Too frivolous, she wondered? But then a white rose was never actually frivolous; that was for scarlet and fuchsia flowers; a white rose was like the unattainable.

When she was through Mildred examined herself carefully in the mirror. A *young* thirty, she thought, hardly looking like the mother of two school-age children, the wife of a "college-trained" farmer. Indeed, she had once been told she had a mouth like Gene Tierney's. She moved it back and forth in smiles and sneers into the glass. Again she touched with her finger tips the one white rose; yes, that was just right, that was absolutely the perfect touch.

Mildred had forgotten how hot it was outside until she stepped from the front door and the sun struck her whole body with the force of a physical blow. The faint touch of perspiration starting underneath the arms irritated her as though it were an insult; its presence was incongruous with the cool clothes, the flower in her hair. There was a wind blowing but it was as hot as sunlight; it was like the air that billows out of floor registers in the wintertime. She started from the house, feeling the wind and the crunch of dry grass underfoot and the pelting sunlight all as one sensation, some personal thing that was being done to her directly.

As she came down the hill and drew closer to where the men were working they began to watch her furtively, not lifting their heads. A thought struck her suddenly that was far more earthy than either the lady or the condescending angel: that perhaps they had not seen a woman in a long time, some of them for years. She became acutely conscious of the hot wind that was whipping her skirt between her legs, outlining her thighs sharply; she realized that the sun was behind her and everything must be transparent (the lacy nylon slip and the thin brassiere and pants) so that all of them could see her—the swell of stomach and the curve of breast and the shadowy suggestion of nipple, navel, triangle.

Mildred almost turned and ran when a man detached himself from the group and stepped out toward her, until she saw the gun propped carelessly across his arm.

"Hello, ma'am," he said. He did not seem pleased to see her. It was all wasted on him, she thought, even the flower.

"Hello," she said pleasantly. "It's awfully hot down here."

The man didn't offer any answer to this, as if such an obvious remark was beneath his comment, and Mildred began to feel chastened. He thinks I have no business here, she thought.

After a pause she said rather coldly, "Are you in charge?"

"Yessum, I'm the guard." He smelled of beer and she reflected that he was just the kind of man to have a thermos of cold beer while the prisoners worked thirstily in the hot sun. All the time she stood there with him she was aware of their eyes stealthily upon her and almost involuntarily she threw back her head so that the wind could show her dark hair, the contrast of the rose; she tilted her chin so they could see the string of pearls and the Gene Tierney mouth. Then she did an amazing thing. She did it very quickly as if that would keep anyone from noticing it was deliberate, even herself; she spread her feet so that the skirt clung to her legs and rushed in billows in between her thighs. I won't be prudish, some corner of her mind said to some other corner. It's really an act of compassion.

To the guard, without any change in her tone, Mildred said, "I wanted to tell you to bring the men up to the house late in the afternoon. I'll have ice water on the back porch." She decided to make some concession to the man's vanity; people in his position were usually strong on vanity. "And a piece of cake for you," she added, glancing up at him.

She observed that the man was fat and gross; there was stubble all across his face and streaks of light and dark where sweat ran down and had been wiped. There was something faintly obscene about him, as if he had absorbed all the contamination from his charges so that it clung to him in dirt and fat and whiskers. Mildred thought for one minute the lips slid back on the soiled teeth in something that was very like a knowing grin, but it was gone too fast. She could not tell. I do not like this man, she thought sharply. I do not like anything about him.

Almost jovially (with a tone of familiarity?) he said to her, "Yes, ma'am," and nodded his head. "Yessum, we'll be pleased to come. It's mighty hot." He ran his eyes along her hip and into the curve of waist insolently, and her face hardened. "Mighty generous of you," he added slyly.

Mildred nodded coolly to him and moved back up the hill, feeling the eyes as hot upon her as the ends of cigarettes. There had been two, she thought with a delicious shiver; there had been two striped suits among them. The guard had stepped over to the men; she heard the whispering and talk; somebody snickered, like a little boy. It seemed to her she must make a handsome picture as she moved away—the sun falling brightly about her head, pinpointing the white-and-greenness of her for one instant on the long brown hill. She forced herself to walk slowly so all of them could see that she was not afraid.

Back in the comparative coolness of the house Mildred swept the kitchen floor like a careful hostess in anticipation of callers, checked the ice cubes and added some jars of water to the refrigerator shelves. The thought of what she had done filled her with youthful excitement, so that she hummed snatches of old songs she had not thought of in years. For a minute she stopped by the telephone, debating whether to call Carrie about it; then she realized how much better it would sound when they had come and gone and all the dirty glassware sat around the kitchen. It would have to be boiled, she supposed, all of it boiled after they had handled and drunk from it. Carrie would say how typical it was that Mildred should have done such a thing. "I should never have had the courage, you may be sure of that," Carrie would tell her admiringly.

Mildred felt quite exhilarated by the whole afternoon. Looking down the long hill now was like watching a group of acquaintances whom she was soon to know better. This sense of familiarity sent her back upstairs to see herself in the long, cool mirror. The rose had wilted and she cast it down, making a disappointed face. Perhaps it was better not to wear it for the second time. Perhaps it was better to leave that bare wisp of memory so that they could argue about it later: "She had a flower in her hair, I'm sure of that."

"A flower, sure, a white one. I think it must have been a lily."

It seemed to Mildred that the waiting afternoon dragged by. She walked through the house nervously, poking at the unfrozen ice with an impatient finger, opening and closing the cabinet door where the glasses were. The jam-jar glasses would do, she thought, and the odd ones from a broken dime-store set, and after that the ones someone had given her that had the rather hideous painted vines. They would none of them notice the glasses anyway. They would all want to remember how she herself had looked.

By three o'clock she was nervous. Perhaps after all this had been a very foolish thing; perhaps once they got near the house they would all unite, grab her as hostage, take her in a group to the woods back of the house and there shred her of her clothes, savagely, like men who have nothing to lose any more, like starved men taking the skin from oranges. Mildred cringed at the thought of herself in their midst, naked and afraid, the brutal hands that would touch her, twist her, bend her back. Her shoulders jerked as she ran to pull the curtains and look at the men working harmlessly in the sun, their minds busy with the Lord knew what unspeakable plans! And where was the gun; what had George done with the foolish gun?

Mildred felt quite faint with her terror. What had she done after all? It had been an insane gesture, a moment of madness that had come upon her when she stepped into the sun. For a minute she was almost convinced that the thought had never entered her head until she stepped into the yard and had some sort of blind attack that left her senseless in the heat.

Once she began to be afraid, the hours flew; the hands of the clock seemed to circle wildly before her eyes and the echo of one quarter-hour striking would hardly die away before the next was starting. Like a death bell tolling, she thought nervously. Like the death bell in "Barbara Allan."

At five o'clock the men began to move and collect their tools. Mildred had been clenching her fists all during that last half hour, half believing the school bus would draw up in front of the house before they came and Peter and Margaret would come clattering in ahead of them. She sat thinking all this and yet a little ashamed of her willingness to involve the children in her danger. I could still call Carrie, she thought frantically, but she made no move toward the phone.

When the men began finally to shuffle into an awkward line and the mustard brown truck edged toward them down the highway (as if it had been waiting all this time drawn off the road somewhere), she gave up hoping for the school bus or for Carrie and went stiffly to the kitchen, where she stood against the refrigerator as if for a firing squad. They would be here in a minute, she thought; it would not take long, loading the truck and driving it up the narrow road and around the back yard to the porch, dropping the mesh door for the men to climb out. She pictured them riding up the hill, sitting quietly along the narrow benches like the carefully arranged dead, not saying anything or giving anything away but locking eyes now and then knowingly.

Mildred squared her shoulders, placed her palms against the coolness of the refrigerator. In a few minutes she would hear the wheezing of the motor as it brought them (the men in the striped suits) nearer to the house, nearer to where she waited. She closed her eyes in resignation, flattened her back to the door as though it were her marble slab.

She stood that way, waxen as a painted saint, for a few more minutes and then her eyes flew open and she was sharply aware of the silence about her. Even when she strained both her ears she could hear nothing but the buzzing of bees against the mat of honeysuckle in the yard and the closer hum of electric current at her back. She could not hear the truck coming at all, not even when she took a step forward and cocked her head.

In another minute she had walked to the back screen and from thence to a side window, and after that she ran through the house to the living room and flung the front door wide.

They were gone. The long brown hill stretched ahead of her to the deserted highway; there was not even a puff of dust to show where they had been or where the truck had passed. Unbelievingly she looked up the little road to the house, searched the trees for the outline of a sinister parked vehicle, looked for the blobs of stealthy men that might be anywhere, watching her.

But they were truly gone, the striped suits and the furtive glances and even the unshaved foreman—gone off in the truck without a word to her. She waited still another minute in case they had driven down the road for gasoline or turned the truck around, but when three shiny cars came round the curve and flicked brightly out of sight, she knew none of them was coming. They had all climbed into the truck in an orderly line and driven off and none of them was coming.

When she went back into the house Mildred slammed the door viciously behind her and stood motionless for an instant between the door and the faintly blowing curtains. She turned then on her heel and opened the door and slammed it a second time, louder than the first, so that the delicate china ash trays quivered on the coffee table and a magazine slithered to the rug. She said aloud: "The scum. The filthy scum."

After a while she worked purposefully through the house and back to the kitchen again, talking to herself. What could you expect from people like that? If they were decent they wouldn't be where they were, would they? She thought for one wild moment she might burst into outraged tears, like a teen-ager cheated out of a party.

But by the time Margaret and Peter came in from school she was much calmer. She didn't say anything about it to the children. As for them, they were too busy eating peanut-butter cake to see the ice cubes melting in the sink.

Before this story appeared in *Mademoiselle* and in *Best Short*

*Stories, 1957,* two known writers sensed Mrs. Betts' talent. In an unpublished letter, Pearl Buck wrote, "Mrs. Betts' stories are immature and have an obsession with death, but the writing itself reveals a perceptiveness which speaks well for the future." Marjorie Kinnan Rawlings said, "The Doris Betts stories are completely mature and effective, as fine as any published stories I have read in a long time."

*Mademoiselle* also published a first story by Louise Hardeman. Read Miss Hardeman's "The First Supper," and judge it for yourself. Do you believe an editor would consider it a story which, as Aldous Huxley suggests of all good writing, "gives meaning to life"?

# THE FIRST SUPPER

LOUISE HARDEMAN

They had lived in a house that a gargoyle might have designed. It sat on the top of a hill and all around it slanted untended shrubs and flower beds like things somebody had thrown out.

He had left that house in hatred and he had made a vow never to enter it again.

He was their only child who had offered them his love and trust and they had given it the same attention that they gave his school report card, which they looked at with one bored eye, anxious to return to their quarreling.

He had spun with them in a circle of purposeless rage. They had made wounds in him that he contained like his own rib cage. Every Sunday afternoon they said that everything was going to be different and that he need not worry any more. They had torn him apart and put him clumsily back together until, finally, he had hated them both.

He had gone away desiring vengeance. He would educate himself and in forgetting them, would become a Robert Frost or an Albert Schweitzer, living in dignity and quiet. Eventually, his life would be well-known and his parents would see themselves for what they were. If they survived that knowledge, they would come to him and implore his forgiveness.

But the years and the distance and the sacrifices he had made had brought about a change in himself he had not foreseen, so great that the man on the train and the boy who had been born to his parents might never have met each other. The man saw that his parents were not responsible for what they were, and saw also neither of them would ever be any different. His mother was a psychopath, a drunk. His father was just a plain drunk.

Because of that he was going to do the thing he had vowed never to do. And what propelled him was the heart of his transformation. Without having been asked, he was prepared to forgive his parents.

And so he had begun this long journey at the end of which waited a homecoming.

He had a compartment in the train (it was both his first as well as his last luxury) and he sat pressed against the window envisioning the life that would commence when the train left him and he would enter the small, antiquated station and face his parents.

His mother would have on a black dress with stains on it like polka dots and she would be wearing a lot of costume jewelry and a pill box hat with a torn veil lighting uncertainly on top of it. His father might still be wearing the grey gabardine suit that looked always as if it had just come from the bottom of a trunk. Probably they would both be drunk.

But that would not upset him the way it once did. Forgiveness would shield him. Gently he would greet them and patiently he would tell them of his plans for the coming year—that he had been accepted for a teaching position in the local high school and that he had rented a room in a boarding house near the school in order that he might walk to school and not deprive them of their car.

And immediately he saw the room in which the most important year of his life would be lived. He knew every part of it, as he had insisted that his landlady send a detailed description of it.

It was a room fit for a person divested of illusions. It was situated on the third floor and at the back of what was once a fine house. A bay window looked out on an old rose garden. A trash burner was its single means of heat and he planned to use that only in the coldest weather, for this was to be a year of self-denial and discipline and silence. A spiritual year.

He would rise early, before the sun, and cook his own meager breakfast on a hot plate. Then he would read or study until it was time to go to school. Each afternoon he would walk to his parents' house and work there. He would work in the yard or he would repair the house. If they were fighting or drinking he would continue with his work, like a servant pretending not to see or hear what was going on. And all the time into the soil of that yard and into the foundation and rafters of that house he would fuse his forgiveness.

Because he was free of illusions, he knew that nothing would change them. At the end of the year they would be the same, but for him it would end things properly. Almost, it would end things happily and he could go away again knowing that he had made of his vision a truth and he could begin to build something solid and good for himself.

Never would he in anger or sorrow say the words. Forgiveness would be his breath. It would come down like snow and cover everything, all the ugliness, and he would live in its midst—clean and cold and bright.

He reached into his coat pocket and brought out a worn copy of a letter which he had written his parents at least a month before and which they had never answered or may never have read.

"Dear Mother and Father," it began (he had always called them "Mama" and "Daddy" but that was not the sort of thing you could write down, not when you had undergone a transformation), "I'm sure you will be surprised to hear that I am coming home. It has been a long time since I left and, as you probably remember, I said I was never coming back. I acted very childishly then, but I think I have become a man since I've been away. I have had many enlightening experiences and I will never be the same again, for which I am grateful. I do not think many people ever really mature.

I have been working in a book store here and going to school when I could. Last month I graduated and I also got a teacher's certificate. What I plan to do is to teach at home for a year and then come back here to Graduate School so that I can teach on the college level. Don't bother about my room because I think it will be better for me to rent a room closer to the school. I would either have to buy a car or use yours if I lived at home. I am planning to come down on July 18. I'll see you then."

The few other letters he had written them had been very emotional. He was proud of the dispassionate quality of this one. He had signed it, inappropriately "As ever," because he could think of no other way.

Reading it over again, he realized he had forgotten to say which train he was taking so that they could not meet him at the station after all. He was surprised at the feeling of relief this gave him because he had made all the preparation that could be made, but, at least, this would give him a chance to get settled in the room before meeting his parents.

For the last four hours of the trip he dozed and when the train stopped to let him off, he awoke refreshed and feeling singularly competent.

He descended the steps onto the platform and looked back nostalgically at the departing train. When he turned around to pick up his baggage, there were his parents, protecting themselves with a folded newspaper from the light of the late afternoon sun.

The smell struck him like a rock—whiskey and cologne from his mother, whiskey and cigars from his father.

"Why didn't you tell us what train you were coming on?" asked his father, "we've been meeting trains all day."

"You look fine," said his mother, glaring at his father.

"You sure do," said his father, trying unsuccessfully to smooth out his irritated frown.

He couldn't speak.

"Well," said his mother after a while, putting her words cautiously together, "Let's go home. We've got a mighty good supper waiting."

He saw the old-fashioned kitchen with the single light that left most of the room in darkness and the table they ate on, covered in green plaid oilcloth and pushed up into a corner so that even as a child he had had to hold in his stomach in order to squeeze in his chair.

They got to the car and he spoke for the first time.

"I'll drive."

It was a long breath for such a short sentence and it was not what he had meant to say.

"I can drive," said his father defensively.

"Let him drive," interposed his mother.

"I can drive," said his father loudly and finally, his head beginning to tremble as he looked at his wife.

They got in and drove off. His mother smiled unsurely from one to the other, the enthusiasm beginning to leave her face like sand from an hourglass.

She said, "We're glad you're home, Son."

"You don't have to say that," he said.

His father, in the suit that appeared to be made of bats' skin, was driving the car with an exaggerated carefulness.

"She knows she don't have to say it," he said, not looking around.

They rode in silence. He could tell his mother was trying to think of something else to say.

They had not asked him one word about himself or mentioned his graduating from college or his plans for the coming year. All that full and rich life he had had meant nothing to them.

"Why didn't you tell us what train you were coming on?" his father asked again. "We've been meeting trains all day."

An intensely controlled voice said, "That's not all you've been doing all day."

Shocked, he looked beside him to see who had said that and there was no one beside him.

He saw them both stiffen.

He had the strange sensation that a mean little man was darting around inside him, setting fires.

"Here we are," his father said coldly, parking the car three feet away from the curb.

He opened the door and got out and looked up at that house.

The hair rose on his neck like briars.

He retreated a few steps along the sidewalk swallowing hard to try to put out those fires.

"Didn't you get my letter?"

He retreated a few more steps.

As politely as he could, he said, "I think I better go over to my room and unpack."

"I'll be damned," said his father, dropping the suitcase he had, surprisingly enough, been carrying.

"We bought a steak and wine and your Mama's got it all fixed up."

His father began to come after him down the street and all the time he kept inching backward.

"That's all right about the supper," his mother called from her position halfway up the hill.

He and his father both turned and looked at her.

"What a fool," his father said wearily to himself.

Tears came to his mother's eyes. (She was talented that way.)

"I heard you," she said to his father. "You're such a bully, I don't blame him for leaving home. I'd of left too if I'd of had some place to go."

"Aw well, Hell." His father began to try to paste things back. "Let's forget it."

"Come on, Son," said his mother attempting to get him on her side. "Let's us go in the house."

The flames rose from his bowels and opened every wound he thought had healed.

"I wouldn't go in that house if my life depended on it," he yelled. "I hate that house, I hate everything I remember about it including the damned soap opera that goes on inside it."

They stood there. People passing by looked at them. He lowered his voice.

"You haven't asked me one word about myself," he said.

He looked at his mother's face expecting and wanting to see the pain he felt reflected there. What he saw was that she was not even surprised. It was like coming across a room in your own house that you hadn't known was there.

"I was going to, Son," she said.

She smiled at him sadly and he turned and ran down the street like a little boy.

When he got to the house across town lights were coming on everywhere as if in panic over the lost day.

There was no one in the front hall so he went on up the two flights of stairs and into the room he knew so well.

It was in partial darkness but he could see it was like his landlady had described.

Without turning on the light, he went over to the huge iron bed and lay down across it. It spun like a whirlpool.

When it stopped, he was still nauseated. He looked up at the strange shadows he had never seen before.

Night birds went across the ceiling and each one brought a more terrible message than the one before. Ignorance, said one, and instability, said another, and pride and hatred and deception, they said, until all of them flew wildly together, crying failure, failure, failure.

Horror-stricken, he grabbed the iron foot of the bed and pulled himself up. When he opened his eyes it was his own shadow he saw prostrated across the floor.

"You God-awful fool," he said to it.

It lay there.

"You're just like them," he said to it.

He moved across the room and it confronted him at the door.

"You're just like everybody else," he said.

He looked at his hand on the doorknob waiting for a signal from him. He flexed his fingers and turned the knob back and forth without opening the door. Then he turned and slid down the wall to the floor. There was a table by a window and in his mind he could see the other table with the two people leaning over it. There was no cheer in that room. The people ate cold food and drank warm, bitter wine and they were alone.

In their own way, they loved him. They were the only people who did love him. The least he could do was go and quarrel with them.

He looked up at the ceiling. The night birds were gone and in their place was just the shape of summer leaves.

When he got home he discovered that he was enormously tired —and it was like a privilege. He turned into the gravel path that led up the hill to the house, rising like a nightmare above it. It was so familiar. He saw himself as a child during one of the periodic woundings to which he was constantly subjected, standing alone in the neglected but mercifully secluded yard, and swearing aloud to some dark tree or company of stars that when he was a man . . . .

He waited outside the house for something to come and rescue him.

Nothing came.

He walked up the steps, through the open door and down the hall to the kitchen.

Narrow the space and cold the meal that waited for him. Nevertheless, he entered the room and took his place at the table.

Of her work, Miss Hardeman says, "You asked me how it came to be. In attempting to revise a story in which the central character was a young boy, discovering in a time of crisis that his love for his mother was not the guarantee of happiness he believed it was, I began to wonder what kind of adult this boy would become. 'The First Supper' is the result of that speculation."

.  .  .

The story is finished, but finishing the story is not the end of the trail. If the author begins with an urge to communicate, as we have said, he ends with the search for an audience which can understand his language. Miss Hardeman sent "The First Supper" out on its own, submitting it for publication, and—as one of the results—you have become part of its audience.

You may now want to send out a narration of your own in hope of publication. You may decide to try a campus magazine, join other students in mimeographing and distributing the stories written in your class, or perhaps approach a publishing house or a magazine with national distribution, in the hope of competing with established writers. Bear in mind that you yourself should keep a copy of your manuscript, as a reference and as insurance against possible loss, and that an editor normally expects a manuscript to be cleanly typewritten, double-spaced, on one side of the sheet.

The avenues for publication are extremely varied and are also subject to change. New publications come into being, others die out, and editorial personnel may shift. The suggestions which follow are therefore rather general in nature. They can be supplemented by more detailed advice from your instructor and by your own study of current information sources.

If you decide to seek publication directly, you have several alternatives. You can address a letter of inquiry to an editor, giving a synopsis of the story or novel and perhaps a sample of the writing but withholding the manuscript itself until it is actually requested. Or you might send an entire copy of the completed manuscript to an editor without preliminary inquiry, in which case you should forward with it a stamped and self-addressed envelope. You will find editorial staff names listed in a number of the handbooks for writers available on any newsstand. These handbooks also list the lengths of stories and types of fiction various editors require. *The Writer, Inc.*, published at 8 Arlington Street, Boston 16, Massachusetts, is one of the better-known literary guides. *The Writer's Digest*, 22 East 12th Street, Cincinnati, Ohio, offers information for the beginner. Another very useful directory, which should be available in your school or city library and which lists book publishers, magazines, and newspapers, is *Literary Market Place*, published by R. R. Bowker Company, 62 West 45th Street, New York 36, New York.

If you mail your work directly to a magazine or book publisher, it will be assigned to a reader. If he finds the manuscript unsuitable because of quality or because it falls outside the areas in which his firm publishes, he will return it to you with a rejection which may be either a printed form or a personal letter. A letter generally indicates that the manuscript has aroused some interest. If the interest is strong enough, the reader may pass your work along to other readers or to an editorial committee for final decision. The machinery by which a publishing house arrives at a decision can be quite complex and accounts for the fact that notice of rejection or acceptance may be a long time in coming. The young writer, in particular, should realize that if his manuscript is rejected by one publisher it may still be accepted by another. The history of publishing is full of instances in which works which later became famous were rejected ten, fifteen, or even twenty times before final publication.

If you would prefer to work through a literary agent, you might begin by writing the Fisher Bindery, 74 Union Place, Hartford 3, Connecticut, for a free pamphlet called "What

Is a Literary Agent?" Part of this pamphlet, which lists a number of reputable authors' representatives, is quoted below.

### What an Author's Representative Can Do for Him

An agent's functions vary in emphasis with the needs of each individual author.

The agent agrees to offer for sale such manuscripts as he believes to be publishable.

He may or may not offer editorial advice on form or content before sending the material out.

He selects the markets which seem to him best suited for the material. In the event of a sale, he negotiates the terms. He collects the monies due, deducts his commission, and forwards the balance to the author. He then handles any other rights in the literary property which are reserved for the author after the initial sale.

Since the market for good writing is world-wide, there are literary agents in all principal publishing centers. American literary agents maintain working relationships with agents abroad, through whom the work of their clients is offered in all appropriate markets. A literary agency is therefore essentially a service organization for the systematic marketing of literary properties wherever they can be sold.

Some agencies handle an author's work in all fields, including publishing, motion pictures, radio and television. Other agents, specializing in literary material only, work in close association with agencies that handle properties for theatre, the motion pictures, radio and television. On no occasion does their combined fee exceed ten per cent.

The agent may be delegated by the author to act for him, in his absence, in signing contracts and performing similar functions pertaining to his work.

An agent is a shield between the author and the constant discouragement of rejections. He protects him from the petty annoyances of requests for permission to quote, for autographs, for advice. He takes care of many details which must be promptly and properly handled.

Above all else, a good agent is, in the words of one author, "someone to help you fight the Indians." The agent is, in short, not only a literary business manager but also advisor, encourager and friendly critic.

### What an Agent Cannot Be Expected to Do

An agent is not a miracle worker. He cannot sell an unsaleable manuscript—he can only find the best markets and the best terms for a saleable one.

An agent is not an instructor in writing. He cannot afford the time to give detailed critical help to authors whose work has not reached a professional level.

An agent is not a rewrite man. He can direct an author to reputable people when he thinks the material warrants it, but he cannot be expected to do more than minor editing of manuscripts himself.

### Standard Practice of an Agent

1. He takes only ten per cent commission on domestic sales and no more than twenty per cent on foreign sales.

2. He pays out the author's share of monies as soon as possible after receipt.

3. He charges the author with no expense incurred by the normal operation of his office, such as postage or local phone calls. He does charge the author for such things as copyright fees, manuscript retyping fees incurred at the author's request, copies of books for submission overseas.

4. He may charge a reading fee for unsolicited material but refunds this in the event of his acceptance of the material.

5. He does not advertise his services.

### How to Find a Good Literary Agent

Any of the following will supply a list of reputable agents:
1. The Authors Guild of America, 6 East 39th Street, New York.
2. Any nationally known book publisher.
3. Any national magazine.

Although it is not standard practice, a reputable agent will sometimes comment on the work a talented new writer sends him even though he may not think the author can yet compete in the professional field. Shirley Fisher, in an article on "The Writer and His Agent" has offered the following comments to the beginner.

I know most new writers are under the impression that they must be published before an agent will agree to look at their material. This is a workable enough public yardstick for many good agents, either because their business is small and personal with a limited number of clients or simply because they like it that way. A large percentage of our authors, almost all of the younger ones, are people for whom we placed their first published work.

Agents, of course, can no more teach writing than an editor or even an English department can. But when they see the unmistakable signs of talent in a manuscript, even if the manuscript itself has no promise of being made publishable, they will do everything they can to suggest and guide the young writer as he searches among many styles and areas for his own writing self.

You may not yet have found your own writing self but if you do there is a good chance that a discerning editor or agent will encourage you. Malcolm Cowley, the well-known critic and writer, says,

My essential advice is to write a lot and get published—even if what the young writer gets published isn't the great work he wants to do. Publication is the function usually omitted in writing courses. I never know what to tell young writers about literary agents, who serve a useful purpose—but it's almost as hard to find a literary agent as it is to find a publisher. The agent is looking for publishable work. One other point is the importance of word-of-mouth. Somebody—a teacher, a professional writer—reads the young writer's work and tells somebody else, who tells an agent or an editor, and then the manuscript receives a prompt and attentive reading.

While you are seeking an editor who will promptly and attentively read what you write, submit your stories through any avenue you can find. For just as each writer must find his own style, he must—or so many of us believe—make his own path to the editor who will recognize him.

## SUBMITTING YOUR MANUSCRIPT: Assignment 34

When your second story, or any narrative of your own that you believe is worth sending out, has been revised, hand the correctly typed copy to your instructor and discuss with him where it should be sent. Mail the story to the publication of your choice.

## *14*

# The Writer Speaks for Himself

After he had become one of the finest American writers, Thomas Wolfe sent a letter to Professor Koch, his former teacher at Chapel Hill, repudiating the work he did as "a careless boy."

I am very proud to call myself one of the Playmakers and to remember that I belonged to the first group you ever taught at Chapel Hill, and had a part in writing and producing some of the first plays. I want to tell you also that no one is prouder than I of the great success the Playmakers have achieved and of the distinguished work which has been done by them. The fact that I was associated with that work at the very beginning, even in an obscure and unimportant fashion, is another fact I am proud of. I am also proud to remember that the two little one-act plays that I wrote were among the first plays put on by the Playmakers and that I acted in them and helped produce them. I was a boy of eighteen years when I wrote those plays and I wrote each of them in a few hours because I did not then understand what heartbreaking and agonizing work writing is and I think those plays show this and are fair samples of the work of a boy who did not know what hard work was and who wrote them in a few hours. But I do not think they are fair samples of the best which the Playmakers can do and have done, nor of the best in me. I therefore want to ask you, as my old friend, who will not misunderstand my plain and sincere feeling in this matter, that you do not allow either of these plays to be used again for production.

I should like to be remembered as a Playmaker and as one who had the honor to be a member of that pioneer first group, but I do not want to be remembered for the work which a careless boy did.

From   "Tom Wolfe on the Drama,"
in *The Carolina Quarterly*

Norman Mailer, the author of *The Naked and the Dead*, wrote *Advertisements for Myself*, in which he cast a cold eye on his early work at Harvard.

## ADVERTISEMENT FOR
## "A CALCULUS AT HEAVEN"

Before I was seventeen I had formed the desire to be a major writer, and this desire came upon me rather suddenly in the last two months of my sixteenth year, a time I remember well because it was my first semester at Harvard. All through December 1939 and January 1940 I was discovering modern American literature. In those sixty days I read and reread *Studs Lonigan*, *U.S.A.*, and *The Grapes of Wrath*. Later I would add Wolfe and Hemingway and Faulkner and to a small measure, Fitzgerald; but Farrell, Dos Passos and Steinbeck were the novel for me in that sixty days before I turned seventeen.

In my sophomore year I wrote a great many stories which were influenced by Ernest Hemingway. Although I was more excited by Dos Passos and Farrell, it was Hemingway I imitated—probably because he seemed easier. To write like Farrell or Dos Passos would have required more experience than I could possibly have had at eighteen—to sense what is real in the commonplace is not easy when one is young, shy, half in love and certainly self-loved, sex-ridden, yet still weeding out the acne—no, it is more attractive to conceive of oneself as (and so to write about) a hero who is tall, strong, and excruciatingly wounded.

"A Calculus at Heaven" is about just such a hero. It is probably the best of the ambitious pieces I tried at Harvard, and it was the next to last thing I did—I finished it for my twentieth birthday. "A Calculus at Heaven" was printed in Edwin Seaver's *Cross-Section*, which first appeared in 1944, and Marjorie Stengel who was his reader came across it first and liked it very much. She was to help me more than once over the years, and always deftly, but she was generous in her praise then, and Edwin Seaver was most decent—I remember that I saw him for a few minutes about a month before I went into the Army, and I muttered in a small voice that "A Calculus at Heaven" had been influenced by *Man's Fate*.

"You admire Malraux greatly?" Seaver suggested.

"I'd like to be another Malraux," I blurted.

"Well," Seaver said, with real kindness, "maybe you will, maybe you will."

Tennessee Williams has talked about the cell in which each writer is confined for the duration of his life. "The Field of Blue Children," which follows his comments, is a story that sends out its own whispering sounds of solitude.

Of course it is a pity that so much of all creative work is so closely related to the personality of the one who does it.

It is sad and embarrassing and unattractive that those emotions that stir him deeply enough to demand expression, and to charge their expressions with some measure of light and power, are nearly all rooted, however changed in their surface, in the particular and sometimes peculiar concerns of the artist himself, that special world, the passions and images of it that each of us weaves about him from birth to death, a web of monstrous complexity, spun forth at a speed that is incalculable to a length beyond measure, from the spider mouth of his own singular perceptions.

It is a lonely idea, a lonely condition, so terrifying to think of that we usually don't. And so we talk to each other, write and wire each other, call each other short and long distance across land and sea, clasp hands with each other at meeting and at parting, fight each other and even destroy each other because of this always somewhat thwarted effort to break through walls to each other. As a character in a play once said, "We're all of us sentenced to solitary confinement inside our own skins."

Personal lyricism is the outcry of prisoner to prisoner from the cell in solitary where each is confined for the duration of his life.

I once saw a group of little girls on a Mississippi sidewalk, all dolled up in their mothers' and sisters' castoff finery, old raggedy ball gowns and plumed hats and high-heeled slippers, enacting a meeting of ladies in a parlor with a perfect mimicry of polite Southern gush and simper. But one child was not satisfied with the attention paid her enraptured performance by the others, they were too involved in their own performances to suit her, so she stretched out her skinny arms and threw back her skinny neck and shrieked to the deaf heavens and her equally oblivious playmates, "Look at me, look at me, look at me!"

And then her mother's high-heeled slippers threw her off balance and she fell to the sidewalk in a great howling tangle of soiled white satin and torn pink net, and still nobody looked at her.

I wonder if she is not, now, a Southern writer.

Of course it is not only Southern writers, of lyrical bent, who engage in such histrionics and shout, "Look at me!" Perhaps it is a parable of all artists. And not always do we topple over and land in a tangle of trappings that don't fit us. However, it is well to be aware of that peril, and not to content yourself with a demand for attention, to know that out of your personal lyricism, your sidewalk histrionics, something has to be created that will not only attract observers but participants in the performance.

I try very hard to do that.

From Introduction to *Cat on a Hot Tin Roof*,
by Tennessee Williams

# THE FIELD OF BLUE CHILDREN

## TENNESSEE WILLIAMS

That final spring at the State University a restlessness came over Myra which she could not understand. It was not merely the rest-lessness of superabundant youth. There was something a little neurotic about it. Nothing that she did seemed quite satisfying or complete. Even when she returned from a late formal dance, where she had swung from partner to partner the whole evening through, she did not feel quite ready to tumble exhausted into bed. She felt as though there must be something still further to give the night its perfect fullness. Sometimes she had the almost panicky sensa-tion of having lost or forgotten something very important. She would stand quite still for a moment with tightened forehead, try-ing to remember just what it was that had slipped from her fingers —been left behind in the rumble seat of Kirk's roommate's roadster or on the sofa in the dimly-lighted fraternity lounge between dances.

"What's the matter?" Kirk or somebody else would ask and she would laugh rather sharply.

"Nothing. I just felt like I'd forgotten something!"

The feeling persisted even when every article was accounted for. She still felt as though something were missing. When she had returned to the sorority house she went from room to room, ex-changing anecdotes of the evening, laughing at them far more than their humor warranted. And when finally everyone else had gone to bed, she stayed up alone in her room and sometimes she cried bitterly without knowing why, crushing the pillow against her mouth so that no one could hear—or else she sat in pajamas on the window seat and looked out across the small university town with all its buildings and trees and open fields a beautiful dusky blue in the spring night, the dome of the administration building like a snowy peak in the distance and the stars astonishingly large and close—she felt as though she would strangle with an emotion whose exact nature or meaning she could not understand.

When half-drunken groups of serenaders, also restless after late dances, paused beneath her house, she turned on the bed lamp and leaned above them, patting her hands together in a pantomime of delighted applause. When they left, she remained at the window, looking out with the light extinguished, and it was sad, unbearably sad, to hear their hoarse voices retreating down moon-splashed ave-nues of trees till they could not be heard any longer or else were drowned in the noise of a starting motor whose raucous gravel-kicking departure ebbed quickly to a soft, musical hum and was succeeded at length by the night's complete blue silence.

Still seated at the window, she waited with tight throat for the sobbing to commence. When it did, she felt better. When it did not, her vigil would sometimes continue till morning began and the restless aching had worn itself out.

That spring she took Kirk Abbott's fraternity pin. But this did not radically change her manner of living. She continued to accept dates with other men. She went out almost wherever she was asked with almost whoever asked her, and when Kirk protested she didn't try to explain the fever that made her behave in this way, she simply kissed him until he stopped talking and was in a mood to forgive her for almost anything that she might conceivably do.

From the beginning of adolescence, perhaps earlier, Myra had written a little verse. But this spring it became a regular practice. Whenever the rising well of unexplainable emotion became so full that its hurt was intolerable, she found that it helped her a little to scribble things down on paper. Single lines or couplets, sometimes whole stanzas, leapt into her mind with the instant completeness of slides flashed on the screen of a magic lantern. Their beauty startled her: sometimes it was like a moment of religious exaltation. She stood in a frozen attitude; her breath was released in a sigh. Each time she felt as though she were about to penetrate some new area of human thought. She had the sensation of standing upon the verge of a shadowy vastness which might momentarily flower into a marvelous crystal of light, like a ballroom that is dark one moment and is the next moment illuminated by the sunlike brilliance of a hundred glass chandeliers and reflecting mirrors and polished floors. At such times she would turn out the light in her bedroom and go quickly to the window. When she looked out across the purple-dark town and the snowy white dome above the quadrangle, or when she sat as in a spell, listening to the voices that floated down the quiet streets, singers of blues-songs or laughing couples in roadsters, the beauty of it no longer tormented her, she felt instead a mysterious quietness as though some disturbing question had been answered and life had accordingly become a much simpler and more pleasurable experience.

*"Words are a net to catch beauty!"*

She wrote this in the back of a notebook toward the close of a lecture on the taxing powers of Congress. It was late in April when she wrote this—and from then on it seemed that she understood what she wanted and the hurt bewilderment in her grew less acute.

In the Poetry Club to which Myra belonged there was a boy named Homer Stallcup who had been in love with her for a year or more. She could tell this by the way that he looked at her during the club sessions, which were the only occasions on which they met. Homer never looked directly at her, his eyes slid quickly across her face, but something about his expression, even about the tense pose of his body as he sat gripping his knees, made her feel his awareness of her. He avoided sitting next to her or even directly across from her—the chairs were usually arranged in a circle—and because of this she had at first thought that he must dislike her, but she had come gradually to understand that his shyness toward her had an exactly opposite meaning.

Homer was not a fraternity member. He waited on tables at a campus restaurant, fired furnaces and did chores for his room and board. Nobody in Myra's social *milieu* knew him or paid him any attention. He was rather short, stocky and dark. Myra thought him good-looking, but certainly not in any usual way. He had intense black eyes, a straight nose with flaring nostrils, full, mobile lips that sometimes jerked nervously at the corners. All of his movements were overcharged. When he rose from a chair he would nearly upset it. When he lighted a cigarette his face would twist into a terrible scowl and he would fling the burnt match away like a lighted firecracker.

He went around a great deal with a girl of his own intellectual type, a girl named Hertha something or other, who was rather widely known on the campus because of her odd behavior. In classes she would be carried away by enthusiasm upon some subject, either literary or political, and she would talk so rapidly that nobody could understand what she was saying and she would sputter and gasp and make awkward gestures—as though she were trying to pluck some invisible object out of the air—till the room was in an uproar of amusement and the instructor had to turn his face to the blackboard to conceal his own laughter.

Hertha and this boy, Homer, made a queer picture together, she nearly a foot taller, often rushing along a foot or more in advance of him, clutching him by the coat sleeve as though afraid that he might escape from her, and every minute or so one or both of them bursting into violent laughter that could be heard for a block.

Homer wrote poetry of a difficult sort. It was uneven. Parts of it were reminiscent of Hart Crane, parts were almost as naïvely lucid as Sara Teasdale's. But there were lines and phrases which stabbed at you with their poignant imagery, their fresh observation. When he had given a reading at a symposium, Hertha would always leap out of her chair as though animated by an electric charge, her blinking, near-sighted eyes tensely sweeping the circle of superciliously smiling faces, first demanding, then begging that they concur in the extravagant praise which her moist lips babbled.

Only Myra would say anything when Hertha had finished. The rest were too baffled or too indifferent or even too hostile. And Homer's face, darkly flushed, would be turned to his lap throughout the rest of the meeting. His fingers would fold down corners of the neat pages as though the poetry had been erased from them or had never been written on them, as though these pages were simply blank pieces of paper for his fingers to play with.

Myra always wanted to say something more, but her critical vocabulary was slight.

"I think that was lovely," she would say. Or, "I liked that very much." And Homer would not lift his eyes, his face would turn even darker, and she would bite her tongue as though in remorse for an unkind speech. She wanted to put her hands over his fingers, to make them stop crumpling the neat pages, to make them be still.

It was not till the last meeting of the year, in early June, that Myra had the courage to approach him. After that meeting she saw him standing by the water fountain at the end of the corridor. She rushed impulsively up to him and told him, all in one breath, that his was the best unpublished verse she'd ever heard, that he should submit it to some of the good literary magazines, that she thought the other members of the club were absolute fools for not understanding.

Homer stood with his fists clenched in his pockets. He did not look at her face the whole time she was speaking. When she had stopped, his excitement burst through. He tore a sheaf of manuscripts from his brief case and thrust them into her hands.

"Please read them," he begged, "and let me know what you think."

They went downstairs together. On the bottom step he tripped or slid and she had to catch his arm to prevent him from falling. She was both touched and amused by this awkwardness and by his apparent delight in walking beside her. As they went out of the white stone building the late afternoon sun, yellow as lemon, met their faces in a beneficent flood. The air was filled with the ringing of five-thirty bells and the pliant voices of pigeons. A white feather from one of the stirring wings floated down and lighted upon Myra's hair. Homer lifted it off and thrust it in his hatband, and all the way home, after leaving him, Myra could feel that quick, light touch of his fingers. She wondered if he would keep the pigeon's feather; treasure it, possibly, for a long while afterward because it had once touched her person.

That night, when the sorority house was submerged in darkness, she took out the sheaf of poems and read them through without

stopping. As she read she felt a rising excitement. She did not understand very much of what she was reading, but there was a cumu-
lative effect, a growing intensity in the sequence. When she had
finished she found herself trembling: trembling as when you step
from warm water into chill air.

She dressed and went downstairs. She didn't know what she was
planning to do. Her movements were without any conscious direction. And yet she had never moved with more certainty.

She opened the front door of the sorority house, ran down the
brick-paved walk, turned to the left and continued swiftly through
the moonlit streets till she had reached Homer's residence. It startled
her to find herself there. There were cicadas burring in the large
oaks—she had not heard them until this moment. And when she
looked upward she saw a close group of stars above the western
gable of the large frame house. The Seven Sisters. They were huddled together like virgin wanderers through a dark forest. She
listened and there was not a voice anywhere, nothing except the
chant of cicadas and the faint, faint rustling of her white skirt when
she moved.

She went quickly around the side of the house to the door that
she had seen Homer come out of in the mornings. She gave two
short, distinct raps, then flattened herself against the brick wall.
She was breathing rapidly. After waiting a while, she knocked again.
Through the glass pane she could see down a flight of stairs into the
basement. The door of a lamplit room was open. She saw first a
moving shadow, then the boy himself, catching a heavy brown
robe about his body and frowning up at the door as he mounted
toward it.

As the door came open she gasped his name.

For a whole minute, it seemed, he said nothing. Then he caught
her arm and pulled her inside the door.

"Myra, it's you."

"Yes, it's me," she laughed. "I don't know what came over me.
I've been reading your poetry and I just felt like I had to see you
at once and tell you. . . ."

Her breath gave out. She leaned against the closed door. It was
her eyes this time, and not his, that looked for concealment. She
looked down at the bottom of his ugly brown bathrobe and she
saw his bare feet beneath it, large and bony and white, and the
sight of them frightened her. She remembered the intense, fleeting
way of his eyes sliding over her face and body and the way he
trembled that afternoon when she came up to him in the corridor,
how those large feet had tripped on the bottom stair and she had
been forced to catch him to keep him from falling.

"There was one thing in particular," she went on with a struggle.

"There was something about a field of blue flowers. . . ."

"Oh, yes," he whispered. "The blue children, you mean!"

"Yes, that was it!" Now she lifted her eyes, eagerly.

"Come down to my room, Myra."

"I couldn't!"

"You couldn't?"

"No, of course not! If anyone caught me. . . ."

"They wouldn't!"

"I'd be expelled!"

There was a slight pause.

"Wait a minute!"

He ran down three steps and turned.

"Wait for me just one minute, Myra!"

She felt her head nodding. She heard his running down the rest of the steps and into the basement room where he lived. Through the door she saw his shadow moving about the floor and the walls. He was dressing. Once he stepped into the portion of the bedroom that she could see through the half-open door and he stood in her sight naked from the waist up, and she was startled and strangely moved by that brief glimpse of his full, powerful chest and arms, strikingly etched with shadows thrown by the lamp. In that moment he acquired in her mind a physical reality which he had never had before. A very great physical reality, greater than she had felt in Kirk Abbott or in any of the other young men that she had gone with on the campus.

A minute later he stepped out of the door and closed it and came quietly up the short flight of steps to where she was standing.

"I'm sorry I took so long."

"It wasn't long."

He took her arm and they went out of the door and around to the front of the house. The oak tree in the front lawn appeared gigantic. Everything was peculiarly sharpened or magnified; even the crunch of gravel under their two pairs of white shoes. She expected to see startled, balloon-like heads thrust out of all the upstairs windows, to hear voices calling a shrill alarm, her name shouted from rooftops, the rushing of crowds in pursuit. . . .

"Where are we going?" she asked as he he led her south along the brick walk.

"I want to show you the field I describe in the poem."

It wasn't far. The walk soon ended and under their feet was the plushy coolness of earth. The moon flowed aqueously through the multitude of pointed oak leaves: the dirt road was also like moving water with its variations of light and shade. They came to a low wooden fence. The boy jumped over it. Then held out his arms. She stepped to the top rail and he lifted her down from it. On the other side his arms did not release her but held her closer.

"This is it," he told her, "the field of blue children."

She looked beyond his dark shoulder. And it was true. The whole field was covered with dancing blue flowers. There was a wind scudding through them and they broke before it in pale blue waves, sending up a soft whispering sound like the infinitely diminished crying of small children at play.

She thought of the view from her window at night, those nights when she cried bitterly without knowing why, the dome of the administration building like a white peak and the restless waves of moonlit branches and the stillness and the singing voices, mournfully remote, blocks away, coming closer, the tender, foolish ballads, and the smell of the white spirea at night, and the stars clear as lamps in the cloud-fretted sky, and she remembered the choking emotion that she didn't understand and the dread of all this coming to its sudden, final conclusion in a few months or weeks more. And she tightened her arms about the boy's shoulders. He was almost a stranger. She knew that she had not even caught a first glimpse of him until this night, and yet he was inexpressibly close to her now, closer than she had ever felt any person before.

He led her out over the field where the flowers rose in pale blue waves to her knees and she felt their soft petals against her bare flesh and she lay down among them and stretched her arms through them and pressed her lips against them and felt them all about her, accepting her and embracing her, and a kind of drunkenness possessed her. The boy knelt beside her and touched her cheek with his fingers and then her lips and her hair. They were both kneeling in the blue flowers, facing each other. He was smiling. The wind blew her loose hair into his face. He raised both hands and brushed it back over her forehead and as he did so his hands slipped down behind the back of her head and fastened there and drew her head toward him until her mouth was pressed against his, tighter and tighter, until her teeth pressed painfully against her upper lip and she tasted the salt taste of blood. She gasped and let her mouth fall open and then she lay back among the whispering blue flowers.

Afterward she had sense enough to see that it was impossible. She sent the poems back to the boy with a short note. It was a curiously stilted and formal note, perhaps because she was dreadfully afraid of herself when she wrote it. She told him about the boy Kirk Abbott whom she was going to marry that summer and she explained to Homer how impossible it would have been for them to try and go on with the beautiful but unfortunate thing that had happened to them last night in the field.

She saw him only once after that. She saw him walking across the campus with his friend Hertha, the tall, weedy girl who wore thick-lensed glasses. Hertha was clinging to Homer's arm and shaking with outlandishly shrill laughter; laughter that could be heard for blocks and yet did not sound like real laughter.

Myra and Kirk were married in August of that year. Kirk got a job with a telephone company in Poplar Falls and they lived in an efficiency apartment and were reasonably happy together. Myra seldom felt restless any more. She did not write verse. Her life seemed to be perfectly full without it. She wondered sometimes if Homer had kept on with his writing but she never saw any of it in the literary magazines so she supposed it couldn't have amounted to very much after all.

One late spring evening a few years after their marriage Kirk Abbott came home tired from the office hungry for dinner and found a scribbled note under the sugar bowl on the drop-leaf table.

"Driven over to Carsville for just a few hours. Myra."

It was after dark: a soft, moony night.

Myra drove south from the town till she came to an open field. There she parked the car and climbed over the low wooden fence. The field was exactly as she had remembered it. She walked quickly out among the flowers; then suddenly fell to her knees among them, sobbing. She cried for a long time, for nearly an hour, and then she rose to her feet and carefully brushed off her skirt and stockings. Now she felt perfectly calm and in possession of herself once more. She went back to the car. She knew that she would never do such a ridiculous thing as this again, for now she had left the last of her troublesome youth behind her.

Jean Stafford, the novelist and short story writer, made the following comments on fiction to a group of students at the Woman's College of the University of North Carolina.

I do not advocate, in fiction, a sedulous addiction to the truth: far from it. And especially not in fiction that is drawn from personal experience. All fiction is of necessity autobiographical to a degree, but it should never be too frankly so. Shifting the scene from the west to the south or changing the sexes and ages of characters does not deflect the course of the truth, but it gives the writer liberty and allows him therefore to embellish and invent. One time I made a disastrous attempt to write a novel about an act of violence in which I had been peripherally involved when I was in college. I had been witness to a suicide that had come at the end of a frenzied and squalid life, but a life so illustrative of the thirties that it was a crystallization of the manners and morals of those days. The actions were motivated by the dislocations of the twenties that had still not been set right, by the depression, by the end of prohibition, and by the New Deal. It involved that famous song of our times, "Gloomy Sunday" that was said to have started an epidemic of suicide amongst college students all over the world; the game Monopoly figured in it and the Young Communist League, *Ulysses*, and the undergraduate vogue of swallowing goldfish. It concerned a boy who had sat next to me in Latin Comedy and had made a tolerable sum of pocket money for himself by renting out at a dollar and a half a day an unexpurgated copy of *Lady Chatterly's Lover* which he had smuggled in from France on a tramp steamer. There were medical students who went on ether jags, chemistry students who stole grain alcohol from the laboratories and made it into bathtub gin; professors who were open advocates of the USSR; German exchange students who created incidents in classes in political economy.

In addition to its being typical of my generation, my story had universal elements and an urgent drama and compelling implications and for many years I had toyed with the idea of writing it down. I did write it once in a long story but the story was a failure because I did not know what my own feeling toward the people was. Ten years after the shocking event, I believed that the emotional experience had sunk deeply enough to rise again as literary experience, and now that the immediacy was removed, I thought I could examine its components judiciously and disclose the meanings. I had been so out of touch with all the people who had been involved that I was certain I could contrive a whole new dramatis personae.

But from the very start I faced more perplexing problems than I had ever done before. The matter was extremely personal and interior and was, I discovered, quite as painful in recollection as it had been in its genesis. I found that I had, after all, *not* forgotten the people I had known then, and I reproduced all the miseries of those days with pitiless accuracy. I am reminded here of another occasion when I wrote directly out of my own life: I wrote a story about an automobile accident I had been in, in which my skull had been fractured. In describing the pain that assailed my heroine, I so perfectly revived my own past pain that each time I sat down at my typewriter, I acquired a shattering headache. But that was only a physical distress, and the canvas I had set out to cover was not a large one.

I imagine that in the next three and a half years, as I worked on the suicide story, I accumulated twenty pounds of manuscript and destroyed an equal amount. I completed two versions, one in the first person and one in the third; I tried and rejected the omniscient observer. By actual count, I wrote twenty-three versions of the first chapter with twenty-three different accentuations. But the book continued to be heavy, flat, oppressively factual, cumbrously emotional. My prose ailed. I was writing about people I knew nearly as well as I knew myself, about a setting as immediately before my eyes as the room in which I worked, about a sequence of events I had thought about and talked about for years. And even so, every page, every sentence bore the signature of a liar. I told lies right and left not only about my characters but about humanity in general, but they were not good lies—they were tiresome, malicious and transparent. . . .

The clever reasons why I could not progress with the book varied as I thought them up: college was too remote for me, I told myself, so I went for some months to Columbia University to study systematic botany, and I became so absorbed by what I saw under my microscope that often I stayed in the laboratory until after sundown. I saw no students. I was instructed by a geneticist in his own laboratory, and I saw him and his colleagues who were breeding mice with tails like bolts of lightning and mice that danced in circles counter-clockwise. I learned a little about botany and something about genetics and a lot about the kind of jokes that make zoologists laugh, but these acquisitions did not further the work-in-progress on my desk at home.

I hit upon another explanation: the fault lay in my living in New York, an improbable place for contemplative work; moving out of the city would not have solved the problem, of course, but I was given an excuse to study brochures issued by real estate brokers advertising country properties and to acquaint myself with the rural regions of Ireland exuberantly described in guide books. To escape the noise of my apartment building where radios and children blared, I used to go with my notebooks to a small subscription library, thinking that in the quiet there I would come to terms with my book. But I tended to come to terms with the books Mrs. Wharton had written rather than with the one I had not. Occasionally I spent whole mornings in the zoo in Central Park; frequently I walked across Brooklyn Bridge, sometimes I sat for hours on a bench on the East River Drive staring across at Welfare Island. I took sightseeing boats around the island of Manhattan and I lunched one Saturday in Hoboken where, in a single block, I counted twenty-two saloons. In the worst periods of guilt, I consoled myself by saying that this was all grist to the mill and that in time I would make use of the sights and the sounds and the smells in these byways of the city. There were sometimes stretches when I wrote for ten hours a day, but these were followed by long famines when I avoided the sight of the manuscripts on my desk as if they were a source of physical pain and I fled my apartment, seeking a fresh affection. The light at my desk was bad, so I had lengthy consultations with people who might remedy it; I rearranged my books and my spices; I took up needlepoint.

And then finally one afternoon after a morning when I had started on page one again for the twenty-fourth time, the reason I could not write the novel came to me. It was ever so simple: I hated my material. The years I had elected to write about had not been attractive for me or for any of my characters and we emerged, in my merciless pages, unappealing to a degree in our despondency; we were humorless, morbid, self-seeking, unworthy of any but the dreary fates I meted out to us. I had used all the standard tricks—had elongated people who in real life were short, had turned men into women and teachers into priests, had stricken hale men with heart disease and invested imbeciles with intelligence.

But while the disguises might have fooled my readers, they did not take me in for a minute, and behind the fake mustaches and the plaster noses, the wigs, the wooden legs and bogus passports, I saw my friends and foes and kinsmen. But most of all, I saw only my own ubiquitous self practicing ventriloquism to no purpose. I was everywhere hampered by my irrational feeling that I must tell the truth and must, moreover, tell nothing *but* the truth, that every act must come in its proper chronological order. That day I riffled through the enormous pile of typewritten paper and concluded that every page of it was bad. Whether the architecture of the book and the writing of it and its conception were really as bad as I thought them to be, I shall never know because I burned the whole thing up, leaving not a word of it behind. As the last feather of smoke curled up my chimney, I underwent a dreadful shock that lasted several days. But when it had passed, I knew that I had acted wisely. I had been for all these months the victim of an absurd delusion; I had believed that because the events of my story had been important to me and had influenced my thought and my behavior, they were therefore of literary use and significance. . . .

I do not advocate the rejection of first-hand experience, of course, for if I did and practiced what I preached, I would have to stop writing tomorrow. But I do argue against the case history, and particularly the case history that is long on psychological analysis and short on action and plot. There are times when I wish we might return to the reticences of my parents' era when people kept their secrets; sinners might beat their breasts and scream out their trespasses at revival meetings, but one didn't meet those people socially; now they are on hand at every cocktail party, fresh from the couch. It was ridiculous and beastly to hide away relatives of unsound

mind in upstairs bedrooms, but it was more becoming than to brag
in public of the heritage that can explain our own misdeeds.


## THE STORY AND ITS PARTICIPANTS:   Assignment 35

Describe the subject matter you think most pertinent for use in a
new story or novel of your own, and then tell why you feel that what
you have to say will make your readers want to participate in your
work rather than merely observe it.

# 15

# The Deeper Sources

How do I keep on writing, you may ask in trying to form a working cycle. Where are the deep sources in which a story or a novel lies waiting? How can I take one road from among the many that might be taken? Or perhaps I have only one road and in taking it will come to a dry spring. How do I sense, as every writer who keeps on working must, the right time and the right place?

Some people do seem to be born to write one book, or even just one story. If your single piece of work is art, then you are fortunate. Emily Brontë, blowing the winds of Wuthering Heights across the world and giving the force that was Heathcliff a life of its own, performed her voyage as an artist—and what a voyage. She wrote her book while others write what they think is theirs and then wake up to find themselves famous for what they will always believe is their lesser work.

Conan Doyle, for instance, created one character and then in turn seemed to have been created by him. Doyle could never escape Sherlock Holmes although he tried to kill him more than once, apparently made an end of him at Reichenbach Falls, resurrected him, and finally had to retire him as a beekeeper in Sussex. Even today there are people who believe that the detective is at work among the bees while only Conan Doyle is dead.

Like many writers, Doyle was a bad judge of his work and Mark Twain was another. Twain had a sentimental faith in his own vision of Joan of Arc but could find few people to share it. On the other hand he never seemed to understand the transcendent beauty of his stories of the Mississippi and his boyhood. Once he spoke of pigeonholing the manuscript of *Huckleberry Finn* or perhaps even burning it on what would have been a dark day for the novel in America.

But all of them, Emily Brontë, Conan Doyle, and Mark Twain, wanted to keep on writing. Their problem was the one you face, for once you have acknowledged your urge, you have the recurrent need to recognize what is meaningful in your own experience and then find the language that will communicate the story you want to create. The matter of selection of events and language, as Gore Vidal says, is one of the main problems of the writer in our time.

For every Scott Fitzgerald concerned with the precise word and the selection of relevant incident there are a hundred American writers, many well-regarded, who appear to believe that one word is just as good as another and that everything which occurs to them is worth putting down. It is an attitude unique to us and deriving, I would suspect, from a corrupted idea of democracy: if everything and everyone are of equal value then any word is as good as any other word to express a meaning which in turn is no more valuable than any other meaning.

Gore Vidal

In his best work, Scott Fitzgerald did know how to find the precise word and also how to select the events that would show the rootless society of which he was a member. Part of his own problem as a writer lay in being able to keep writing in that society after he became emotionally bankrupt. But even in the dark night of the soul he did keep on writing.

As a young writer, you yourself probably cannot go very far back in years for your material. This book, in attempting to start you on your way, and keep you on your way, can only say again that the deep sources from which you have drawn originally are those to which you must return. As James Joyce says, "The same remains." But for the writer and for those to whom he is appealing, the vision and the world that emerges from the vision are new each time.

—As we, or mother Dana, weave and unweave our bodies . . . from day to day, their molecules shuttled to and fro, so does the artist weave and unweave his image. And as the mole on my right breast is where it was when I was born, though all my body has been woven of new stuff time after time, so through the ghost of the unquiet father the image of the unliving son looks forth. In the intense instant of imagination, when the mind, Shelley says, is a fading coal that which I was is that which I am and that which in possibility I may come to be.

James Joyce in *Ulysses*

Time is the great foe, especially of the writer, but through his work it can become his great ally. Marcel Proust, the author of *Remembrance of Things Past*, recorded free-floating images in time and place that emerge and fade and emerge again. He made the web of his work out of moments in space that obliterate themselves only to re-form and find their permanent place at last in a work of art.

What was lost and what is found is not just time, but a fragment of time to which clings a fragment of space; and in the interior of this small universe, the self, the individual is indivisibly bound by its faith and its desire to this moment of time and to this point in space. From a feeling of existence detached from times and places, the being finds himself brought back by deep remembrance to a first feeling, truly original, constituent of himself and of the world, the act of faith by which the sentient being adheres instantaneously, locally, to sensible reality.

Georges Poulet in *Studies in Human Time*

The sensible reality of the stream-of-consciousness writer is multiple, associative, protean. For him life is not "a series of gig lamps, symmetrically arranged; but a luminous halo, a semitransparent envelope surrounding us from the beginning of consciousness to the end." This credo, set down by Virginia Woolf, gives the stream-of-consciousness writer access to a time scheme of his own.

In using time much more simply than a Woolf, a Proust, or a Joyce, a young writer may take a crucial moment from his childhood or adolescence and from that moment project a narrative. Through the power of memory he may create again a typical day in his early life, giving an artistic form to emotion he knew in time gone. He may remember a relationship with a person he loved and from remembrance create a fiction, turning time past into time now and giving it a new significance.

A story or a novel may start from a recognition of the place from which you came. Through fiction, you may create a place that resembles the one from which you came and yet has a spirit of its own. Or again, as in the representation of Africa in the following passage, you may use a particular locale to give a book its whole lifelike movement.

From the bow of the ship she saw Table Mountain rising like a monster from the sea. Ahead, too, was the harbor with seals and penguins, a mountain with a lion's head and a wharf where the ship would dock for one night only before moving forward again out of the Atlantic and into another sea.

"Come back to the deck with me." Dannie spoke from beside her.

As they left the bow, the harbor was closer with each forward dip of the *Belle* through the sea. Over the prow the water that was like snowdrops broke and fell; from the stern appeared a light blue wake, and almost 7,000 miles behind it lay the home in Steeple Hill she hoped to find again when the journey was over. Everywhere the birds flew over the sea that with land so close was no longer terrible.

Standing then in the shade of the lifeboat above her, with its canvas-covered engine that might not last through the first rough sea, she watched the water where a seal swam by. Behind the sea was the mountain, brown in the sun, and on its slopes the protea she would see in the flower market in the town. Africa was a giant, and strange. Quiet, she watched the harbor. Ahead lay the Indian Ocean. Beyond that the Pacific. And then that point beyond which any direction was home.

Jessie Rehder, in *Remembrance Way*

To observe is to perceive, to listen, to pay attention, to play the role of watcher. But in writing from observation, or from the "mustard seed" given you for a story, you become a participator in spite of yourself.

... Conrad, in an Eastern port, saw a young officer come out from a trial, in which he had been found guilty of a cowardly desertion of his ship and its passengers after a collision. The young man had lost his honour and Conrad realized all at once what that meant to him, and he wrote *Lord Jim* to fix and communicate that discovery in its full force.

For that he had to invent characters, descriptions, a plot. All these details, as with the painter, had to enforce the impression, the feeling that he wanted to convey. The reader had to *feel*, at the end of the tale, 'That is important, that is true'. It's no good if he says, 'I suppose that is true, but I've heard it before'. In that case Conrad has failed, at least with that reader. For his object was to give the reader the same discovery, to make him feel what it meant to that young man to lose his honour, and how important honour is to men.

Joyce Cary in *Art and Reality*

A plot is much more than observation. A good plot, born out of invention, deals with a selected rather than a natural order of events. Into whatever category it falls, realistic or fantastic, plot asks us to accept something that is less than life and yet more. One function of a plot is to hold a reader, to keep him going ahead in the story.

As a plot progresses, it arouses various expectations in the audience or reader about the future course of events. An anxious uncertainty about what is going to happen, especially to those characters with whom we have established bonds of sympathy, is known as *suspense*. If what in fact happens violates the expectations we have formed, it is known as *surprise*. The interplay of suspense and surprise is a prime source of the magnetic power of a plot; but the most effective surprise is that which turns out to have been thoroughly grounded in what has gone before, even though we have hitherto made the wrong inference from the given facts. As E. M. Forster put it, the shock of the unexpected, "followed by the feeling, 'oh, that's all right,' is a sign that all is well with the plot."

M. H. Abrams, *A Glossary of Literary Terms*

As for the theme of a story, Daphne Athas points out that the same theme handled by different authors is not the same at all: "Its cities, its eyes, its burdens, its proofs, its spokesmen, its leaves, and its stones are all different." Your theme can be revealed through action, character, symbol, atmosphere, or a fusion of these. But every writer, whatever means he uses to give his own revelation to others, starts with a challenge and an action. Out of this action something results. In discovering the implication of that result, you find your theme.

Each story, with its constituent parts, grows out of its own particular soil and in its own individual climate. But the permanent cast of a writer's work, as Joyce Cary points out in *Art and Reality* is often given to his mind and feelings by early environment and experience. Cary believes that the genius of Dostoevsky, Tolstoy, James Joyce, and many others, lay in using their early religious training to make new and original works of art. But for each of them, as for Henry James, experience had its own individual meaning.

> The power to guess the unseen from the seen, to trace the implication of things, to judge the whole piece by the pattern, the condition of feeling life in general so completely that you are well on your way to knowing any particular corner of it—this cluster of gifts may almost be said to constitute experience, and they occur in country and in town, and in the most different stages of education. If experience consists of impressions, it may be said that impressions are experience, just as (have we not seen it?) they are the very air we breathe. Therefore, if I should certainly say to a novice, "Write from experience and from experience only," I should feel that this was rather a tantalizing monition if I were not careful immediately to add, "Try to be one of the people on whom nothing is lost!"
>
> From "The Art of Fiction," by Henry James

As a young soldier, Ernest Hemingway saw war and dying everywhere, and it thus became part of his own experience. Out of what he saw he created a *nothing* world in fiction. His books say for him that you will never know what life is about, for God is not there to tell you. You can only learn to stand up to what every man must face before he dies. Hemingway was able to recreate his own *nothing* or *nada* vision so well in fictional terms that his editor said of one of the later novels:

> I cabled you this morning after I read what you sent of the ms. The impressions made by it are even stronger after the lapse of time. The scenes are more vivid and real than in the reading. This has always happened to me after reading your novels, and it is true of mighty few writers. . . . Last night, I had to talk about forthcoming books to the people in the bookstore, and I ended by saying what a simple thing it is to be a real writer, the easiest thing in the world, and I was going to give them an example to show it, how anybody could do it, and then I read them, without saying who had written it, the first three pages, through the point where Jordan gets his glasses adjusted, and sees the mill and the waterfall and all. Having him do that makes the whole scene jump out at you as real as real. I said, "Why couldn't any of us do that? It's perfectly simple." But of course nobody can do it.
>
> *Editor to Author: The Letters of Maxwell E. Perkins*

Every good writer, in making his work as real as real, may seem, and only seem, to be writing simply, as Ernest Hemingway does. He may have the conceptual approach of a Henry James or the passionate feeling of a D. H. Lawrence. But he must have a vision. Not expecting justice, one author gives us a character who believes that you must learn to love without the help of anything on earth. Another, creating his own morality in fiction, keeps a vision of the joy, the hope, the uncertain fate which bind men to each other and all mankind to the visible world.

These writers are people on whom nothing is lost. They are also people in whom something is found.

# Index of Selections

*(Asterisks are used to denote student authors)*

273